WEST ACADEMIC PUBLISHING'S LAW SCHOOL ADVISORY BOARD

DRAFTING ORGANIZATIONAL DOCUMENTS

■ ■ ■

James J. Kelly, Jr.
Clinical Professor of Law
Notre Dame Law School

AMERICAN CASEBOOK SERIES®

WEST ACADEMIC PUBLISHING

444 Cedar Street, Suite 700
St. Paul, MN 55101
1-877-888-1330

Printed in the United States of America

ISBN: 978-1-64020-210-8

To Lisa,

with deepest love and gratitude

PREFACE

This book teaches drafting as an analytical process, of which constructing sentences that have legal effect is merely the final step. In teaching the production of articles, bylaws, and operating agreements, this book introduces students enrolled in transactional clinics, simulation courses and advanced legal writing classes to the basic tools they will need to prepare any type of contract, will, or statute as well.

The book's introductory chapter sets out and develops the foundational image for legal drafting: the construction of a machine made of words. In comparing the drafting of text that generates legal consequences to the writing of legal prose, the introduction calls on students to take the time needed to understand the conceptual and language choices they make as practicing transactional lawyers. For complex documents, such care requires separation of the drafting process into checklist, outline and sentence-drafting stages. Chapter 1 places the drafting of organizational documents at the core of the representation of a start-up enterprise. It introduces the three benefits of entity formation that drive drafting decisions for every type of basic organizational document.

Chapters 2 and 3 lead lawyers through the checklist, outline and drafting phases for nonprofit articles of incorporation and nonprofit corporate bylaws respectively. Chapter 2 shows how clearly a typical nonprofit corporation statute lists the subjects to be addressed in articles of incorporation. Chapter 3, by contrast, examines the outlining of bylaws as a reciprocating inquiry of legal requirements and client circumstances.

Chapter 4 concentrates on the drafting of the sentences that make up any of the organizational documents studied in the book. As such, its lessons can be learned at any point in the study of drafting and apply outside the context of corporate documents as well.

Chapter 5 introduces students to the documents needed to organize a limited liability company, the most popular form for profit-making small businesses. It walks students through the creation of articles of organization and operating agreements, respectively the charter and governance documents for the LLC. Chapter 6 focuses on legal documents that address the transfer of for-profit ownership interests, examining the construction of three different types of option mechanisms.

Chapter 7 instructs readers on how to prepare the certificate of incorporation and bylaws for a Delaware for-profit corporation. The final chapter explores the charter and governance documents that create the most popular of the business entity forms that, in some ways, are hybrids of the nonprofit and for-profit structures. The benefit corporation allows for-profit entities to commit themselves legally to public benefit. The chapter discusses their formation under the Pennsylvania statute and offers an original set of bylaws provisions unique to the benefit corporation model used in that state and many others.

The book's appendix reprints excerpts from the Revised Model Nonprofit Corporations Act (1988), federal tax law regulations governing the formation of 501(c)(3) organizations, Indiana's LLC statute, the Delaware; General Corporation Law and Pennsylvania's Benefit Corporation's statute. Although only the federal and Delaware materials may be directly useful to a wide range of student lawyers, their inclusion allows for practicing the application of relevant law to the drafting of charter and governance documents for new enterprises. Further exercises, teaching ideas and discussion of integrating drafting pedagogy into the seminar portion of a transactional clinical course are available to adopting instructors through West's website.

JAMES J. KELLY, JR.

March 1, 2018

ACKNOWLEDGMENTS

James J. Kelly, Jr. is Clinical Professor of Law at Notre Dame Law School, where he teaches and directs the Community Development Clinic. Prior to beginning his clinical teaching career at the University of Baltimore School of Law in 2004, he represented nonprofit community-based organizations in Baltimore and tenants and tenant associations in New York City.

This book prepares students to engage legal forms and other precedent documents critically by teaching them how to draft from scratch. As such, its original material benefits from the inclusion of reprinted form documents and statutory provisions. The forms and statutes in this book appear with the permission of the Community Law Center, Thomson Reuters, and the American Bar Association.

The author would like to acknowledge all the encouragement, support and assistance he has received in writing this book. After benefitting from years of road testing by seminar students in Notre Dame's Community Development Clinic, the core pedagogical concepts were presented at the 2015 and 2017 Transactional Clinical Conferences held at the Kauffman Foundation Conference Center and Penn Law School respectively. Special thanks go to those who read full drafts of the manuscript and offered insightful feedback and encouragement, especially Lloyd Mayer, Bill Klimon, Jennifer Prusak, Kristine Dunkerton, Susan Bennett, and Brian Krumm. Joe Nugent, Allison Cho, and Luke White provided valuable research assistance.

The book's journey from its origin as a collection of clinical seminar teaching materials would not have even gotten under way without the patient and persistent encouragement of West Academic Acquisitions Editor Austin "Mac" Soto. Finally, the author's own contributions to this volume were made possible by the support of his faculty colleagues at Notre Dame Law School, especially Associate Dean Bob Jones and Dean Nell Newton and the author's family, particularly his wife, Lisa Buonaccorsi Kelly, to whom this work is dedicated.

SUMMARY OF CONTENTS

TABLE OF CONTENTS

DRAFTING ORGANIZATIONAL DOCUMENTS

INTRODUCTION

■ ■ ■

A. LEARNING LEGAL DRAFTING BY CREATING ORGANIZATIONAL DOCUMENTS

Of all the skills that a lawyer must develop to be successful, drafting is the least familiar to any law student. Interviewing, counseling, and negotiating are frequently learned during law school, but also before. High-school debate and other pre-law public speaking opportunities prepare lawyers for oral argument in the courtroom. Instruction in direct examination and cross-examination may wait until after the first year of law school, but few aspiring attorneys have not watched lawyers, or at least actors pretending to be lawyers, practice their craft on TV or online. Legal writing may not get the same popular media attention as trial work, but first-year students build upon prior research and writing training in preparing memoranda and briefs. On the other hand, the process of creating statutes, contracts, deeds, and corporate documents is unknown to them and can remain so throughout all three years of law school and beyond.

This book teaches drafting by focusing on the legal documents that law students are most likely to be called upon to create before graduation: basic organizational documents. Students in transactional clinics frequently help new businesses and charities get started. Nearly all these ventures form as nonprofit corporations, limited liability companies (LLCs) or for-profit corporations. Each of these entities come into existence with an officially accepted filing of a charter document: articles of incorporation[1] or articles of organization. But, to function, each also needs a governance document. Corporations generally have bylaws. An LLC has an operating agreement. In laying the foundations for their organizational clients, transactional clinic students can also establish a knowledge base for all their future legal drafting.

In Chapter 3, you will learn what you need to know to draft bylaws for a nonprofit corporation. Bylaws work like statutes or court rules. They create the <u>legal relationships</u> and <u>procedures</u> that are the working parts of an institution. Public institutions, such as government agencies, are created by constitutions and statutes. Private entities like businesses or charities are shaped by their bylaws. Mastering the language tools used to create

[1] As shown in Ch. 7, Delaware refers to the corporate charter document as a "certificate of incorporation." Other states do the same, but many more use that term to refer to the document attesting to the state's acceptance of the filed articles of incorporation.

corporate bylaws will put you in a position to draft rules and procedures for all manner of institutions.

Chapter 5 focuses on the most popular legal form for new businesses: the limited liability company or LLC. An LLC operating agreement takes the form of a contract signed by all the owners of the new business. Much of it functions and reads very much like bylaws. But it and other agreements among business owners studied in Chapter 6 create powers, rights, and duties in and among business founders. Like other business agreements, basic organizational documents also subject procedures, rights, duties, and discretionary authority to conditions and/or limitations. These provisions are written and enforced in the same way as those found in any business contract. By learning how to draft bylaws, operating agreements, and buy-sell arrangements, you will be able to create and assemble the building blocks of all manner of legal documents.

Drafting legal documents from scratch requires a rigorously logical approach to organizing and articulating provisions. Frequently, drafters with very different prose styles will produce markedly similar legal documents. As you will see in Chapters 3 and 4, provisions of the same type will all be built around the same verb structure. The tendency towards, as well advantages of, standardization in legal documents are particularly strong in the creation of organizational documents.

Drafting incorporation and governance documents involves working with existing templates known as forms. So why then bother to learn how to draft organizational documents from scratch? A thoughtful selector and adapter of legal forms needs the analytical tools of the drafter in order to choose the right form and make it work for the project at hand. Beginning with the penultimate section of this chapter, this book will teach you how to use your drafting skills to adapt forms to your use. The rigorous analytics involved in drafting from scratch and editing forms will not only help you now but also serve you well into a future of profound and rapid change. Imminent advances in the technology of document creation make a conceptual understanding of drafting more important rather than less important to the lawyer of tomorrow.

B. DRAFTING, A DISTINCT FORM OF LEGAL WRITING

1. DRAFTING LANGUAGE THAT HAS LEGAL EFFECT REQUIRES SPECIAL CARE

In the legal writing classes that you took soon after starting law school, you learned to write legal memoranda and briefs that carefully analyzed the law. Using this book, you will write documents that *are* law. Legal writing required you to understand thoroughly what you were writing about. A good research memo depended on mastery of both law and the facts in controversy. Drafting demands that you know how the law impacts your document. A document that contains provisions that meets the client's needs can be put together only if the lawyer knows his or her client's objectives. But finishing the document involves taken that knowledge of the relevant law and understanding of the client's circumstances and crafting legal provisions. In drafting words that have direct legal effect, you must take special care in how you put your sentences together properly. When creating law, your word choices will be subjected to a scrutiny more intense than with any other writing you will engage in.

A lawyer engaged in drafting is not describing something so much as creating something. Essentially, he or she is building a machine out of words. For this machine to work, the lawyer must make sure to have all the right parts and to fit them together. To function exactly as expected, a legal document must be **complete**, **correct**, and **clear.**

By looking at the differences between typical prose writing in the legal context and writing that has actual legal effect, we can better understand what legal drafting is generally. But, more importantly, we can learn how careful drafting of a legal document differs from strong legal writing in briefs and memoranda.

2. HOW GOOD LEGAL DRAFTING DIFFERS FROM GOOD LEGAL PROSE WRITING

Just about any type of prose writing involves describing something. Sometimes, the author is trying to explain a complex idea to the reader. Often, the author attempts to convince the reader to agree with the author's position on a controversial subject. He or she will introduce a main idea and then develop that main idea by providing relevant detail and compelling imagery. To engage the reader, a good prose writer will repeat key points but vary the language used so as not to seem repetitive.

The need for precise clarity deters a legal drafter from varying his or her language in the way the prose writer does. Rigorous consistency flows from the drafter's need to be clear: the good legal drafter always says the same thing the exact same way. For example, the individuals on a board of directors can be referred to as "directors" or "members of the Board." In a legal memo about corporate governance, the author might encourage the reader's attention by alternating between the synonymous terms. But, in writing the actual bylaws, the drafter will pick one expression, probably "directors," and stick with it throughout. Otherwise an interpreter will be tempted to think that the two terms used, though similar, are not meant to be identical in meaning and that there is some crucial significance to the drafter's choice to use one term in some parts of the document and the other elsewhere. The need to avoid ambiguity in a legal document is so demanding that boring the reader with repetitive language does not compete as a concern.

Covering the subject completely and correctly is the hallmark of any good memo or brief. But a set of bylaws, a statute, or a contract drafted by someone who has misunderstood the related law or left critical questions unanswered fails in a way not found in a flawed memo or brief. Appellate advocates must judge which arguments to focus on and which to leave to the side. Poor decision making may limit a brief's effectiveness but rarely leads to a complete breakdown. The drafter creating law, on the other hand, must know which issues must be addressed and how existing law shapes the range of possible approaches. Logical gaps or substantive mistakes of law in a set of bylaws, a contract, or a statute may grind the entire machine to a halt.

The difference between writing prose and drafting becomes even starker when we move from outlining to actual word choice. Good persuasive legal writing requires an attention to tone that can be accomplished only through careful use of language. But virtually every word in a legal provision will be selected by the drafter with the exclusive goal of clearly expressing the precise rule or standard the document outline calls for. Only such a precise approach to crafting provision language can allow a complete and correct plan for a document to result in a working verbal machine. In this way, drafting a legal document is similar to writing code for a computer program.

3. HOW GOOD LEGAL PROSE WRITING AND GOOD LEGAL DRAFTING ARE ALIKE

Computer software, however, is written in special languages designed to be read by machines as a sequence of 1s and 0s. Legal documents use the same language that memos and briefs do. What makes good legal prose and strong legal documents alike is arguably more important than what sets them apart.

Even though a memo is organized differently than an operating agreement, it is crucial that both be well-organized. The logical structure of an analysis of an argument must be apparent to any knowledgeable person reading a memo or a brief. Even more so, the structure of a governance document must be apparent to any reader. Both memos and legal documents make liberal use of headings to signal the various topics addressed. Both legal prose and legal documents cater to the so-called "fly-over" reader as well as those who read the entire piece from beginning to end. Legal drafters do well to use sub-headings too. Leaders of an incorporated entity may need to consult the organization's bylaws to answer a particular procedural question. A drafter that sorts and labels subsections sensibly serves these reference readers.

Both those who write about the law and those who write the law have a professional obligation to be inclusive in their use of language. An organizational document that refers to an entity director or officer as "he" sends a signal that the leadership position is expected to be held by a man. Prose writers, including the author of this book, will employ the somewhat awkward "he or she" pronoun construct or will alternate between the two gender-specific pronouns. But drafting's dedication to consistency eliminates the latter option when writing rules. Most legislative style manuals instruct drafters to avoid use of gendered pronouns altogether. Even though most states have enacted a rule of construction that encourages either personal pronoun to be interpreted inclusively, style guides promote the repeated use of generic nouns such as "a person" or "an individual" over use of personal pronouns.

Inclusivity also entails the avoidance of jargon. Having bylaws or an agreement written in plain language will not give a layperson client the same understanding of it that a lawyer will have. Legal knowledge goes far beyond fluency in legalese. Good drafting cannot make up for a reader's unfamiliarity with how legal provisions interact with statutes, regulations and common law. But the needless use of legal jargon should not render a charitable corporation's governance documents unintelligible to those who need to follow them. As a rule of thumb, a lawyer should never use in a document any word that he or she did not know the meaning of before entering law school.

Even strict adherence to this rule may not sufficiently stress the importance of plain language. Clarity in writing means making the document work for the reader regardless of background. Many of my clinic students know that a quorum means the minimum number of decision makers needed to be present at a meeting in order for decisions made at the meeting to be binding. Many of their client constituents do not know that. That difference in sophistication does not lead a good drafter to sidestep the issue of quorum in drafting bylaws or even to avoid the use of the word "quorum." But, rather than simply stating "A quorum for any meeting of the Board of Directors shall consist of a majority of the Directors eligible to vote." and moving on, the thoughtful drafter could reframe it as follows: "Quorum. Any meeting at which the Board conducts business must involve a majority of the Directors eligible to vote." The latter provision sets the quorum without assuming the definition of the word "quorum" is known to the reader. The use of the subheading educates the reader as to the meaning of the term. "Quorum" is an example of useful but not indispensable legal shorthand. Almost all legal terminology is shorthand for a concept that can be expressed without jargon. Since so much of legalese is rarely useful even among lawyers, the drafter should avoid it always.

Plain language does not render structurally complex documents simple. Making the vocabulary of a document accessible does not necessarily make the document accessible. Good drafting never eliminates the need for good client counseling. There are no general rules about when and to what extent a legal document should be complicated in its mechanics. Such decisions need to be made as part of the planning stages of the drafting process. In the next section, you will learn more about the planning that precedes the writing in the drafting process.

But the most important element of good legal drafting is every bit as important to good legal prose writing: review and revision. The adage "There is no such thing as great writing, only great rewriting." applies to document drafting and briefcraft alike. Writers do not achieve their goals by engaging raw talent in a moment of intense concentration. They go back and look at their work as a reader. Thoughtful writers know their objectives and can find the opportunities to improve upon what they have already written.

Even with careful outlining followed by meticulous sentence composition, the drafter does well to read the completed provisions, both together and in isolation, checking for ambiguity, testing for consequences, and sharpening where needed. Where the author of memos and briefs will normally edit his or her own work, the legal drafter making judicious use of forms will frequently start with someone else's text. As discussed further in the penultimate section of this chapter, the legal drafter, in the real world, is an editor who adapts a template, usually created by someone else, to meet the needs of the project at hand.

C. COMPLEX DOCUMENTS: THE DRAFTING LAWYER AS ENGINEER

1. A COMPLEX LEGAL DOCUMENT IS NEITHER A TREATISE NOR A NOVEL—IT IS A MACHINE MADE OF WORDS

The charter document for a new business or charitable entity can often fit on a single page. But bylaws and operating agreements frequently run a dozen pages or more. Certain sections of these governance documents can take up several pages by themselves. Some parts of these documents are so significant and so involved that they can be drafted as separate legal documents. For instance, conflicts-of-interest procedures for nonprofit corporations are sometimes written into the bylaws. But they can also be adopted by way of a standalone document. Likewise, the buy-sell arrangements examined in Chapter 6 can be drafted as part of or apart from foundational governance documents. But no amount of document subdivision will free the drafter from having to face a large-scale drafting project.

Organizational documents, long or short, are often even more complex than they appear. In the case of an LLC, for instance, the operating agreement, as the main governance document, has to relate to the buy-sell agreement, which governs the ability of the founders to transfer their ownership interests. These documents must be **complete** in themselves and complete as a pair. There cannot be gaps in either document, nor can there be issues allowed to fall in the cracks between the two documents. When the operating agreement is drafted, it may be assumed that the possibility of an owner losing his or her share to a foreclosing creditor will be dealt with in the buy-sell agreement rather than in the operating agreement. For reasons that will be discussed in later chapters, that may not be a good idea. But it will clearly be a problem if the subsequent drafting of the buy-sell agreement then proceeds on the mistaken assumption that the issue of involuntary ownership interest transfer to a creditor has already been addressed in the operating agreement. Covering all the issues requires careful planning and attention to detail.

Similarly, complex provisions and documents must be coordinated to be **correct** and **clear.** Substantively, the answers they provide to the questions asked must not be invalid under existing law. More to the point, the provisions must not work against each other much less explicitly contradict one another. Going back to our previous example, an operating agreement and a buy-sell agreement that provided opposing answers to the issue of transfer to a creditor could create a bigger problem than leaving the question unanswered by either document. Lack of consistency among provisions creates ambiguity, which, as you will read in later chapters, is the enemy of clarity.

With any complex drafting project, you should not begin by writing out the finished provisions in order from first to last. You need to be prepared and organized before you begin creating the actual wording of the document. No responsible engineer would build a physical machine without drawing a detailed plan first. Before fitting together the verbal components of your legal document, you need an outline, which itself comes from a checklist.

2. THE STAGES OF DRAFTING

In the case of a simple, standalone document, the three steps that make the finished product **complete**, **correct**, and **clear** can be done together or, at least, may be accomplished in one sitting: The drafter needs to:

- ask all the right question(s), then
- find the right answers, and then
- get the wording just right.

But a complex document or suite of documents should be constructed in three phases, one for each of these indispensable steps. If you don't separate the stages, you're skipping the planning and jumping right into the wordsmithing. Before you can get the right wording for the answers, you need to have a clear understanding of the answers. Before you can know the answers, you need to identify the right questions. For the completion of one segment to support the work of the next, each of step must produce a written record. With the questions written down, you can give the proper attention to sketching the outline of each answer. With all the answers summarized, you have a clear idea of what you are trying to articulate in the finished legal language of the document.

- When you have written out a record of all the right questions to be answered, then you have a **complete <u>checklist</u>.**
- When you take that list of questions and then sketch out the right answers in general terms, then you have a **correct <u>outline</u>.**
- With that outline organized to match the sections of your document, you can then fashion the precise wording into a **clear <u>draft</u>** of the full document.

Doubts about the necessity of checklists and outlines are understandable. You've written long exam answers and essays before without writing an outline, much less a separate list of the questions the outline answers. But transactional practice is complex. If it were simple, no one would hire a specialist like you to do it. Atul Gawande makes the case for experienced professionals creating and following checklists for complex procedures in his bestselling book, The Checklist Manifesto. Following procedures carefully and thoroughly should not be left to trusting your gut.

To illustrate how important following checklists can be to a client, Gawande recounts an anecdote from the memoir of David Lee Roth, original lead singer for the rock band Van Halen, about a concert in Colorado that was cancelled because the promoter had failed to provide backstage a bowl of M&Ms with the brown ones removed. The band's state-of-the-art stage show required rigging procedures far more complex than typical concert venues had previously seen. To ensure that the band would know if the steps in the contract rider had been strictly observed, a clause requiring the edited candy bowl was inserted amidst them. "When I would walk backstage, if I saw a brown M&M in that bowl", he wrote, "well, we'd line-check the entire production."[2] The cancellation of the Colorado show may have begun with the discovery of brown M&Ms, but it was caused by the subsequent confirmation that the stage would likely have collapsed had

[2] Atul Gawande, The Checklist Manifesto: How to Get Things Right 80 (2009).

the concert gone forward as planned. Even experienced professionals need checklists.

The chart below shows the entire process of drafting complex legal documents from scratch. The middle column describes the work of legal and factual research needed to make sure the checklist and outline together plan a document that meets the client's legal needs. The work of the drafting stage will be described in more detail in the first section of Chapter 4.

Drafting from Scratch		
<u>Stage</u>	**<u>Work</u>**	**<u>Goal</u>**
Checklist	Identify every issue and question required by the law. Identify every issue and question req'd by client's goals and circumstances.	**Complete Checklist** of every issue and question to be addressed by the document
↓	↓	↓
Outline	Research how law limits possible answers to questions. Identify those answers remaining that best address client's goals and circumstances. Learn client's preferences and counsel client to identify best answer for each issue.	**Correct Outline** sketching out each answer to every issue and question on the **Checklist**
↓	↓	↓
Draft	Build sentences that have legal effect using steps in Ch. 4, Sec. A.	**Clear Draft** of provision language expressing each answer in the **Outline**

Drafting legal documents is about delivering value to the client. Organizational documents create formal business entities. Business entities are vehicles for holding, managing, and growing resources. As will be discussed in more detail in Chapter 1 and beyond, well-designed business entities provide **liability risk limitation, an effective decision-making structure,** and **favorable tax treatment.** The value the organizational documents deliver will guide you in creating checklists, outlines and finished provision language. These same client objectives more broadly conceived as risk management, control of value and tax efficiency will continue to demand your attention in any form of transactional legal work for an enterprise. This book's methods for identifying issues and developing options for the provisions of basic organizational documents will not translate directly to those same process steps in drafting contracts or real estate documents. But your checklist, outline and provision writing for the core documents of business entities will be a foundation upon which your other drafting skills can be built.

In litigation, the content of memos and briefs comes from the facts and the law about the events in controversy. With transactional documents, the key facts are the client's goals and circumstances. In organizing a start-up venture, a thorough understanding of the basic benefits listed above will get you started in posing the right questions and finding the right answers that make up your **complete checklist** and your **correct outline** respectively. In each chapter, the material in this book will assist you in finding the relevant law for each document. You will also learn how the interviewing and counseling skills you are developing will help you shape the documents you draft to your client's unique goals.

D. FORMS: THE DRAFTING LAWYER AS EDITOR

As alluded to earlier, you may only rarely draft a legal document completely from scratch. The use of already existing documents—whether they are called precedents, templates or forms—saves time and promotes standardization. But uncritical selection and use of forms is simply bad lawyering. You cannot truly judge the quality and suitability of a precedent for your client's legal need unless you can create, in due time, the needed document from scratch. If, however, you have the tools to know the right questions, find the right answers and express them clearly, you will not have to write your document from scratch. You will be able to compare forms confidently and efficiently, selecting the right one for adaptation.

A precedent may be clearly written but not have the right answers. For example, a nonprofit corporate bylaws provision on quorum may express with perfect clarity that only 10% of the directors need be present at a meeting to conduct business; but that provision conflicts with most states' statutory minimum for quorum. The provision is **clear,** but it is not **correct.** A precedent may have answered all the questions covered correctly but neglected to cover some important issues, or it could tackle matters that are not appropriate for that type of document. The document's answers are **correct,** but the document is not **complete.** For instance, certain governing statutes require that certain types of provisions appear in the charter document (articles of incorporation or articles of organization) filed with the state instead of in a governance document (bylaws or operating agreement). If you take a fully drafted set of bylaws and focus only on word choice and sentence structure problems, you are assuming that the document you are starting is already complete and correct.

The stages of legal drafting are just as important when working with forms as they are when drafting from scratch. But, if you had to write something up for each of the three stages—checklist, outline, and draft—just to judge the quality of the form you found, you would not be saving much time by starting with a precedent. The first two starting-from-scratch steps—writing out a checklist and then an outline—need to be modified for the work of form adaptation.

If you are new to an area of document drafting practice, you should still go ahead and list the issues that you know the adapted form will need to address. You should do this even if you are fairly confident that the form you have found covers all the right issues. In writing the checklist out the first time, you should put the form you have found to the side to give yourself the space to cover all the bases. After taking a first stab at it, you will undoubtedly discover issues addressed by the form that should be added to your list. On the other hand, you should not be afraid to question whether or not some subjects covered in your form are superfluous or even inappropriate for what your client requires. As a rule, if a form does not cover the right set of issues, it's probably best to try and start with a different form. If the form fits your checklist, it's time to make sure it is substantively correct.

If a set of bylaws contains a section that violates the statute under which it is drafted or has provisions that contradict one another, it should be a warning to start over with a different form. In the outline phase of adapting a form, there should be no need for you to create your own set of answers to the questions on your checklist. Instead, you should use that checklist to go through the document section by section to see if the rules, procedures, and obligations that the drafter was creating work for your client under the applicable law.

Once you have assured yourself that the form, as found or as you have marked it, is **complete** and **correct,** then you are basically in the same position you would be in after completing a first draft. The only difference between form adapting and drafting from scratch is that you did not write out the first draft. But the revision process is fundamentally the same. You are trying to make sure that your draft is **clear** in expressing the **correct** answers to the **complete** set of questions. The chart below revises the previous depiction of the drafting-from-scratch process.

<table>
<tr><th colspan="3">Adapting Forms</th></tr>
<tr><th><u>Stage</u></th><th><u>Work</u></th><th><u>Goal</u></th></tr>
<tr><td rowspan="3">Checklist</td><td>Identify every issue and question required by the law.</td><td rowspan="3">Complete Checklist of every issue and question to be addressed by the document <u>and/or</u>
a form that either addresses each issue or notes the need to</td></tr>
<tr><td>Identify every issue and question required by client's goals and circumstances.</td></tr>
<tr><td>Compare your checklist to the headings of the form you found. Revise both as needed.</td></tr>
<tr><td>↓</td><td>↓</td><td>↓</td></tr>
<tr><td rowspan="3">Outline</td><td>Research how law limits possible answers to questions.</td><td rowspan="3">Correct Outline sketching out each answer to every issue and question on the Checklist <u>and/or</u>
a form edited to reject flawed or otherwise inferior answers in favor of preferable options</td></tr>
<tr><td>Identify those answers remaining that best address client's goals and circumstances.</td></tr>
<tr><td>Learn client's preferences and counsel client to identify best answer for each issue.</td></tr>
<tr><td>↓</td><td>↓</td><td>↓</td></tr>
<tr><td>Draft</td><td>Build and revise sentences that have legal effect using steps in Ch. 4, Sec. A.</td><td>Clear Draft of provision language expressing each answer in the Outline</td></tr>
</table>

This book is written for student lawyers drafting their first organizational documents. You will have many forms available to you in creating your charter and governance documents. As such, this book follows the form-adaptation approach to the three drafting stages described above. It will first teach you and then, through exercises, prompt you to create checklist items from scratch. Likewise, for the outline stage, it will call upon you to apply given facts about the law and the client to address vital organizational document issues. When it comes to the actual provision language, the book will show you how to put the sentences together. But it will then prompt you to make needed changes to sample sections provided.

While the book emphasizes the distinct tasks of each phase of creating an organizational document, the reality of drafting in stages will rarely be so cut and dried. You may have a well-constructed checklist that you discover needs revision only after you have begun looking to the substantive answers. Likewise, you may find out that the sketches of the procedures that you thought were so clear are not so perfect when you sit down to actually put them into language that has legal effect. Some of these returns to earlier drafting stages will be due to upstream mistakes. But some of them will be due to the difficulties inherent in learning the relevant law, understanding client objectives, reconciling the two and working with a language that, by its nature, lacks clarity, precision, and consistency.

If these problems did not need to be confronted, then computers could replace lawyers as drafters in the near future. As it is, technology will not eliminate the need for lawyers that know how to draft. But rapid advances in computing power will impact how lawyers draft and will provide a comparative advantage to those lawyers who understand how a computer would approach the job of putting together a legal document.

E. THE FUTURE OF LEGAL DRAFTING

The experience of drafting is very different now from what it was 50 years ago. Contracts were typed not created using word processing software. But the intellectual process of drafting is very much the same as it was back then. It is almost certain that the process of legal drafting will be as much changed by computers in the next 50 years as word processing has changed the typing of them over the last fifty years.

Computational transformation of legal drafting is already under way with the expansion of word processing. In the 1980s, software such as Word Perfect® and Microsoft Word® made it easier to fix spelling and grammar mistakes. A document no longer had to be written out by hand and then proofread before being typed. Later, word processing programs offered to spot misspelled words and flag them or even correct them automatically. More recently, the computer-as-editor has internalized rules of grammar and style. A user of Microsoft Word® will now receive a prompt to rewrite that last sentence in a more concise way, not because it is "wrong" as written but because the computer thinks it could be written better. Computer software is also rapidly advancing in the creation of interactive legal forms, which even now go far beyond the insertion of labeled blank spaces that characterized the pre-printed legal forms of yesterday.

The rules of legal drafting are not so completely different from the rules of grammar and style as to put them beyond a computer's ability to use them. Already transactional lawyers have the option of using software that will analyze their contracts and other legal documents for internal consistency and flag potential problems. Some of the guidance you receive from this text will be beyond computer's abilities for many generations, but, someday soon, computers will use many of the rules described in these chapters as easily as they use spelling, grammar, and style rules now. Just as you still need to know those rules of good writing to work with the word processers of today, you will need to have knowledge of both the simple and nuanced rules of legal drafting to work in the computer-assisted drafting world to come.

A sign of potentially more disruptive innovations to current transactional practice is the advent of self-executing contracts using the same blockchain technology underlying digital currencies such as Bitcoin®. Earlier in the chapter, you read that a legal document can be conceived of as a machine made of words. A computer program can also be thought of as a machine made of words. Both legal documents and computer programs are composed of interlocking instructions, rules, and conditions. Blockchain contract technology takes advantage of this fundamental similarity and expresses agreements between parties as a set of commands on a peer-to-peer computer network with direct control over the subject assets. Because the networked computers participating in the distributed ledger can move money when certain events called for in the agreement have taken place, these agreements are self-executing. The blockchain program is not only the record of the agreement, it is also the means by which the agreement is carried out. As a lawyer of tomorrow, you need to understand the logical structures that animate your legal documents so that you are an effective user of legal drafting technology.

CHAPTER 1

ORGANIZATIONAL DOCUMENTS

■ ■ ■

A. DRAFTING A START-UP VENTURE'S DOCUMENTS: THE CORE OF THE REPRESENTATION

1. FOUR DELIVERABLES IN THE REPRESENTATION OF A START-UP VENTURE

Every formal business entity is established by the creation of two legal documents: a charter document that creates it and a governance document by which it operates. But the lawyer representing a start-up not only drafts this pair of documents but also helps the founders decide which charter and governance documents they should choose. That is, the lawyer counsels the client about the choice of form options available. As you will read in the next section of this chapter, a lawyer assisting a client in choosing among various nonprofit and for-profit entity options should focus on three entity benefits:

- **Liability Risk Limitation**
- **Effective Decision-Making Structure**
- **Favorable Tax Treatment**

Each of these will be discussed in detail at the end of this section. If the client confirms it wants to form as a corporation, then the lawyer knows to create it by filing articles of incorporation and to set up it governance by drafting bylaws. Likewise, a client who prefers the limited liability company will have articles of organization as its charter document and an operating agreement as its governance document.

As it turns out, the first two benefits, **liability risk limitation** and **effective decision-making structure,** are, respectively, the primary objectives of the charter and governance document deliverables. Acceptance by the state of the drafted and filed articles confers the liability shield sought by the new venture's founders. The governance document is not filed with the government; instead, it provides the decision-making structure of the new business. The fourth and final start-up venture deliverable, counseling and representation on the entity's income-tax classification, focuses on the third benefit, **favorable tax treatment.**

Although the documents that are filed with the IRS to obtain a particular tax status are not the focus of this book, a client's ability to claim a favorable tax classification will often depend on the choices made during one or more of the three earlier deliverables. A charitable nonprofit gets its liability shield from the state's acceptance of its articles and its governance structure from the adoption of bylaws, but even its 501(c)(3) recognition will hinge on the content of each of those documents, especially its articles.

2. CHECKLISTS AND OUTLINES: SKETCHING OUT THE CONTENT OF CHARTER AND ORGANIZATIONAL DOCUMENTS

Articles are rarely complex documents. None of the charter documents that you will learn to create will run more than a page and a half. Articles are simple because **liability limitation** is simple; a venture either has it or it doesn't. The business gets it by having its articles accepted, so the main question becomes: "What does it take for the articles to be accepted?" As you will see in the chapters ahead, the statutes for nonprofit corporations, limited liability companies, for-profit corporations and benefit corporations all list the required item of information quite clearly. If the availability of certain **income-tax classifications** did not hinge on the nature of a nonprofit's purposes or the uniformity of a small business's ownership structure, then the drafting of articles might have very little to do with real lawyering. As it is, separating the checklist and outline phases of charter document drafting is more trouble than it's worth. The whole process of creating articles is over before you know it.

Governance documents, on the other hand, are rarely short and simple. One would think that a governance document for a business owned by just one person would be ridiculously short. But an operating agreement for a single-member limited liability company usually runs at least five or six pages. For every type of formal entity, there is a corresponding set of state statutes that address how they are to be governed. The relevant statute names the primary decision makers for each type of entity. The governance document checklist begins with setting out the selection and collaboration processes of those main leaders of the entity and others needed for an **effective decision-making structure.** Creating the outline involves developing one or more answers to each of the questions on the checklist. The answers cannot be correct if they violate the law. Thus, you will need to know every statutory provision that mandates a certain approach to governance. To be effective, the options you sketch out in the outline phase must not conflict with mandatory provision of the state statute. Within those parameters, you will work to understand the best governance practices not only by reflection on the various facets of an **effective decision-making structure** generally but also by learning from your client's leaders about their particular circumstances and preferences.

3. OTHER TRANSACTIONAL LAWYERING SKILLS CRUCIAL TO START-UP REPRESENTATION

Even as drafting organizational documents stands at the heart of the representation of a start-up venture, other skills are indispensable to creating quality documents and addressing related legal needs of the client. As indicated in the prior chapter's discussion of its three stages, the drafting of organizational documents starts by looking to client goals and the law to form questions and develop answers to those questions. The three benefits common to all formal entities provide the start-up venture's attorney with general guidelines. But, to create documents that truly work for the client, the lawyer for a start-up needs to understand the facts about the venture and the client's unique objectives to a degree that cannot be accomplished without good **interviewing** skills.

The people coming together to start the enterprise need to make any decisions among options as to entity form, purposes or governance provisions. But they will need your **counseling** to make those decisions in an informed way that reflects their views and attitudes. Good counseling involves a clear and balanced presentation of the costs and benefits of the various options available to the client. As noted above, the client's goals and the law strongly shape the relevant costs and benefits. For counseling and drafting to be based on a correct understanding of both elements, **researching** law and facts will be crucial. While some facts will come to you from the client constituents, other vital information may need to be tracked down online or in the field. Fortunately, the law most relevant to determining the content of formal business entity documents is almost entirely statutory. The chapters ahead will help you form interview questions and direct you to key statutory provisions

Representing start-ups can involve **advocating** on their behalf. The secretary of state for your jurisdiction and the IRS play vital roles in your client's obtaining a corporate liability shield and favorable tax treatment respectively. The processing of these filings is rarely contentious much less litigious. But you need to be prepared to make your case for the choices you and your client have made to get the benefits your client expects. You also should anticipate that any advocacy project may require **negotiating** to achieve the best resolution for your client.

Many other skills that neither engage the client's legal needs directly nor are unique to lawyering will be vital to your effectiveness. These include strong time management, cultural awareness, open-mindedness, focus, self-control, stress management and maintenance of work-life balance. One skill that may go also unnoticed by the client, but that is particular to transactional lawyering, is **planning out a transactional representation.** Case planning involves identifying and listing every item you will produce to help the client as a set of <u>deliverables</u>. A good case plan will also coordinate the timing of the client communication, legal and factual research, preparation, review, and presentation involved in generating each deliverable.

An adequate discussion of these transactional lawyering practice skills of interviewing, researching, counseling, advocating, negotiating, and case planning is beyond the scope of a book focused on the equally vital ability to draft legal documents. [1] But, as you move forward in the seemingly solitary work of planning and creating a set of organizational documents, you will see how interviewing and researching will play a vital role in your success as a legal drafter.

4. THE THREE BENEFITS OF A FORMAL BUSINESS ENTITY

a. Liability Risk Protection

With any activity, there is risk. There is, of course, always the chance that a project will not reach its goals, that it will fail to provide all, or even any, of the return hoped for. But there is also the possibility that the failure will be so severe as to leave large debts in its wake. The founders of that or any venture, whether nonprofit or for-profit, will want, from the beginning, protection against personal responsibility for such debts. State incorporation law responds to the client's need by providing the benefit of liability limitation. As you will read in the next chapter, creating a new business entity by filing a charter document with the state can allow the founders to operate the venture without being personally liable for the debts it may incur.

The corporate veil, while not indestructible, allows the creators of a new enterprise to invest their time and/or their money without undue anxiety that they will lose more than they have chosen to put at risk. The state's offer of a liability shield to those forming a new venture is not one that most entrepreneurs require much time or deliberation before accepting. While the fee amounts for filing articles of incorporation vary significantly from state to state, the benefit of liability risk protection frequently makes up for these costs as well as for any other constraints or requirements associated with incorporation.

b. Effective Decision Making

When people work together on a new project or ongoing enterprise, they need to control the resources of the venture and chart a course for its development. The legal entity formed is sometimes called a "vehicle" for the venture's operations and the resources that make them possible. If

[1] Fortunately, transactional clinics have access to a text that ably meets the daunting challenge of introducing students to these indispensable capacities. Alicia Alvarez & Paul R. Tremblay, Introduction to Transactional Lawyering Practice (2013).

incorporation is the entity's bumpers and airbags that keep occupants safe, then its governance structure is what keeps the vehicle on the road moving in the right direction and at the right speed. Like a mechanical vehicle, an entity is only as effective as its steering, acceleration and braking mechanisms allow it to be.

What makes for an effective decision-making structure can vary strikingly depending on the communication styles of the founders and the nature of the venture. While adherence to best practices will promote some standardization among governance documents, the decision-making benefit will be fully realized only if the bylaws or operating agreement of the new entity reflects the client's choices about this indispensable benefit. Even if those starting a new enterprise have no concerns about personal liability or minimization of tax, they will still want to have an agreed-upon structure for making decisions together.

c. Favorable Tax Treatment

Ventures spend money and take effort, but they also attract resources, both human and monetary. Where there are resources of any kind and movement of those resources in and out of an entity, the subject of tax comes into play. Several different types of tax can impact the bottom line of a business or a charity, but income tax is usually the one type that dominates the discussion. A new venture's tax classification and the choices it makes within the relevant tax rules can have a major effect on how much of its income it has to pay over to the federal and/or state government. For various reasons, federal tax law considerations shape the part of organizational planning concerned with tax classification.

Returning to our vehicle metaphor, the tax treatment of a new venture determines its fuel efficiency. The less the taxman takes the more there is left to go to the venture's purpose, which for virtually all for-profit entities is to enrich the owners. Many large corporations pay taxes on their excess revenue every year and then see their owners taxed again when dividends are issued. These companies are making profits but cannot pass all or even almost all those revenues to their shareholders. Smaller business entities seek tax classifications that do not involve this double taxation. Generally, each of their owners just pays personal income tax on his or her share of the taxable revenues. More dramatically, those ventures that form as nonprofits are largely exempt from income taxation altogether. Since nonprofits are generally not owned by those that lead them, their "fuel efficiency" relates to the fact that more of their excess revenues can remain dedicated to their purposes. A great number of nonprofits qualify under tax law as charities and receive a subsidy from the income tax system, which incentivizes donations to them from individuals who can deduct such gifts on their personal tax returns.

Together these three benefits of a well-formed business entity can have a tremendous impact on the ability of the venture to attract and manage investment both of monetary and human resources. Each benefit becomes a primary focus of concern at different stages of the organization's creation. The risk protection afforded by incorporation takes center stage when the charter document is submitted for acceptance by the state. The drafting of bylaws or of an operating agreement is all about creating an effective governance structure for the entity. The process, if any, for formalizing the entity's tax classification with the Internal Revenue Service does not usually occur until after the charter and governance documents are completed. But some of the critical factors that determine eligibility for favorable tax treatment are established when the articles and/or the governance document is written.

You need to know how well-formed entities benefit new ventures because these three factors represent the value you add as a lawyer for a start-up venture. If entrepreneurs did not need risk protection, effective decision making, and favorable tax treatment, you, as a transactional lawyer, would not have work, at least not the paying kind. These three factors drive the drafting choices that you make when building an entity structure. But they also shape your recommendations as to what kind of entity form the venture should choose. The three benefits determine not only the details of each document but also the set of documents to be drafted.

5. OTHER MEANS OF OBTAINING THE SAME BENEFITS, OTHER BENEFITS OBTAINED BY THE SAME MEANS

Drafting the organizational documents is the primary legal service provided to start-ups. Not surprisingly, along with assuring compliance with relevant law, the three benefits—liability risk protection, effective decision making, favorable tax treatment—discussed are the core objectives of the start-up venture representation. But the organizational documents are not the only means by which lawyers help achieve the three benefits.

Besides incorporation, there are other ways for entrepreneurs to limit their risk of personal liability. The new business can buy one or more types of liability insurance policies. Frequently, these policies will include board members, officers and key employees as additional insureds without requiring higher premiums. As you will see in each of the next two chapters, organizational documents can provide for corporate reimbursement to directors, officers and other who incur costs relating to legal claims made against them in connection to their work for the organization. This form of reimbursement is called indemnification. In some states, leaders of charitable ventures receive at least limited statutory immunity from liability arising out of their volunteer service.

More commonly, businesses and nonprofits contract for such absolution by having those participating in their activities sign waivers and releases. Of course, those engaged in commercial or nonprofit activities can best limit their liability by simply being careful. Their lawyers can facilitate this by inquiry about their actual practices, inspection of sites and observation of operations when appropriate, and suggestions for improvement that balance cost and benefit. Each of these liability risk management approaches offers protections to the venture as well as to those who direct its course. Legal counseling has a role to play in a client's decision to use any of them.

Sometimes the entity's charter document not only obtains liability protection but also impacts decision making. When the articles of incorporation for a nonprofit identify certain specific purposes to which the entity's resources must be dedicated, that document is imposing a boundary around the board's decision-making authority. To obtain favorable tax treatment for your client, you may need to prepare a third deliverable to be filed with the Internal Revenue Service. Those IRS forms may not be drafted organizational documents, strictly speaking, but the eligibility for certain tax classification is often determined by the choices made in the charter and/or governance documents.

With for-profit ventures, you will see in chapters 5–7 that the organizational documents will structure not only how owners are involved in **decision making** but also how and what they receive as revenue as well as how they apportion and prioritize their claims on the business's assets. The business owners' claims on profits, losses, and assets as well as the transferability of those rights will be explored more fully as **equity structure.** Just as an effective decision-making structure helps inspire confidence in the effectiveness of organization thereby attracting resources to it, a well-considered equity structure will incentivize current and future owners of the venture to invest in the entity knowing that their voices in the company's operations and their returns from its success will grow proportionately. Control certainly matters, even if it rarely takes precedence over money. For-profit organizational documents must attend to both.

The final chapter will consider yet another facet of organizational form. The choice of a social enterprise to incorporate as a benefit corporation can be driven in part by **branding** considerations. The founders of such a venture may want to signal to investors, consumers and the public at large a commitment to certain social goods. The considerations involved in that public relations strategy as well as the **founders' ideals** may shape not only the choice to form as a benefit corporation but also the content of its articles and bylaws. Those same social ideals may also animate the approval and content of nonprofit articles of incorporation, which is the focus of the next chapter.

B. IDENTIFYING THE RIGHT SET OF DOCUMENTS: CHOICE OF FORM

Before we can focus on the drafting of organizational documents, we must ask, "What, if any, set of organizational documents will meet the client's needs?" This is the question of choice of form: What sort of entity is the best for this new venture? You may not to be surprised to find out the three benefits of a formal corporate entity to which you were just introduced drive the legal analysis involved in the question.

Below is an example of a brand-new community enterprise that frames the question of choice of form as follows: Should this new venture be a separate nonprofit corporation? This apparently simple yes/no question is actually a compound question made of three elements:

- corporation or unincorporated entity?
- separate or part of an existing entity?
- nonprofit or for-profit?

With just a little elaboration, each of these questions can be recast to match up with each of the three benefits.

- Liability Risk Protection—Should the entity be one that provides liability limitation to those involved in the venture?
- Independent, Effective Decision Making—Should the venture have its own entity as opposed to becoming (or remaining) part of an existing entity?
- Favorable Tax Treatment—Should the entity seek exemption from corporate income tax by organizing itself so as to prevent distribution of excess income to those involved in leading the venture?

If the answer is "Yes" to each of these three questions, then you will want to draft nonprofit articles of incorporation as well as bylaws for this venture. If the answer is "No" just to the first question, then a charter document and a governance document for an unincorporated nonprofit association will be in order. If the answer is "No" to the second question, then the venture is going to be part of an already existing organization. In that case, the first and third questions matter only as to what kind of organization the venture should join, and there will be no organizational document drafting project as such. If the answer is "No" to the third question, then you will move from a focus on nonprofit organizational document choices to the options available for for-profit ventures.

DISCUSSION QUESTION 1–A

Liberty City Land Trust (LCLT)—
A New Community Enterprise

You are getting ready to conduct an intake interview with the founders of (the fictional) Liberty City Land Trust (LCLT) and, after consulting with your supervising attorney, have drafted a retainer agreement that calls for your Clinic to advise and represent LCLT in structuring the organization and seeking the most favorable tax status available to it. As you plan out the first part of the representation, you focus on counseling as to choice of entity form and the drafting of appropriate documents. Here is what you learned from the client intake form and the materials attached to it:

> LCLT has grown out of the activities of certain "guerilla gardeners" working in the Near Northwest neighborhood of Middletown, Indiana. This inner-city residential area has a growing number of vacant houses and vacant lots. The activists have been tilling the most visible of these lots to be turned into individual plots for community gardeners. Other lots have been beautified and made into "pocket parks" with simple wooden benches. Although LCLT owns none of the seven lots its members work, it is in the process of acquiring two of them through a tax foreclosure process. Two of the other lots are owned by the City, which has given LCLT permission to cultivate them. LCLT has been working with Neighborhood Resources, Inc., a local intermediary organization for neighborhood groups, to acquire basic donations of materials and money to carry out its work. LCLT is run by a small committee of lead gardeners but has neither incorporated nor set up a bank account. The intake lists the names and addresses of each of the lead gardeners, gives one of these addresses as the contact for the organization, but also references a new post office box address where the group is receiving its mail.
>
> The leadership of LCLT is considering the creation of a nonprofit corporation and the submission of an application to the IRS for 501(c)(3) tax-exemption recognition. One of the lead gardeners wants to know the advantages and disadvantages of LCLT becoming a nonprofit corporation before moving forward.

One way to respond to the question of whether or not LCLT should form a separate nonprofit corporation is by taking each of those three words—"separate", "nonprofit", and "corporation"—as a question to be answered.

Be prepared to discuss in class what you would expect to recommend to LCLT (based on the information you already have) as to the three issues enumerated below and what questions you would ask in the interview to help you be more confident in your actual recommendation. What are the pros and cons of each option that you will present? Do any of the issues involve considerations clearly within a lawyer's area of expertise? Is one or more of the issues more dependent on the client founders' preferences?

1) Separate—Should LCLT have its own entity as opposed to becoming (or remaining) part of an existing entity?

2) Nonprofit—Should the entity be organized so as to dedicate its excess revenue to the organization's stated purposes and to prevent distribution of any of it to those involved in the venture?

3) Corporation—Should the entity be one that provides liability limitation protection to those involved in the venture?

C. COMPLETE AND CORRECT ORGANIZATIONAL DOCUMENTS

For this section, let us assume that the founders of LCLT, Inc. have decided to form a nonprofit corporation that will seek recognition as tax-exempt under § 501(c)(3). We can now explore how the three entity benefits that shaped the discussion of choice of form now contribute to the outlining and checklist. In showing how each document's questions are listed and their possible answers outline, you will see how your understanding of these general client objectives work with statutory research and client inquiry to flesh out the checklist and outline process.

As a corporation, LCLT, Inc. will provide its constituents with full **liability risk protection.** The articles of incorporation as the corporate charter document unlocks this benefit. Basically, as long as the articles are accepted for filing and the incorporation process is completed at the organizational meeting that follows, LCLT will receive its liability limitation. The costs of filing and maintaining the simple formalities needed to preserve the liability shield will be part of your counseling on this aspect of choice of form, as even the clearest advantages have some cost associated with them.

As will be seen in the next chapter, a complete list of the issues for this charter document will be driven by consulting the relevant section of the nonprofit incorporation statute. The specific section on the content of the articles of incorporation will spell out exact what questions the statute mandates be answered by the articles. From there, you will consider what other information, though not required, should still be included in this publicly filed foundational document.

The client's need for **favorable tax treatment** will play a large role not only in the inclusion of a purposes provision in the articles but also in its content. Internal Revenue Code § 501(c)(3) limits its benefits to nonprofits that have purposes limited to those named in that section. The Internal Revenue Service looks to the purposes clause of an organization's articles to determine if that aspect of the organizational test has been met. Looking to the outlining of charter documents more broadly, the answers to the questions that must and should be addressed will largely come from simple factual questions posed to the client founders but will sometimes involve more complex considerations related to **favorable tax treatment** or, in the case of the Delaware for-profit corporation, **equity structure.**

As a separate entity, LCLT, Inc. will need an **effective decision-making structure.** Virtually every fundamental governance question will be addressed in the bylaws. Thus, to come up with a list of all the components of this new organization's decision-making apparatus, the list will start by identifying the various leadership roles and move on to the processes for identifying and empowering them to manage the affairs of the new entity. The state nonprofit statute will get you started by identifying the directors and certain officer roles as indispensable. But even the checklist for nonprofit bylaws can be generated from scratch only by reflection on all the various decision makers and the procedures by which they are identified and the processes through which they contribute to organization leadership.

Creating the outline for nonprofit bylaws, as well as for other governance documents, will require you to draw upon your understanding of decision making, the information you have gained about your client's decision-making preferences, and the mandatory and default governance provisions in your state's nonprofit corporation statute. The nonprofit bylaws chapter will guide you on all three. It will explore the various components of effective decision making, noting that the core benefit involves costs in the form of time and resources. It will list key interview questions to use to find out what costs and other aspects of good decision making are especially important to your client. Finally, the outline section of Chapter 3 will illustrate how widely adopted provisions of the Revised Model Nonprofit Corporation Act constrain and suggest options for nonprofit bylaws provisions.

As a charitable nonprofit, LCLT, Inc. will want to seek the most **favorable tax treatment** possible. To gain not only exemption from taxes but also the ability to receive tax-deductible contributions, LCLT, Inc. will need to meet the requirements of IRC § 501(c)(3). While some bylaws provisions will be affected by these rules, the articles of incorporation must have a purposes section and a dissolution clause that will each pass the strict requirements that the IRS imposes on charitable nonprofits.

These three substantive goals of most effective **decision-making structure**, most **favorable tax treatment** and full **liability risk**

protection combine to support the overarching substantive goal for creating any new entity: to structure it to be the most effective vehicle possible for holding and using resources for the relevant productive activities.

CHAPTER 2

DRAFTING NONPROFIT ARTICLES OF INCORPORATION

■ ■ ■

No drafting project you will ever undertake is likely to be more straightforward than the creation of a charter document for a new organization. One client objective takes precedence above all others: obtaining liability risk protection. Without exception, state law clearly states what you must do to achieve your client's goal. Most states go further and provide an approved, pre-printed form that identifies all the information required. Most of these templates also include space for optional provisions. About half of the states in the U.S. closely follow the structure and provision language in the Revised Model Nonprofit Corporation Act (RMNCA) promulgated in the late 1980s. For illustration purposes, this chapter and the one that follows will refer to RMNCA provisions noting those that have not been widely adopted. [1]

A. CREATING THE CHECKLIST—WHAT HAS TO GO IN AND WHAT SHOULD GO IN

For nonprofit articles as for any charter document, the checklist focuses on the elements essential to get the filing accepted. No part of the list of issues to be addressed is more important than the section that lists the questions that must be answered. But you should also consider what issues, if any, the articles should speak to beyond what the law might require. Likewise, you would do well to identify those questions that could be answered in the articles but may be better addressed elsewhere, such as in another document or by the statute itself.

1. THE ISSUES THAT SHALL BE ADDRESSED IN THE ARTICLES

RMNCA § 2.02(a) provides the following list of required elements for nonprofit articles:

(1) a corporate name for the corporation that satisfies the requirements of section 4.01

[1] Relevant provisions of the RMNCA are reprinted in the Appendix.

(2) one of the following statements:

(i) This corporation is a public benefit corporation.

(ii) This corporation is a mutual benefit corporation.

(iii) This corporation is a religious corporation;

(3) the street address of the corporation's initial registered office and the name of its initial registered agent at that office;

(4) the name and address of each incorporator;

(5) whether or not the corporation will have members; and

(6) provisions not inconsistent with law regarding the distribution of assets on dissolution.

Even states that have not adopted the RMNCA have a list of required articles elements very similar to the one set out above. Those states and many of the ones that have adopted the RMNCA, however, do not follow (a)(2)'s requirement that articles choose one of the three nonprofit corporation types.

Take note that the RMNCA list above does not include a statement of the nonprofit's purposes. Many nonprofit corporation statutes do require this language. Many more states offer approved nonprofit articles forms that include a space for purposes even though their statutes do not require that it be completed. When a business entity does not address a question in its organizational documents, it is relying on the statute to provide an answer.

Many nonprofits wish to be recognized as tax-exempt pursuant to § 501(c)(3) of the Internal Revenue Code. To do so, they must pass that federal tax statute's organizational test, which requires that the corporation's purposes be limited to those covered by § 501(c)(3). These organizations' articles cannot be silent and rely on the broad range of purposes permitted by the state nonprofit corporation statute. A nonprofit that wishes to be recognized under §501(c)(3) as a tax-exempt organization must have a purposes clause limited to those purposes listed in the federal statute. Likewise, any dissolution clause in the articles must also comply with the §501(c)(3) organizational test. [2] Because the dissolution clause is already required by the RMNCA, this federal law requirement for a conforming purposes clause provides the only legally mandated addition to the "SHALL set forth" list of your state statute.

[2] The Appendix to this book includes an excerpt from Treasury Regulation § 1.501(c)(3)–1 setting out the requirements of the organizational test under IRC § 501(c)(3).

2. THE ISSUES THAT MAY AND SHOULD BE ADDRESSED IN THE ARTICLES

Unlike bylaws, articles of incorporation are filed with the state and are publicly accessible. Sometimes that visibility causes certain provisions that would normally be in the bylaws to be included in the articles instead. Even if your state statute does not require (as the RMNCA does not) that the articles provide the address of the organization's principal office, many clients see the benefit of including that information, especially if it is a different address from that of the registered agent. Other provisions are included in the articles instead of the bylaws because the former document is somewhat more difficult to amend. Even, as is often the case, the decision-making procedure for changing the bylaws is the same as the one amending the articles, any change to the articles is effective only once it has been accepted for filing.

Finally, some provisions will be effective if included in the articles but will be invalid if found only in the bylaws. The primary example is a provision that delegates some or all of the power and responsibilities of the board of directors to one or more persons. [3] As will be more fully explored in the next chapter, a state's nonprofit corporation statute has many provisions that govern nonprofits as long as those nonprofits do not adopt contrary rules in their organizational documents. These statutory sections are called default provisions. Most default provisions begin with the phrase "Unless its bylaws or articles of incorporation provide otherwise, ..." But some leave out "its bylaws or" restricting the power to modify the statutory provision to the articles alone. Common examples include any modification of the directors' power to amend the articles and any downward departure from the indemnification provisions found in the state statute.

B. CREATING THE OUTLINE

1. NOT JUST ALL THE RIGHT QUESTIONS, BUT ALSO THE RIGHT ANSWERS

Of the questions that we know must be answered, many seem to have easy answers. With just the various names and addresses required, you will have half of what is needed. But, even with these simple items, you do well to understand the legal parameters for acceptable answers and what issues are worth exploring before the answers are filed. The chart below summarizes these limits and guides client dialogue over each of the items on the RMNCA nonprofit articles checklist.

---

[3] See RMNCA § 8.01(c).

Checklist Item	RMNCA/501(c)(3) limits	Client Inquiry
Entity Name	Distinct; cannot be misleading[4]	Trademark goals:
Nature of Corporation	Should fit purposes	
Registered Agent & Address	Must be the in-state business office address of state resident	Does client know someone willing to provide address?
Incorporator(s) name(s) & address(es)	Any individual or entity	Counseling as to role in incorporation process
Members?	Various governance provisions affected by the presence of members	Will subsequent directors be elected by directors or others?
Post-dissolution asset distribution	If tax-exempt, clause must limit distribution	
Purposes	If to be tax-exempt, limited to those purposes	Limit purposes? Specify purposes?
Principal Office Address		
Amendment	Default: Board majority	

Nearly every question posed by a state's nonprofit articles of incorporation form can be answered by relaying it to the founders of the organization. Some, such as the name and business address of the in-state person or entity that will act as registered agent, may be more difficult to answer than others. But two issues definitely warrant some further explanation. A relatively small number of states follow the RMNCA in requiring that new corporations choose from among three options the type of nonprofit being formed. To choose the correct one, the client founders may need to know a little about how the options listed differ from one another. Religious corporations are not restricted to houses of worship but include any nonprofit formed for religious purposes. A public benefit corporation is any nonprofit that qualifies for tax exemption under § 501(c)(3) not already covered by the former category. Likewise, a mutual benefit corporation is any nonprofit not covered by one of the other two categories.

The other issue presented by the RMNCA and many states' nonprofit corporation statutes deals with the involvement of members in nonprofit governance. Corporation statutes mandate the existence of a board of

[4] The RMNCA does not require that the legal names of nonprofit corporations include corporate identifiers such as "Corporation", "Incorporated" or their abbreviations, but many states do require them.

directors and vest governance authority over the entity in that board. By declaring a role for members in its articles, a nonprofit corporation allows for persons other than directors to take part in the control of the entity. Members' responsibilities, set forth in the bylaws, consist of electing all or part of the board and often approving any changes to the articles and bylaws.[5] Most charitable nonprofits in the United States are not membership nonprofits. They are run by self-selecting boards, which look to existing board members to elect new directors. But certain nonprofits—such as resident associations, labor unions, religious bodies, and political organizations—that act in a representative capacity may benefit from forming as membership corporations.[6]

DISCUSSION QUESTION 2–A

For each of the following nonprofits briefly described below, explain which type of nonprofit corporation you would recommend the founders select in the articles and whether or not the corporation will have members:

1) A neighborhood residents' association and a nearby church wish to work together to create a community development corporation that will work to build affordable housing, promote opportunities for youth and reduce crime in this economically distressed inner-city community.

2) A small group of concerned citizens wishes to raise money to help low-income pet owners pay for necessary veterinary services.

3) Several cycling enthusiasts want to form a club that will promote development and use of bike trails in their metropolitan area.

---

2. THE ISSUES THAT MAY BE ADDRESSED IN THE ARTICLES BUT PROBABLY SHOULD BE ADDRESSED ELSEWHERE

In general, articles should be simple and straightforward. You should be careful to avoid provisions that your client will need to change in the future. Some required items, such as registered agent information, may need to be updated as circumstances change. States typically allow such information updates to be filed without a formal adoption process and sometimes without charge.

---

5 RMNCA § 1.40(21) defines "member" as a person having "the right to vote for the election of a director or directors."

6 The discussion of articles in this chapter and of bylaws in the next will focus on nonprofit corporations that do not have members.

Among the most common optional sections found in nonprofit articles are powers and prohibited activities. For a description of corporate powers, entities increasingly rely on the statute. RMNCA § 3.02 lists sixteen specific corporate powers and adds "to do all things necessary or convenient, not inconsistent with law, to further the activities and affairs of the corporation." This residual clause adds any power legally available to the corporation. Given the completeness of the RMNCA and many other statutory approaches, the principal reason for including a powers provision in the client's articles might be to prohibit the corporation from engaging in certain actions.

§ 501(c)(3) of the Internal Revenue Code not only restricts the purposes of nonprofits seeking tax-exemption under it but also prohibits such charities from engaging in certain activities, such as supporting or opposing candidate campaigns for public office. A prohibited activities provision is fairly common in 501(c)(3) entity articles even though it is not required by state or federal law. Federal tax law merely prohibits any provision in the articles from expressly empowering the organization to engage in a limited or prohibited activity to a degree that would violate the restrictions that come with its tax-exempt status. Nothing, however, requires that the articles repeat the prohibitions already in the statues and regulations. [7] Restating existing law in articles may remind organizational leaders of such legal obligations, but since bylaws are more frequently consulted they may provide a better opportunity for continuing instruction.

DISCUSSION QUESTION 2–B

Find the statutory provision for your jurisdiction that corresponds to RMNCA § 2.02(a) (reprinted above). How does its list of required elements in nonprofit articles of incorporation differ from the one in the provision above? Now, find the form your state provides for nonprofit articles of incorporation. How does it differ from the sample form reprinted below that Indiana uses? (Indiana's statutory counterpart is identical to RMNCA § 2.02(a)) Which parts of each form are not mandated by that state's statutory provision? Would you fill them out anyway? in all cases? in some cases? If the latter, which cases?

[7] Before including such a provision in your articles, take care to make sure that it does not unduly restrict your organization. Some versions of the prohibited activities provision limit "attempting to influence legislation" to "no substantial part" without reference to the corporation's ability to take advantage of an alternative test for that restriction under IRC § 501(h). Unfortunately, the prohibited activities provision offered by the IRS itself is defective in this way. See Internal Revenue Service, Suggested Language for Corporations and Associations (per Publication 557), available at https://www.irs.gov/charities-non-profits/suggested-language-for-corporations-and-associations. If used at all, the sentence in the Fifth Article there that begins "No substantial part . . ." should be amended to begin "Except as authorized by section 501(h) of the Internal Revenue Code, no substantial part . . ."

Articles of Incorporation for a Nonprofit Corporation

Reset Form

ARTICLES OF INCORPORATION FOR A NONPROFIT CORPORATION
State Form 4162 (R13 / 5-14) Corporate Form No. 364-1 (October 1984)
Approved by State Board of Accounts, 2014

CONNIE LAWSON
SECRETARY OF STATE
BUSINESS SERVICES DIVISION
302 W. Washington Street, E018
Indianapolis, IN 46204
Telephone: (317) 232-6576

INSTRUCTIONS:
1. Use 8 1/2" x 11" white paper for attachments.
2. Present original and one copy to the address in the upper right corner of this form.
3. Please TYPE or PRINT in INK.
4. Please visit our office at www.sos.in.gov.
5. Make check or money order payable to Secretary of State.

Indiana Code 23-17-3-2
FILING FEE: $30.00

NOTES:
1. Nonprofit corporations must qualify with the Internal Revenue Service and the Indiana Department of Revenue. It is strongly suggested you do not complete or file this form before contacting both agencies.

2. Article VII must be completed appropriately. Please see (1) above.

ARTICLES OF INCORPORATION

The undersigned, desiring to form a Corporation *(hereinafter referred to as the "Corporation")* pursuant to the provisions of the Indiana Nonprofit Corporation Act of 1991 *(hereinafter referred to as the "Act")*, execute the following Articles of Incorporation:

ARTICLE I - NAME AND PRINCIPAL OFFICE

Name of the Corporation: *(The name must include the word Corporation, Incorporated, Limited, Company or an abbreviation thereof.)*

Address of Principal Office *(number and street)*	City	State	ZIP code

ARTICLE II - PURPOSE

The purposes for which the Corporation is formed are:
Specific language is required by the IRS in this article in order to be approved for 501(c) status. Contact the IRS for assistance.

ARTICLE III - TYPE OF CORPORATION *(CHECK ONLY ONE)*

The Corporation is a:

☐ public benefit corporation, which is organized for a public or charitable purpose;
☐ religious corporation, which is organized primarily or exclusively for religious purposes; or
☐ mutual benefit corporation *(all others)*.

ARTICLE IV - REGISTERED AGENT AND REGISTERED OFFICE

Registered Agent: The name and street address of the Corporation's Registered Agent and Registered Office for service of process are:

Name of Registered Agent *(cannot be the corporation itself.)*

Address of Registered Office *(number and street) (PO Box not accepted)*	City	State	ZIP code
		IN	

Required:

☐ By checking the box, the Signator(s) represents that the registered agent named in the application has consented to the appointment of registered agent.

ARTICLE V - MEMBERSHIP

Indicate if Corporation will have members:
☐ Yes ☐ No

(Continued on the reverse side)

ARTICLE VI - INCORPORATOR(S)
(INCORPORATORS MAY NEVER BE AMENDED)

Name(s) and address(es) of the incorporator(s) is/are as follows:

Name	Number and Street or Building	City	State	ZIP code

ARTICLE VII - DISTRIBUTION OF ASSETS ON DISSOLUTION OR FINAL LIQUIDATION

Refer to Indiana Code 23-17-22-5 for permitted activities following Dissolution:
Specific language is required by the IRS in this article in order to be approved for 501(c) status. Contact the IRS for assistance.

* Please note this section must be completed.

ARTICLE VIII - INCORPORATOR(S)
(INCORPORATORS MAY NEVER BE AMENDED)

In witness whereof, the undersigned incorporator(s) of said Corporation execute(s) this document, and verify(ies) subject to penalties of perjury that the facts contained herein are true this ________ day of ________, 20____.

Signature	Printed name
Signature	Printed name
Signature	Printed name

This instrument was prepared by: *(name)*			
Address *(number and street or building)*	City	State	ZIP code

C. WRITING OUT THE PROVISIONS

If your client's articles are restricted to the sections listed above, only two will require you to write sentences: the dissolution clause and the purposes section. For tax-exempt organizations, the content of these provisions is restricted by the relevant section of the Internal Revenue Code. Although a handful of states have statutory default provisions for distribution upon dissolution that satisfy the requirements of the 501(c)(3) organizational test, most articles will not be to rely on the statute. When trying to draft language to match a regulatory requirement, the best approach often it to track the actual language of the law in your provision. For dissolution clauses, the IRS offers a form provision that does just that:

> Upon the dissolution of this organization, assets shall be distributed for one or more exempt purposes within the meaning of section 501(c)(3) of the Internal Revenue Code, or corresponding section of any future federal tax code, or shall be distributed to the federal government, or to a state or local government, for a public purpose. Any such assets not so disposed of shall be disposed of by a Court of Competent Jurisdiction of the county in which the principal office of the corporation is then located, exclusively for such purposes or to such organization or organizations, as said Court shall determine, which are organized and operated exclusively for such purposes. [8]

If you put this provision into your articles, you do so with complete confidence that it will pass the § 501(c)(3) organizational test.

For purposes, this one-size-fits-all approach may not work. You could simply state that the organization's purposes are any and all § 501(c)(3) purposes. This approach would pose no problems under the § 501(c)(3) test. The fact that the organization would not pursue many of its permitted purposes also poses no legal problem.

But your client may wish to limit its purposes. Why would it want to do so? Most nonprofit enterprises benefit from having a well-defined mission. But that does not mean the business entity must be constrained to following that focused operational plan. Mission statements frequently define not only goals but the means of achieving them. It may be difficult and problematic to draft a purposes clause that tries to achieve that same level of specificity. Nevertheless, some nonprofits wish to make a public commitment that their resource will used for some § 501(c)(3) purposes and not others. Conservations organizations such as the Liberty City Land Trust may wish to let potential donors know that any land given to them will be used to promote the environment rather than to support affordable housing or any other worthy cause. If an entity is to limit its purposes, then the articles must specify those purposes.

IRC § 501(c)(3), together with its attendant regulations and administrative materials, provides language that can be tracked when articulating particular purposes. If you are incorporating a community development organization, you will see that the regulatory definition of "charitable" includes "combatting community deterioration" and "relief of the poor and distressed or underprivileged." Neither of these purposes will ever cause an organization's purposes clause to fail the § 501(c)(3) organizational test.

---

[8] Internal Revenue Service, Suggested Language for Corporations and Associations (per Publication 557), available at https://www.irs.gov/charities-non-profits/suggested-language-for-corporations-and-associations.

If your client is best served by specifying its primary purposes but not restricting itself to those purposes, a residual clause may be the best solution. After listing purposes that clearly fit within the statute, the last item might allow "any other purpose within the meaning of Section of 501(c)(3) of the Internal Revenue Code . . ."

CHAPTER 3

DRAFTING NONPROFIT CORPORATION BYLAWS

■ ■ ■

Just as the core benefit associated with articles of incorporation was the liability risk protection that state law offers, bylaws provide the structure for effective decision making so central to a nonprofit's ability to carry out its mission. To review a form set of bylaws with a critical eye, you should first look at how the objective of decision making combines with relevant law to generate the checklist. Articles of incorporation provided a simple benefit, but effective decision making is a more complex goal than liability limitation protection. The corporate veil, which protects principals from having to pay the debts of the entity, is either there, or it is not. It works the same way for all incorporated businesses and nonprofits. But effectiveness in decision making has multiple elements:

- fairness
- accountability
- timeliness
- risk protection
- resiliency in times of strong conflict
- inclusivity
- commitment to excellence
- transparency
- confidentiality
- resistance to corruption
- accurate identification of issues
- mission focus
- access to relevant information
- communication among decision makers.

While these are hardly exclusive of one another, some may be more important to a client than others. Just as the client goal identified with bylaws is complex, so too is the law related to corporate governance.

In Chapter 5, you will learn that law defining the governance of limited liability companies is relatively simple and very flexible. But the sets of statutes that authorize the creation of corporations are noticeably stricter and more complex.

A. CREATING THE CHECKLIST—COMPLETE

1. WHAT DECISION-MAKING AND OTHER LEADERSHIP ROLES WILL THERE BE

To construct a **complete checklist** for nonprofit bylaws, you first need to understand the framework of nonprofit decision making. Decision making in the nonprofit corporation involves governance, corporate administration, and management. State law makes the directors responsible for the governance of the corporation. The directors are ultimately responsible for the nonprofit's policies and major decisions. Like the legislative branch in government, they deliberate, make policy, and oversee the functioning of the organization's operations. The directors' decisions set the program focus of the nonprofit and the budget under which it operates. The management of day-to-day and even month-to-month operations, on the other hand, is usually handled by the hired staff led by the Executive Director, who is hired by the board but normally takes the lead in hiring the rest of the staff.

To fulfill its governance role, the board needs certain individuals to perform certain administrative functions. The board needs a leader to preside at meetings and carry out authorized actions in between sessions. If the board has not delegated management functions to an Executive Director, then this elected executive role can be quite substantial. The board also needs someone to keep the corporate records and someone else to oversee the nonprofit's finances. These three corporate administrative roles are carried out by the three most commonly elected officers: the president, secretary, and treasurer respectively.

While bylaws typically have little to say about management, they set out every aspect of governance and corporate administration. If the governance process goes beyond the board of directors, then the bylaws will be more complex. Those organizations that have some or all of the directors elected by members will need procedures regarding membership, including other governance decisions that might require membership approval. Boards can delegate deliberative and oversight work to committees. Nonprofits sometimes create advisory boards that have no official governance role but volunteer helpful expertise.

The table at the top of the facing page provides a summary of the basic nonprofit corporation structure:

Authority Type	Description	Persons Responsible
Governance	Sets all policies, authorizes all programs and budget, oversees management	Directors
Corporate Administration	Takes on tasks needed for Board to function	Officers
Management	Day-to-day decisions and execution of policy	Directors usually delegate to Staff or Officers

Our checklist then begins with a list of those involved in the decision-making structure of the nonprofit:

- Directors
- Officers
- Executive Director (if any)
- Members (if any)
- Committees (if any)
- Advisory Board (if any)

Even this simple list including possible roles for members, committees and paid staff can help you re-evaluate your interview questions to see if you are asking your client contacts the kinds of questions about the leadership resources and the finances to help you understand whether the bylaws will provide for any or all of the optional roles listed.

2. HOW DECISION MAKERS AND OTHER LEADERS IN EACH CLASS WILL BE IDENTIFIED

For the directors and officers in particular, the bylaws will need to address a range of questions as to how the roles are filled. For instance, for directors, the bylaws should address:

- Numbers of positions on the Board
- Qualifications for serving as a Director
- Selection: Nomination, Election & Vacancies
- Terms
- Removal

The optional roles can also be created with the same level of detail. But even bylaws that reference the creation of committees, for instance, frequently will simply authorize the board to oversee their formation. If formal structures are needed later, a governance document other than bylaws, such as a committee charter, can be drafted.

3. HOW DECISION MAKERS WILL MAKE THEIR DECISIONS

Each role will also generate questions as to how they fulfill their roles. For directors, this involves:

- Duties
- Meetings
    - Frequency
    - Notice
    - Quorum
    - Voting
    - Conflict of Interest
- Executive & other committees
- Action without meeting

When developing the list for other roles, you might find the lists for other deliberative roles, such as members, to be remarkably similar to the one above, while the checklist for officers may begin and end with "Duties."

Reflecting on how nonprofits work generally will only bring you so far in filling out your checklist. To be sure you have covered all the bases, you need to consult the relevant statute as to issues that must be addressed in the bylaws. RMNCA § 8.05(a), for instance, requires that nonprofit bylaws specify the terms that director serve, if that issue is not already covered in the articles of incorporation.

Bylaws generally do not legislate how management runs the nonprofit on a day-to-day basis. Who reports to whom, who in the community qualifies for what kind of assistance, and how the organization pursues resources are all core policy questions. Each matters enough to be brought before the organization's board of directors for review and approval. But the answers required by them are too detailed and too frequently in need of updating for them to be addressed in a foundational document. Instead, these and other important guidance are more likely to find their way into a policies and procedures manual or an employee handbook.

EXERCISE 3–1

For each of the nonprofits described below, identify which types of leadership roles should be established in the corporation bylaws. For each group of decision makers, list any issues that the bylaws will need to resolve regarding their selection and how they make their decisions.

a) A neighborhood church and the neighborhood residents' association wish to work together to create a community development corporation that will work to build affordable housing, promote opportunities for youth and reduce crime in this economically distressed inner-city community.

b) A small group of concerned citizens wishes to raise money to help low-income pet owners pay for necessary veterinary services.

c) Several cycling enthusiasts want to form a club that will promote development and use of bike trails in their metropolitan area.

---

4. COMPLETING THE CHECKLIST—OTHER ISSUES

Although the core processes of governance, administration and management constitute the focus of bylaws provisions as a whole, there are a sizeable number of ancillary issues covered in bylaws. These other provisions can be grouped into five categories:

- Preliminaries: Reiteration of Articles or law from statute:
  - Name
  - Office Address
  - Purposes
  - Governance vested in Board (often left to statute)
- Board Policies:
  - Indemnification
  - Compensation
  - Prohibited Transactions (often left to articles or statute)
- Records:
  - Fiscal Year
  - Books/Records
  - Budget/Annual Reports
  - Bank Account
- Corporate Policies:
  - Nondiscrimination
  - Other core policies
- General:
  - Amendment of Bylaws (no need to state governing law)

- Effective Date
- Severability/Savings

B. CREATING THE OUTLINE—CORRECT . . . AND READABLE

1. GETTING THE ORDER RIGHT

To outline the bylaws for a readable draft, the checklist items must be arranged in a sensible order and the provisions must be organized into appropriate sections and subsections. As with contracts, bylaws should start with the fundamentals and end with the boilerplate. Looking at who will select whom among the decision makers can give a chronological order to the bylaws:

- Preliminaries
- Membership & Meetings of Members (if applicable)
- Directors
- Meetings of Directors
- Officers
  - Elected
  - Appointed (Staff Leadership hired directly by Board)
- Committees
- Advisory Board (if any)
- Board Policies
- Books and Records
- Corporate Policies
- General Provisions

As you sketch out the provisions, you will get a sense of which subjects should be separated from one another into different sections just as you see the need to break a prose discussion into several paragraphs. Likewise, some sections will be so complex as to justify further subdivision into subsections. By organizing provisions that clearly belong together in this way, you can create a hierarchy of sections and subsections, constructing a document that is not only easier to read from start to finish but also better suited for quick consultation on a particular issue.

2. ANSWERING THE CHECKLIST QUESTIONS: KNOWING THE LAW

The next step, then, is to transform this comprehensive checklist into an **outline** that will lead to a **readable** draft that is **correct** in that it both complies with relevant law and meets the client's substantive goal of having an effective governance structure. Knowledge of state law is crucial to completing the outline. The drafter cannot know the substantive answers to the checklist questions without understanding the parameters set out in the statute. The bylaws provisions cannot contradict either the law or the corporation's articles. In sketching out the substance of your bylaws provisions, you will want to make sure that they will not be invalid under your state's nonprofit corporation statute. When drafting bylaws sections, you do not want to insert (or fail to fix) a provision that contradicts a mandatory rule in the state nonprofit corporation statute.

The table below summarizes those provisions of the RMNCA that are relevant to the most common bylaws checklist issues. The first column includes the specific RMNCA reference sketched out in the two columns to the right. The middle column offers captions for those mandatory provisions in the RMNCA that are commonly adopted. These provisions apply to all nonprofits incorporated in the jurisdiction regardless of what the articles or bylaws might provide. The table's third column lists provisions that create rules for nonprofit corporations "unless the articles or bylaws provide otherwise." These are called default rules because they apply when the corporation's documents are silent on the issue.

Notice that some of the mandatory rules actually contain the verb "may" in them. These provisions in the center column are all mandatory in the sense that they cannot be changed by the bylaws, but some of the rules, such as the ones dealing with resignation, tell people what they may do as opposed to what they must or must not do. Similarly, some of the default rules, such as those dealing with board meeting quorum and notice of special meetings, impose requirements on the corporation, but only if the governing documents do not override them. These mandating default rules are listed **in bold** because you may want to give particular attention to the requirements that you can change.

Checklist	Mandatory Provision	Default Provision
Directors		
Duties—§8.30	Statutory version of Bus. Judg. Rule	
Number—§8.03	Must have ≥ 3 (or ≥ 1 in many states)	Range permitted w/ # set by board
Term—§8.05	≤ 5 years	1 year
Removal—§8.08	Board may w/o cause by . . .	. . . 2/3 vote (or greater)
Resignation—§8.07	May w/ written notice	
Vacs.—§8.11		Board may fill vacancies
Officers		
Req'd?—§8.40	Must have Secretary	Pres., Treas. & Sec.
Removal—§8.43	Board may w/o cause	
Resignation—§8.43	May w/ notice	
Committees—§8.25	Must include ≥ 2 dirs. (or 1 in many states); may not approve dissolution or fill vacancies	May be created only by board of directors
Board Meetings		
Action w/o Meeting—§8.21		Any action if approved in writing by all directors
Call & Notice—§8.22		**Sp. mtgs.: ≥ 2 days' notice; Pres. or 20% directors may call**
Waiver of Notice—§8.23	Written always possible; actual attendance at meeting w/o objection = waiver	
Quorum—§8.24	Must be ≥ greater of 2 or 1/3 of directors in office	**Majority of directors in office**
Voting—§8.24		Majority of directors present
Records—§16.01	Various provisions about what to keep and where	
D&O pay—§8.12		Board may set compensation
Indemnification—§8.51	May indemnify if acted in good faith & reas. believed conduct was in org's best interests; may not if found liable	**Shall indemnify director successful on merits in defending lawsuit (unless articles)**
Conflicts of Interest—§8.31	*No required process but safe harbor protecting validity of action if standard C of I procedure is followed*	

EXERCISE 3–2

Consult your state's nonprofit corporation statute and see what, if any, mandatory provision you can find on the following three subjects:

a) Minimum number of directors

b) Quorum for meetings of the board of directors

c) Indemnification

Make your own table with just those mandatory provisions and use it when adapting a bylaws form for use in your state.

Some statutory sections, like those dealing with conflicted directors, may not be drafted in the same way as mandating rules or prohibitions, which respectively feature verb phrases beginning with "shall" or "shall not." RMNCA § 8.31 does not explicitly mandate the exclusion from a board decision of a director who has a personal financial interest in the outcome of that decision. Instead, it states the board may legitimately make that decision after learning of the director's conflict as long as every director approving the action believes it to be in the best interests of the nonprofit. As written, the statute provides a "safe harbor" for board decisions involving conflicts of interest. That is, the statute describes a process that is definitely legitimate without declaring that there are no other valid ways of proceeding. Typical conflicts of interest provisions are even more restrictive than the statute cited. They generally subject a director who has disclosed a conflict of interest to recusal from deliberating or voting on the matter. In any case, before drafting a conflicts of interest provision for your nonprofit client, you need to know what the statute has to say on the issue.

Since a default provision can be overridden by a bylaws provision addressing the same issue, it may not seem worthwhile knowing any default provision's content once you have decided to address that issue in your bylaws. But knowing the default provision can offer you an initial option for your outline. Ultimately, you may reject in favor of one or more alternatives that you think will better meet your client's needs. But the default provision is worth consulting as a middle-of-the road norm.

Looking at it from the other side, discovering a default provision that works well for your client may lead you to the conclusion that you should not address the issue in your bylaws. After all, the default provision will still apply even if you do not recite it in your bylaws. Keep in mind, however, that you chose to include that issue, be it quorum or the number of director on the board, in your checklist because you felt it a vital part of the governance structure. If that is so, you not only want a clear answer to the question, but you also want that answer to readily available to the leaders of your client organization. Thus, you're not likely to want to leave the question unanswered in the bylaws nor do you want to simply refer your client's leadership to the statute, which the client's leadership may not find accessible.

3. ANSWERING THE CHECKLIST QUESTIONS: KNOWING THE CLIENT'S NEEDS

Once we understand the limits that the nonprofit corporation statute places on the governance provisions in the bylaws, we are free to explore the various permissible options that might best suit the client's approach to decision making. By recalling the elements of effective decision making listed at the beginning of the chapter, we have a sense of the governance concerns common to most clients:

- fairness
- accountability
- timeliness
- risk protection
- resiliency in times of strong conflict
- inclusivity
- commitment to excellence
- transparency
- confidentiality
- resistance to corruption
- accurate identification of issues
- mission focus
- access to relevant information
- communication among decision makers

DISCUSSION QUESTION 3–A

Some of these aspects of good corporate decision making are so fundamental that they are relevant to nearly every core bylaws provision. Others, while still important, are promoted by just one or two provisions in the typical set of nonprofit bylaws. Upon review of the list above, you may even be able to identify one or two items that are not addressed at all by most sets of bylaws. In preparation for classroom discussion, sort the list above into each of these three categories: fundamental, specific, and unaddressed.

DISCUSSION QUESTION 3–B

Consider if any of the identified aspects of good decision making are in tension with other qualities listed. See if you can find at least one item listed above that could be promoted only to the detriment of some other item on the same list. Which sections of the bylaws would be implicated in balancing these aspects of good governance? What would you want to know about your client before creating and presenting options?

Shaping the process of corporate decision making will require you to focus on your client's own approach to communication among its leadership even as you are aware of the constraints imposed and suggestions offered by the statute. Since the law also addresses corporate decisions made for improper reasons, it may be worthwhile not only to inform your client leaders about how civil rights laws constrain their decision making but also to explore any discrimination policy commitments they wish to adopt freely.

Beyond those characteristics that you believe every nonprofit would seek out as part of its quest for good governance, there may be bylaws choices that a new nonprofit will make based on its particular limits or traits. Every benefit has its costs, and effective decision making is no different. Good governance, even when optimally structured, requires time, communication and information gathering. Counseling your client on the content of the bylaws means helping them compare the costs and benefits of certain provisions. This comparison of alternate approaches to a specific section of the bylaws is best handled at the outline stage of the drafting. The different options you provide a nonprofit with regard to certain provisions may be shaped by what you have learned about the client's resources and the way its leaders communicate with one another.

DISCUSSION QUESTION 3–C

Review the following connections made between facts learned about the client and sections of the bylaws that may be impacted by those realities. In class, discuss how the former might shape the provisions listed.

1) The client's volunteer resources ⟶ # of directors, officer roles, committees
2) The leaders' preferred modes of and times for communicating ⟶ meetings, action without meetings
3) Size of the organization's anticipated budget ⟶ treasurer, budget/annual report, bank account, conflicts of interest

---

As fiduciaries to the corporation, nonprofit directors and officers have a duty not to abuse their authority to benefit themselves personally. Both state law and federal tax law provide sanctions and remedies that respond to such self-dealing. A thoughtful approach to corporate governance, however, is not limited to these reactive measures. Conflict of interest provisions proactively promote the duty of loyalty by procedurally isolating directors with personal interests in a particular corporate matter from deliberations and decisions regarding it. Typically, the process requires that a director or officer disclose any personal interest in a corporate matter, which disclosure is followed by a decision as to whether the disclosing director or officer should be excluded from any discussion or vote on the matter. Following these recusal procedures does not guarantee compliance with federal tax law, which requires that directors and officers never receive undue benefits from the organization no matter who approved them. But, RMNCA § 8.31 describes a method of making decisions free of conflicts of interest sufficiently robust to prevent those corporate decisions from being overturned as tainted by self-dealing.

EXERCISE 3–3

a) Review RMNCA § 8.31 and outline a conflicts of interest provision that, if followed, would take advantage of the safe harbor offered.

b) How would a bylaws quorum provision be applied to a vote in which multiple directors recused themselves? Does RMNCA § 8.31 address the issue of quorum? How does it affect the outlining of any provision related to board quorum?

c) Compare RMNCA § 8.31 to the analogous provision, if any, in your state's nonprofit corporation statute. How, if at all, are your answers to the questions above affected?

C. WRITING OUT THE PROVISION LANGUAGE

Whether you are writing out the full legal language of your provisions from scratch or revising a form, your focus at this final stage must be clarity. When learning prose writing, you were certainly taught to be clear and economical in your use of language, but you were also encouraged to keep your reader's interest by, among other things, varying your word choice. As already noted in the Chapter 1, ambiguity in a document intended to have legal effect must be avoided at all costs.

A basic rule of drafting is: <u>If you mean the same thing, say it the same way</u>. It applies to word choice. Do not identify the same concept with one word or phrase in one part of your document and then use a different word or phrase to refer to the same concept. For instance, if you use the word "directors" or the defined term "Directors" in your bylaws, do not use the phrase "Board members" elsewhere. Likewise, do not use the same word to refer to different things. This precept encourages not only consistency within and among documents but also standardization across related types of legal drafting.

For now, let's focus on the most important word choice any legal drafter makes in creating a sentence: Which verb to use? To understand the proper verbs for bylaws provisions, you need to understand what kind of legal effect each type of provision has. Like statutes and the organization's articles of incorporation, the bylaws, for the most part, make legal declarations and outline procedures, both mandatory and discretionary, for valid action. The former are the kind of statements that might have been preceded in ages past with the clause "It is hereby declared that . . .". The plain language movement has succeeding in eliminating this preamble. When making a legal declaration, the drafter simply states the declaration in the present tense: "The name of the Corporation is Liberty City Land Trust, Inc."

Far more commonly, bylaws set out what is and what is not a valid way of making decisions, including which people should serve as decision makers. These provisions either mandate a particular way of proceeding by using the word "shall" or permit, without requiring, a procedure by using the word "may." Because these types of provision focus on how something should be done rather than who should be obligated to act in a particular way, these procedure provisions are generally written in the passive voice.

Sometimes though, bylaws do identify a particular person or persons and give them a responsibility. When a bylaws provision imposes a responsibility and/or a duty to act in a certain way, the provision's verb structure will use "shall" but be cast in the active voice. The subject of the sentence will be the person who has the responsibility or duty. Likewise, if a specific person or role is given some power or discretionary authority, then the verb used is "may", but again in active voice with the empowered person as the subject.

When a mandated procedure is ignored in the process of making a decision or taking an official action, the result may be that the decision or action lacks legal validity. When a corporate official disregards a duty he or she has under the bylaws, it is possible that he or she may have some liability to the corporation as a result. You should write personal obligation provisions in the active voice so as to be **clear** about who is obligated. The passive voice, on the other hand, is used for procedures because those provisions are not concerned with imposing duties on certain people but instead with setting out how valid decisions are to be made.

Bylaws can also place limits on a discretionary procedure or power. Sometimes the limit or condition imposed on the organization or someone within it may do is expressed by adding an "only if" clause to the provision itself. But another way to impose a condition is to write an additional sentence that contains the word "must." For example, the following provision allows for compensation of officers: "The Officers of the Corporation . . . may be paid a reasonable salary." But the next sentence might limit that discretionary procedure as follows: "Should the Board of Directors ever wish the Corporation to pay the Officers a reasonable salary for the time, services, and expertise provided to the Corporation in their capacity as Officers, a Compensation Committee must be convened to set such salaries." The table below sets out the various types of bylaws provisions along with the verb structure particular to each.

Bylaws Provision	**Provision Type**	**Standard Verb (Voice)**	**Bylaws Provision Example Language**
Classes of Directors	Self-Executing Declaration	"is", "are" or other present tense verb (linking verb or active or passive voice)	There **is** only one class of Directors.
Members	Statement of Legal Fact		The Corporation **has** no members. (restating Articles)
Nomination & Election of Directors, Regular Meetings, many others	Mandatory Procedure	"shall" (passive voice)	Regularly meetings of the Board **shall be held** at least quarterly.
Removal	Permissive Procedure	"may" (passive voice)	An officer **may be removed**, with or without cause, as determined by a two-thirds vote of the Board present at any meeting at which there is a quorum.
Officers	Imposed Duty/ Responsibility	"shall" (active voice)	The Secretary **shall keep** accurate records and minutes of all meetings of the Corporation.
Conflict of Interest, Indemnification Limit	Prohibited Action	"shall not" (active or passive voice)	Such person **shall not be counted** in determining the existence of a quorum at any meeting where the contract, [etc.] is under discussion or is being voted upon.

Committees, Discretionary Indemnification	Permitted Action/ Discretionary Authority/Power	"may" (active voice)	The Board of Directors **may create** such committees with such power as it deems wise to have.
Resignation	Limit on Permitted Action/ Discretionary Authority/Power	"may . . . only if" (active or passive voice)	A Director **may resign only** by submitting a written resignation to the President, the Secretary or to the other Directors.
Director Qualifications, Procedural Requirement for Officer Compensation	Specific Requirement or Limitation	"must" (active or passive voice)	Should the Board of Directors ever wish the Corporation to pay the Officers a reasonable salary for the time, [etc.] . . . a Compensation Committee **must be convened** to set such salaries.

EXERCISE 3–4

Before using a legal form as is, you should review it to make sure it is **complete**, **correct** and **clear.** The bylaws form below contains one instance each of falling short of these core legal document qualities.

a) As part of your checklist review, find the provision below that has been erased and use process of elimination to guess the heading of the blanked-out provision.

b) For your outline review, find the one provision below that runs afoul of the RMNCA by contradicting a mandatory provision. What method did you use to find it in a document six-pages long?

c) Look over the verbs in each of the provisions. See if you can find the one sentence that has two instances of incorrect verb structures given the types of bylaws provisions that are being expressed in that one sentence.

Nonprofit Corporation Bylaws[1]

Bylaws of

1. **NAME AND PURPOSES:** The name and purposes of the Corporation ("the Corporation") are set forth in the articles of incorporation.

2. **PRINCIPAL OFFICE OF THE CORPORATION:** The principal office of the Corporation shall be designated by the Corporation's board of directors ("Board of Directors" or "Board").

3. **MEMBERSHIP:** The Corporation has no members.

4. **DIRECTORS:**

(a) Classes: There is only one class of Directors.

(b) Role/Number/Composition: The management of the Corporation is vested in a Board of Directors which shall be composed of no more than eleven (11) persons and no less than seven (7) persons. The Board shall determine the specific number of Directors from time to time.

(c) Election/Vacancies: At each annual meeting, the Directors to serve for the ensuing year shall be elected by the existing Directors. Vacancies occurring between annual meetings may be filled for the balance of the term by election by the remaining members of the Board of Directors.

(d) Term: Each Director shall hold office for a term of three years. The initial Directors shall be divided into three approximately equal groups: one-third (1/3) of the members to serve for an initial term of one (1) year, one-third (1/3) to serve for an initial term of two (2) years, and one-third (1/3) to serve for an initial term of three (3) years. There is no limit to the number of successive terms an individual may serve as Director.

(e) Voting: Except as otherwise provided in these Bylaws, decisions of the Board of Directors shall be by vote of a majority of those present and voting, but not less than one-half of the Directors then serving. Each Director shall have one vote.

(f)

(g) Resignation: A Director may resign only by submitting a written resignation to the President, the Secretary or, if the Resigning Director is the President, to the other Directors.

[1] Reprinted as adapted from Anne Blumenberg, et al., How to Start a Nonprofit Organization in Maryland with permission of the Community Law Center. This form has been altered for purposes of the exercise.

5. OFFICERS:

(a) Election/Vacancies: The Corporation's officers ("Officers") shall consist of President, Vice-President, Secretary, Treasurer, and such additional officers as the Board may from time to time appoint. The Officers shall be elected by the Board of Directors. The Board of Directors shall fill any vacancy occurring in any office, for whatever reason, and any Director so elected shall fulfill the term of his/her predecessor.

(b) Term: Officers shall serve for an unlimited duration of time and until their successors are elected, or until they are removed by the Board of Directors.

(c) Removal: An Officer may be removed, with or without cause, as determined by a majority vote of the Board present at any meeting at which there is a quorum.

(d) Resignation: An Officer may resign only by submitting a written resignation to the President or Secretary, or to the other Directors if the resigning Officer is the President.

(e) Authority and Duties: The Officers shall have the authority and responsibility delegated by the Board and as follows:

(i) The President ("the President") shall preside at and conduct all meetings of the Board of Directors, and of the Executive Committee. The President shall sign all contracts and agreements in the name of the Corporation after the Board has approved them, serve as the representative of the Corporation in meetings and discussions with other organizations and agencies, and otherwise perform all of the duties which are ordinarily the function of the office, or which are assigned by the Directors.

(ii) The Vice-President ("the Vice-President") shall perform the duties of President if the President is unable to do so or is absent; perform such other tasks as may be assigned by the Board and, at the request of the President, assist in the performance of the duties of the President. In the event that the office of the President becomes vacant, the Vice-President shall automatically become President.

(iii) The Secretary ("the Secretary") shall keep accurate records and minutes of all meetings of the Corporation; make available copies of the minutes of the previous meeting and distribute them in advance of each meeting; cause to be delivered all notices of meetings to those persons entitled to vote at such meeting; and maintain the Minutes Book of the Corporation and a current listing, with phone numbers and addresses, of the Directors at the office of the Corporation.

(iv) The Treasurer ("the Treasurer") shall oversee: the deposit of funds of the Corporation into the proper accounts of the Corporation;

the recordation of all receipts and disbursements from such account or accounts; the preparation of the books and records of the finances of the Corporation; the preparation of financial reports of the accounts for each Board meeting; and the preparation and filing of all end of the year financial reports including, among others, federal and state tax reports.

(v) Other Officers appointed by the Board shall perform such duties as may be specified by the Board or by officers given authority over them.

6. MEETINGS:

(a) Annual Meeting: The annual meeting of the Corporation shall be held in the month of January of each year; or at such time as soon as practical thereafter as determined by the Board of Directors.

(b) Regular Board Meetings: Regular meetings of the Board may be held at least quarterly and shall be scheduled more often by the President.

(c) Special Meetings: Special meetings of the Board shall be held at any time and at any place when called by the President or by at least three Directors. Business transacted at special meetings shall be confined to the purposes of the meeting stated in the notice of the meeting.

(d) Notice of Meetings: Notice of regular Board meetings, including the annual meetings, shall be provided, either in writing or orally, at the prior regular Board meeting or at least 10 days before the day of the meeting. Notices of special meetings shall state that it is a special meeting being called and shall be given orally or in writing at least 48 hours prior to the meeting time. Notice of special meetings shall also include the reason(s) for calling the meeting.

(e) Who Gets Notice/Waiver of Notice: All persons entitled to vote at the meeting shall be given proper notice. Failure to provide proper notice to any member shall not invalidate the meeting or any action taken at the meeting as long as any Director who did not receive notice subsequently waives his or her right to notice.

(f) Quorum: For any meeting, a quorum consists of two (2) of the Directors then serving taking part in the meeting.

7. COMMITTEES: The Board of Directors may create such committees with such power as it deems wise to have. The President shall appoint persons to chair and serve on those committees, including persons who are not Directors of the Corporation. All such appointments shall be approved by the Board either prior to the appointment or be subsequently ratified at the next Board meeting.

(a) Executive Committee. The Executive Committee ("the Executive Committee") shall consist of the President, Vice-President, Secretary, and

Treasurer. The Executive Committee shall develop recommendations with respect to various matters pertaining to the affairs of the Corporation and shall report such recommendations to the Board of Directors for action. In instances where special circumstances require expeditious action between meetings of the Board of Directors, the Executive Committee shall have the power to take the necessary actions, subject to limits imposed by law and any prior limitation imposed by the Board of Directors. The minutes of the Executive Committee shall include a summary of the circumstances requiring any expeditious action taken by the Executive Committee and the minutes shall be submitted to the Board of Directors.

(b) Compensation Committee. Should the Board of Directors ever wish the Corporation to pay the Officers a reasonable salary for the time, services, and expertise provided to the Corporation in their capacity as Officers, a compensation committee ("the Compensation Committee") must be convened to set such salaries. The Compensation Committee shall consist of at least two (2) individuals and shall be made up exclusively of independent directors and/or any other independent individuals the Board may appoint. Members of the Compensation Committee shall evaluate and ascribe a reasonable value to the time, services, and expertise provided by the Officers to be compensated. The Compensation Committee shall consider, among other things:

(i) the market value of the time, services, and expertise;

(ii) the amounts paid to Officers at similar nonprofit corporations; and

(iii) the Corporation's ability to pay.

(c) Standing Committees. The President may establish such standing committees as the President determines are appropriate for the conduct of the business of the Corporation. The President shall appoint members of the standing committees.

(d) Special Committees. The President or the Board of Directors may establish such special committees as they shall determine are necessary for the functioning of the Corporation. Each such committee shall be given a specific charge and term. No special committee shall have a term extending beyond one (1) year unless reappointed. The Board of Directors and the President shall each respectively name the members of special committees the Board of Directors or the President has established.

8. **CONFLICT OF INTEREST:** Any Director, Officer, employee, or committee member having an interest in a contract or other transaction or determination presented to the Board of Directors or a committee of the Corporation for recommendation, authorization, approval, or ratification shall give prompt, full, and frank disclosure of his or her interest to the

Board of Directors or committee prior to its acting on such contract or transaction.

The body to which such disclosure is made shall thereupon determine, by majority vote, whether the disclosure shows that a conflict of interest exists or can reasonably be construed to exist. If a conflict is found to exist, such person shall not vote on, nor use his or her personal influence on, nor participate in discussion of (other than to present factual information or to respond to questions in the discussions or deliberations with respect to such contract, transaction, or determination) the issue. Such person may not be counted in determining the existence of a quorum at any meeting (neither in the number taking part in the meeting nor in the number then serving) where the contract, transaction, or determination is under discussion or is being voted upon.

The minutes of the meeting shall reflect the disclosure made, the vote thereon, and, where applicable, the abstention from voting and participation, and whether a quorum was present.

9. INDEMNIFICATION: The Corporation may indemnify Directors, officers, employees, and agents of the Corporation to the fullest extent required or permitted by the laws of Indiana.

10. COMPENSATION: The Board of Directors shall serve without compensation for their services but may be reimbursed for all expenses reasonably incurred on behalf of the Corporation. The Officers may be reimbursed for all expenses reasonably incurred on behalf of the Corporation and may be paid a reasonable salary as determined by the Compensation Committee.

11. FISCAL YEAR: The fiscal year of the Corporation runs from January 1st through December 31st.

12. ACTION WITHOUT MEETING: Any action which may be properly taken by the Board of Directors assembled in a meeting may also be taken without a meeting, if consent in writing setting forth the action taken is signed by all of Directors entitled to vote with respect to the action. Such consent shall have the same force and effect as a vote of the Directors assembled and shall be filed with the minutes.

13. AMENDMENTS: These bylaws may be amended by a majority vote of the Board of Directors as long as the proposed amendment(s) has (have) been submitted to the Directors in writing with written notice of the meeting to decide on the proposed amendment(s) at least ten (10) days prior to the meeting date.

14. NONDISCRIMINATION: The Officers, Directors, contractors and employees, as well as the organizations and persons served by the Corporation, shall be selected in a non-discriminatory manner with respect to age, sex, race, skin color, national origin, sexual orientation, and religious opinion or affiliation.

Adopted by the Board of Directors this ______ day of __________, 2018

I, the undersigned, being the Secretary of the Corporation, hereby certify that the above is a true, complete, and accurate copy of the bylaws adopted by the Board of Directors.

______________________________ ______________________

Secretary Dated

Reprinted with permission of the Community Law Center.

Please note that the above form has been altered to conform to guidelines offered in the book but also to conflict with those guidelines for the purposes of the chapter's final exercise. Because the alterations of the latter kind may make it unsuitable as a precedent for practice, DO NOT USE the above form as altered in your practice of law.

CHAPTER 4

DRAFTING AND REVISING PROVISIONS FOR CLARITY

■ ■ ■

A. DRAFTING SENTENCES FROM AN OUTLINE

When studying the process of outlining nonprofit bylaws in the previous chapter, you learned that every sentence drafted is an example of one or more different types of provisions. The chart at the end of the chapter showed that each provision type has a unique verb structure. The provision types mapped by that chart describe the building blocks of every charter and governance document. By identifying the provision type, you can select the correct verb for the sentence. In those instances in which the verb is an action verb as opposed to a linking verb, you will also know whether to write the sentence in the active voice, in which the subject of the sentence carries out the action described by the verb. Thus, the critical first step to moving from the outline element to the drafted language is to identify what type of provision does the term you have sketched out in your outline require.

Once you have the core of the sentence, you will be ready to mark out the conceptual boundaries the provision is establishing. The critical conceptual words will often already be in your outline sketch, but this step will allow you to reflect on how the interpretation of those words will shape the effectiveness of the provision. Later in the chapter, you will learn to test complex provisions by mapping the full range of their outcomes. With the provision's core and conceptual terms set, the writing of the actual sentence becomes a careful exercise in grammar.

1. IDENTIFY THE PROVISION TYPE

<u>Declarations and Legal Facts</u>: Sometimes the best way to create a legal relationship or status is just to proclaim it—to speak it into existence. Your charter documents will do quite a lot of declaration. Articles of incorporation will declare the organization's legal name and its purposes. The articles will identify the resident agent and the incorporator. Sometimes, the articles will also identify the initial board members. All of these statements have legal effect. Bylaws will frequently restate the name of the corporation, along with other facts established in the articles. These statements of legal fact differ from the declarations that they merely

reiterate in that they themselves are not the provisions that actually have legal effect. They simply echo the original declarations found elsewhere.

<u>Mandatory and Discretionary Procedures</u>: Governance documents, such as bylaws and operating agreements, create the most fundamental moving parts of a new institution. The decision-making procedures of corporations and limited liability companies allow these entities to put their resources—material, financial and human—to work. For a single-member LLC, the governance procedures for that sole owner will be fairly simple. But the involvement of LLC members governing through a manager or of multiple corporate directors requires more elaborate processes.

The process for conferring and voting must be outlined. Neither the sentences that state how decisions are made nor those that determine how the decision makers are selected are declarations of legal facts. They are instead instructions that set out the boundaries for valid action. Nearly every provision dealing with a deliberative body contributes to some form of procedure, be it mandatory or discretionary.

<u>Duties and Prohibitions</u>: Institutions such as businesses and charities depend on well-defined democratic processes. But they also look to leaders charged with certain responsibilities. When a governance document calls on someone in particular to act in a certain manner, the relevant provision generally imposes a duty or a prohibition. Since corporate directors generally act as a group, their provisions often create procedures. The officers' roles, however, are more frequently expressed as a set of responsibilities. As you learn about the obligations of LLC members created in an operating agreement, you will see that the duties they take on give rights not only to the company but also to one another. Thus, those operating agreement promises have the same grammatical structure as those found in any other contract.

<u>Discretionary Actions and Powers</u>: Just as some procedures are discretionary, so are some of the provisions associated with individuals. When an officer or other entity constituent is given the option to act in a certain way, it is frequently as a power instead of as a responsibility

<u>Requirements and Conditions</u>: Mandated procedures and duties are obligatory in all cases. Requirements and conditions set out what must be done to take advantage of particular options described in an organizational document provision. If there are certain qualifications that a prospective board member must meet to be elected as a director, the provisions setting out those requirements are not expressed as mandated procedures. Joining the board is an optional act. But, in order to do it, certain conditions must be met. Just about any of the other provision types discussed above can be modified by or interact with a requirement or limitation.

2. SELECT THE RIGHT VERB STRUCTURE

Nothing frustrates the drafter's goal of creating **clear** sentences more than a lack of consistency in word usage. When you mean the same thing, express it the exact same way. Standardization in provision type verb structures helps achieve that consistency and clarity. If all duty provisions use one kind of verb structure and all standalone condition provisions use a different verb structure, then the drafter can clearly identify the type of provision intended by selecting the right verb phrase. While there is not universal agreement among legal drafting experts as to how the verb in each provision type should be rendered, the table below summarizes a widely shared approach. While it is not essential that you observe these particular guidelines, it is crucial that you create a clear, precise system for matching provision types and verb structures and that you follow it without fail.

Declarations: Like many a prose sentence you might find in an article online, a declaration sets out a description of some small part of the world. Unlike its prose counterpart, a declaration in a legal document creates the reality it describes. But, since the words are still doing the work of description, the grammar that works for declarative sentence in a prose work serves the purpose of the declarative provision in a legal document. The simple declaration uses a linking verb—most commonly, "is" or "are" but sometimes "means", "consists of" or "includes." Some drafters are uncomfortable with using the present tense to describe a state of affairs that exclusively or primarily concerns the future. If articles specified the number of directors on the board but did not name the initial directors, it may seem odd, perhaps even premature, to write "The Board of Directors has seven members." If you use future tense in a declaration, write "The Board of Directors shall have seven members." not "The Board of Directors will have seven members."

Mandatory procedures, very similar to declarations about the future, also use "shall" not "will." Noncompliance with a mandated process will usually affect the validity of the action taken rather than create liability. The use of the passive voice highlights the action and the object of the action instead of the body or person performing the action, which is often not explicitly referenced at all.

Discretionary authority and discretionary procedures use "may" in the active and passive voices respectively. The option to act in a certain way can be thought of as a right. Rights, however, are broader than just the ability to choose between acting or not acting in a certain way. For a right that cannot or should not be expressed as a discretionary authority, use the verb phrase "is entitled to."

Duty-creating provisions use "shall" in the active voice. Contract drafting books and legislative manuals almost universally agree that when creating a duty to act a drafter should use "shall" not "will."[1] Since a duty obligates a specified party, the duty provision needs to be written in the active voice with the obligated party as its subject.

A prohibition has "shall not" as its verb structure. "May not" might seem a reasonable way of obligating someone not to act in a certain way. But "shall not" more clearly creates a duty not to act in a certain way. "May not" can be used to negate permission to do something, but it also could be read as an attempt to provide someone with the option of not doing something (i.e, as equivalent to the preferable phrase, "may elect not to".)

Requirements and conditions can be drafted in one of two ways: as part of the provisions they affect or as standalone provisions. When a condition is part of the provision being qualified, an "if . . . then" structure is frequently used. But what if an entire set of conditions, such as those that must be true for the closing on the sale of stock to take place, are listed in a separate section entitled "Conditions"? You cannot use "shall" because your reader would think the conditions are actually obligations, which they are not. Instead, you should use "must" when drafting standalone conditions.

The table on the facing page summarizes both the descriptions of and the preferred verb structures for the provision types commonly found in organizational documents.

[1] Other than relatively rare instances such as when parties to an agreement wish to express a shared assumption about an event they believe will take place, "will" should not be used in legal drafting. Predictive statements are generally not very useful in legal documents.

<table>
<tr><th>Provision Type</th><th>Description</th><th>Standard Verb (Voice)</th></tr>
<tr><td>Self-Executing Declaration</td><td>Statement creating legal fact or relationship</td><td rowspan="2">"is", "are" or other present tense verb (linking verb or active or passive voice)</td></tr>
<tr><td>Statement of Legal Fact</td><td>Recital of legal fact created elsewhere</td></tr>
<tr><td>Mandatory Procedure</td><td rowspan="2">Instruction for valid action</td><td>"shall" (passive voice)</td></tr>
<tr><td>Permissive Procedure</td><td>"may" (passive voice)</td></tr>
<tr><td>Imposed Duty/ Responsibility</td><td>Provision for an affirmative obligation</td><td>"shall" (active voice)</td></tr>
<tr><td>Prohibited Action</td><td>Provision for a negative obligation</td><td>"shall not" (active or passive voice)</td></tr>
<tr><td>Permitted Action/ Discretionary Authority/ Power</td><td>Provision for a power or right</td><td>"may" (active voice)</td></tr>
<tr><td>Limit on Permitted Action/ Discretionary Authority/ Power</td><td>Limiting Condition on power or right</td><td>"may . . . only if" (active or passive voice)</td></tr>
<tr><td>Specific Requirement or Limitation</td><td>Condition or Limit</td><td>"must" (active or passive voice)</td></tr>
</table>

3. CREATE CLEAR CONCEPTUAL ELEMENTS

Whether the provision you are writing is a declaration of the organization's name or a mandated procedure for electing directors or the responsibilities of the treasurer, that provision is marking out territory on a conceptual map. With something as specific as a legal name, it may be an exact point. But, mostly, the various provisions will be delineating boundaries that tell the reader "This is what is required; this is what is allowed; this is what is prohibited." The verb, as you have seen, sets the nature of this legal marking. Thus, the action word that follows "shall", "must" "may", "shall be" or "may be" can be an important conceptual element, but rarely is it the only one. The extent of the delineated "area" will be established by the relevant concept terms throughout the sentence. More commonly these conceptual terms are adjectives and adverbs rather than verbs. If nouns they are more often encountered in the sentence predicate than found to be part of the subject. Without regard for part of speech, these conceptual terms can be grouped into two rough categories: descriptive and evaluative.

Few terms identify a target or a range more precisely than numbers. Bylaws that require "at least three" directors leave little doubt as to the minimum size of the board. Numbers are examples of descriptive conceptual elements. Descriptive terms are words or phrases that are definite and objective. They give guidance that can be followed by clear observation.

Evaluative words or phrase, on the other hand, always call for some level of interpretation when applied. Normative terms, such as "for cause", "reasonable", "willful", "negligent" and "material" are classic examples of this second category of conceptual terms. Sometimes, words or phrases that seem free of any normative content are still better thought of as evaluative terms, because they will require judgment and interpretation when they are applied to a situation. These include "ordinary" "commonly used", "workmanlike manner", and "market value."

When you are drafting a provision, the choice between these two types of conceptual elements determines whether you are creating a bright-line rule or an interpretive standard. Rules give clear guidance. Standards, on the other hand, succinctly express our moral intuitions. Rules lean on descriptive elements to the displacement of evaluative ones. Standards rely on evaluative words and phrases. Thus, the choice between descriptive and evaluative conceptual terms comes down to the choice between rules and standards.

Why would you as a drafter committed to clarity ever choose a standards approach that uses inherently vague disputed terms over a rule? By using evaluative words instead of relying strictly on descriptive terms, you seem to be paving the way for controversies over the application of the provision. After all, the whole point of **clear** drafting is to minimize uncertainty in the application of the drafted language.

But you also want your provisions to be **correct.** That is, you want any provision that you draft to produce the right answers for all the various situations to which it may be applied. Rules have the advantage of being clear, but they sometimes fail to anticipate certain difficult cases. For instance, the bylaws provision, "Any director who fails to attend four consecutive regular Board meetings shall be removed.", is a clear rule made up exclusively of descriptive conceptual elements. It also may yield proper results in most cases. The presence in the same bylaws document of other provisions for removal may mitigate any criticism that this provision is under-inclusive (i.e., that it fails to remove board members with better attendance who should nevertheless be removed) when it comes to removing board members. But what about the case of a board member who survives a debilitating illness? As written, the rule applies regardless of the reason for missing four consecutive board meetings. By inserting the phrase "without proper excuse" after "meetings", the chance that the provision will be applied unjustly is greatly reduced. But, even though the provision maintains the clear descriptive elements "fails to attend" and "four consecutive regular Board meetings," it now has an evaluative element introduced in the form of the phrase, "without *proper excuse*." That evaluative term is essential in making sure that the revised provision does not force the removal of a director who was not at fault in missing four consecutive board meetings. Even though the client loses a measure of precise predictability, it will gain in terms of application corresponding to intent.

Remember that vagueness is not the same as ambiguity. Any word or provision that is open to two or more distinct and competing interpretations is ambiguous. That result is always a problem that the drafter should be working to avoid. But, as learned from the discussion of the utility of evaluative terms, choosing a conceptual term that depends on those interpreting it to use their own judgment can be more effective than compounding descriptive terms in the hope of anticipating every possible case. Evaluative terms can be vague, but sometimes we need to sacrifice "**clear**" somewhat to ensure "**correct**."

EXERCISE 4–1

For each of the following provisions, circle the verb and use it to identify the provision type (e.g., declaration, mandated procedure, duty/ responsibility, etc.). Then, identify any conceptual terms as descriptive or evaluative.

a) The management of the Corporation is vested in a Board of Directors which shall be composed of no more than eleven (11) persons and no less than seven (7) persons.

b) Officers shall serve for an unlimited duration of time and until their successors are elected, or until they are removed by the Board of Directors

c) The Board of Directors may create such committees with such power as it deems wise to have.

d) All persons entitled to vote at the meeting shall be given proper notice.

e) Business transacted at special meetings shall be confined to the purposes of the meeting stated in the notice of the meeting.

B. REVISING SENTENCES

You now have the basic tools to take your substantive answers sketched in your outlines and convert them into fully drafted provisions. You will have a chance to do exactly this in the exercises at the end of this section. You can use these same steps of checking provision type, verb structure and conceptual elements to revise drafted language, whether you wrote the original sentences or not. This next set of drafting tools is best used only after a first draft of the sentence has been written.

1. KEEP THE VERB NEAR THE BEGINNING OF THE SENTENCE

Both for clarity and readability, a legal provision should not make its reader wait to know its type. As you have already learned the verb structure of a sentence announces the type of provision it is. If you know the verb and you know whether the sentence is cast in the active or passive voice, then you know what type of provision it is. Nearly every sentence begins with the subject, but the verb should follow it immediately when possible. The core of any provision is its subject and verb; keep the core of the sentence together and near the beginning of the sentence.

2. FIND AND ELIMINATE AMBIGUITY

Clarity in legal drafting faces many challenges, but it has only one true enemy: ambiguity. An ambiguous legal provision has two or more competing meanings. If one of the meanings is true, the other is necessarily false, and vice-versa. There may be plenty of uses of the legal provision where the difference between the two meanings never comes into play, but if one party gets an advantage over the other by pushing one interpretation over the other, litigation—litigation that could have been avoided through more careful drafting—may follow. A vague word or phrase, on the other hand, is one that may or may not cover certain cases. To take Hart's classic rule example of "[N]o vehicles may be taken into the park"[2], the ban on vehicles may clearly apply to cars and trucks, but what about bicycles or strollers? How about toy cars and toy trucks? Would ambulances be prohibited from entering? Despite the uncertainties it causes, there may be good reason to use an admittedly vague word or phrase. The alternative might involve attempting to catalog every conceivable mode of transportation with the vain hope of specifying what's in and what's out. Ambiguity, on the other hand, must be always be sought out and eliminated. Drafters focus on three types of ambiguity: semantic, contextual, and structural.

[2] H.L.A. Hart, The Concept of Law 128 (3d ed. 2012) (1961).

Semantic: Just as some words or phrases can be vague, others can be ambiguous. Semantic ambiguity refers to the competition between meanings of a single word or phrase. Take "dollars", for example. How can use of the word "dollars" cause ambiguity? A provision that describes a price in "dollars" (as opposed to "$") leaves open a possible confusion as to U.S., Canadian or Australian. More likely to cause problems for a drafter is the ambiguity of a common word, such as "or." At first, it seems obvious that "or" directs the reader to make a choice; "a or b" means either a or b (but not both a and b). But consider the following: "A Member shall be entitled to indemnification from the Company for any loss, damage, *or* claim incurred by such Member to the fullest extent permitted by applicable law." If a Member faces a money judgment and a direct financial loss as a result of his or her work for the entity, it is not clear whether he or she must choose just one to be the basis for reimbursement. It is entirely sensible that the provision intends for both the claim *and* the loss to be covered by indemnification. Under this reading, we say that the use of "or" in this instance is inclusive—that is, "a or b" means "a, or b, or both a and b." When you actually read legal provisions that use "or," you may come to the conclusion that this inclusive "or" is far more common than the exclusive one, which seemed, at first, so obvious.

Contextual: Sometimes the competing meanings are not created by a single word or by a single provision, but by two conflicting provisions in the same or different documents. In these cases, an interpreter may need to resort to seemingly arbitrary rules (e.g., the provision that occurs later in the document has the last word on the issue) to prioritize one provision over another. Revising for ambiguity requires a complete reading of the document that checks for internal contradiction.

Structural: By far the most common and most vexing type of ambiguity is the one created by faulty sentence structure. Sometimes, structural ambiguity is as simple as the use of a pronoun that could refer to either one of two (but not both) nouns that precede it. A simple fix here might be to repeat the noun rather than use the pronoun. Even if the language sounds clunky when read aloud, style sometimes needs to be sacrificed to the demands for clarity in legal documents. The more difficult instance of structural ambiguity, both to identify and to repair, involves a qualifying word or phrase that follows more than one item to which it might refer. Take the following example:

> Any board member, officer, employee, or committee member having an interest in a contract or other transaction or determination presented to the Board of Directors or a committee of the Corporation for recommendation, authorization, approval, or ratification shall give prompt, full, and frank disclosure of his or her interest to the Board of Directors or committee prior to its acting on such contract or transaction.

Does the underlined portion qualify all four items in the list that precedes it or just the last one? As with many ambiguities, the context can usually provide us with an answer. In this case, the provision creates a duty to disclose an interest; therefore, it is pretty clear that the phrase "having an interest" applies to every item on the list, not just "committee members." One way to be absolutely clear is to tabulate the provision.

> Any:
>
> a) board member;
>
> b) officer;
>
> c) employee; or
>
> d) committee member
>
> having an interest in a contract or other transaction or determination presented to the Board of Directors or a committee of the Corporation for recommendation, authorization, approval, or ratification shall give prompt, full, and frank disclosure of his or her interest to the Board of Directors or committee prior to its acting on such contract or transaction.

After tabulation, there is no doubt that "having an interest" applies to all four items. Tabulation is so useful for making sentences that contain lists more readable and clear that you will learn the process of tabulating legal provisions in the next section of this chapter.

3. AVOID USING ". . . , PROVIDED(,) THAT . . . ."

Although far from the worst offender, "provided" is one of many examples of legalese that appear in legal documents and rarely elsewhere. When used to reference the provisions of another document or statute, as in "as provided by . . .", it is perfectly harmless. The phrase "provided that" presents special ambiguity problems however when used to connect clauses in the same provision, because it can be read as a simple conjunction or as a signal introducing a condition. When used as a conjunction indicating an exception, "provided" and "that" are sometimes separated by a comma and/or "however." But the most common interpretation of "provided that" is to be read it to mean "on condition that." Because "but" and "on condition that" have very different meanings, you should use one of those to connect clauses rather than ever use some variation of "provided(,) that . . . ."

4. CHECK COMPLEX PROVISIONS BY MAPPING OUTCOMES

When you have taken the time to choose the right verb and fashion the most effective conceptual, you may have a high degree of confidence that your provision will work just as intended. But complex provisions may benefit from testing. No drafter wants to discover a flaw in the logic of an adopted bylaws section only after it has led to a dispute among the client's board members. The time to root out and correct such mistakes is before the client ever sees the document.

Any complex provision can be tested by listing all the different scenarios to which it can be applied and then generating outcomes for each. For instance, the best way to find out if a quorum provision functions as intended is to see how it applies to the various possible combinations of numbers of directors in attendance and number of directors serving on the board. Let's say that the quorum provision for board meetings reads "A majority of directors then serving shall constitute a quorum." You could map the possible outcomes onto a table with the number of members serving across the top and those present down the side.

P ↓ S→	3	4	5	6	7	8	9
1	NQ	NQ	NQ	NQ	NQ	NQ	NQ
2	Q	NQ	NQ	NQ	NQ	NQ	NQ
3	Q	Q	Q	NQ	NQ	NQ	NQ
4	—	Q	Q	Q	Q	NQ	NQ
5	—	—	Q	Q	Q	Q	Q

In applying the rule as written to all these cases, you ensure that the provision language reflects the answer you and your client came to when outlining the board quorum section of the bylaws. But you also see how that decision to make majority the quorum cutoff actually plays out. Note that a board of four cannot carry on business if more than one director is missing. If the client is happy with these results, then the original decision is confirmed.

The practice of mapping outcomes applies to other procedural provisions as well as duties and prohibitions. The "Quorum" and "Non-Quorum" notations will be replaced by "Valid" and "Not Valid" or "Compliant" and "Noncompliant." Mapping outcomes systematically may not be necessary for every complex provision, but those with multiple conceptual elements logically connected to one as conditions or limitations can be drafted with greater confidence if properly vetted.

5. WHEN POSSIBLE, SHORTEN SENTENCES THAT RUN MORE THAN THREE LINES

No one likes to read long, uninterrupted blocks of text, in any form of writing. This fact would present no special problem for drafters if not for another undeniable truth: No one likes to read legal provisions, no matter their length. Readers crave narrative. "Tell me a story" is their constant request. Legal provisions do not engage, explain only infrequently, and, certainly, do not entertain. It's OK that they don't; they're not supposed to. But drafters should not compound the pain needlessly.

As you learned in the previous chapter, one of the best ways to avoid mind-numbing blocks of text in an organizational document is through the judicious use of sections and subsections. Gaps, indentations, and headings can help the reader, better thought of as the user, of your document to see the forest as she or he moves through the trees. Careful organization and use of headings and spacing may be particularly helpful to the user who is looking only for a particular provision or set of provisions.

Even at the sentence level, however, there are opportunities to make provisions more readable. When a single sentence goes on for more than three lines of text, the editing drafter should ask "Why?" Usually the verb in the sentence is at most a short phrase. The subject, typically, is also one or two words. If it is much longer, there may be an opportunity to transform it into a defined term. This step might be especially useful if the subject recurs in the document.

Sometimes all the provision's component parts—subject, verb, and conceptual elements—have been found to be just the length that they need to be, yet the sentence still runs long. Even if the sentence cannot be broken apart into separate sentences, it may contain one or more series and thus might be rendered more readable through tabulation.

EXERCISE 4–2

For each of the excerpts from a bylaws outline, draft the described bylaws provision:

a) Quorum for Board meeting—1/2 of the number of Directors currently serving, but in no event less than 3.

b) Qualifications for membership—live in the Association's boundaries; pay dues; support the goals of the Association.

c) Secretary's responsibilities—keep membership rolls and contact information for Directors and Officers up to date; minutes at meetings; official records; send out notices; certify Association documents.

C. TABULATION

For the most part, sentences in legal documents are made excessively long by lists, complex qualifiers, conditions, and objects. Complexity in objects, qualifiers or conditions may be unavoidable, but a series of parallel items in the same sentence presents an opportunity to tabulate that sentence.

You've already seen how separate paragraphs can be arranged hierarchically into sections and subsections. Tabulation takes a list of parallel—that is, grammatically similar—items within a sentence and arranges them as if they were "subsections" of their own sentence. For example,

this sentence:

> The Compensation Committee shall consider, among other things, the market value of the time, services and expertise, the amounts paid to Officers at similar nonprofit corporations, and the Corporation's ability to pay.

can be rendered more readable by tabulating it:

> The Compensation Committee shall consider, among other things:
>
> a) the market value of the time, services, and expertise;
>
> b) the amounts paid to Officers at similar nonprofit corporations; and
>
> c) the Corporation's ability to pay.

Also:

> Any member who has attended, as a member, two of the previous three annual membership meetings, has paid the annual dues assessment on or before the date of the annual meeting for each of the three previous years, and is current on his or her dues payment may be nominated for election as a director or officer.

can be recast to read:

> Any member:
>
> a) who has attended, as a member, two of the previous three annual membership meetings;
>
> b) has paid the annual dues assessment on or before the date of the annual meeting for each of the three previous years; and
>
> c) is current on his or her dues payment
>
> may be nominated for election as a director or officer.

Notice that, while the spacing and the numbering was introduced to make the sentence more readable, the only change in the punctuation was to introduce the items with a colon and to separate the tabulated items by semicolons instead of by commas. Note also that there was no change whatsoever in the capitalization. It is still, word for word, the same sentence, just a lot more readable. The approach to tabulation above is called <u>sentence format</u>.

Both styles of tabulation space apart the items on a list. The sentence format approach to tabulation makes no changes to the wording or capitalization of the untabulated provision. It makes only minimal changes to the punctuation by putting a colon at the end of the introductory language and semicolons at the end of all but the last of the tabulated items. Introductory language applies to all the items that follow. Tabulation thus obviates the need to have each and every item to begin with "shall" or "may." The "shall" or "may" takes its place at the end of the introductory language. But there is an exception. If the provision calls for a list of prohibitions, the "shall not" is repeated at the beginning of each item to ensure the reader does not lose sight of the fact that the provision calls for prohibitions as opposed to discretionary authorities or affirmative duties.

Sometimes a different tabulation approach, known as list format, can work as well or better. For example, the following sentence:

> The Treasurer shall oversee the deposit of funds of the Corporation into the proper accounts of the Corporation, the recordation of all receipts and disbursements from such account or accounts; the preparation of the books and records of the finances of the Corporation, the preparation of financial reports of the accounts for each Board meeting, and the preparation and filing of all end of the year financial reports including, among others, federal and state tax reports.

can be rendered so:

> The Treasurer shall oversee the following:
>
> a) The deposit of funds of the Corporation into the proper accounts of the Corporation.
>
> b) The recordation of all receipts and disbursements from such account or accounts.
>
> c) The preparation of the books and records of the finances of the Corporation.
>
> d) The preparation of financial reports of the accounts for each Board meeting.
>
> e) The preparation and filing of all end of the year financial reports including, among others, federal and state tax reports.

Notice that each item is capitalized and punctuated as if it were a separate sentence, even though none of them happen to be complete sentences. In sentence format, the penultimate item ends with a conjunction, usually "and" or "or." The series of indented items in a list format tabulation is universally preceded by a colon and an introductory signal that serves the same function of showing the logical relationship among the items. The original sentence tabulated above had a list of items joined by "and" so the introductory signal used for the resulting tabulation was "the following," meaning "all of the following." If the introductory signal had been "or," then the options would be "any of the following" (≥ 0 of the listed options), "one of the following" (exactly 1 of the listed options), and "at least one of the following" (≥ 1 of the listed options). As discussed, the ambiguity of "or" makes the list format an attractive alternative for clarifying disjunctive lists.

The following table compares side by side the two approaches to tabulation using as an example this brief provision:

> (f) Quorum: For any meeting, a quorum consists of the greater of either two Directors or 50% of the Directors then serving taking part in the meeting.

Sentence Format	List Format
[Introductory language]: 1) [item 1]; 2) [item 2]; 3) [item 3]**; and (or)** 4) [item 4] [concluding language, if any].	[Intro. language] **the following:** **1)** [Item 1]. **2)** [Item 2]. **3)** [Item 3]. **4)** [Item 4]. [concluding language, if any].
(f) Quorum: For any meeting, a quorum consists of the greater of either: 1) two Directors; or 2) 50% of the Directors then serving taking part in the meeting.	(f) Quorum: For any meeting, a quorum consists of the greater of the following taking part in the meeting: 1) Two (2) Directors. 2) 50% of the Directors then serving.

EXERCISE 4–3

Revise the following provision for clarity and readability:

> This agreement shall automatically terminate on the written agreement of all of the partners, the lapse of the policy subject mentioned above without value; the bankruptcy or insolvency of the partnership, the death of all of the partners within a 90-day period commencing with the date of the death of the first to die, or the liquidation of all of the interest of any partner during the

partner's lifetime within the permissive provisions of Section Fifteen of this agreement, but only as to that partner.

D. DRAFTING SPECIAL PROVISIONS

1. DEFINITIONS

In a legal document, defined terms appear throughout the document capitalized, especially when they are nouns or noun phrases, as they often are. This capitalization of each word in the defined term reminds the reader that the word or phrase is shorthand for a longer reference set out in full in the first instance. Often these shorthand-type of defined terms are specially created proper names such as "Corporation" to refer to the entity being organized. The original longhand version is immediately followed by a parenthetical reference to the shorthand version in quotes. The legalese signal "hereinafter" is not necessary and should be avoided.

Some documents require not just shorthand references but stipulated meanings for words or phrases used in the document. These provision-length definitions are drafted as declarations. Such definitions are particularly useful to avoid semantic ambiguity for terms such as "dollars" (US, Canadian or Australian?) or "members" (of the corporation? of the board of directors? of committees?) or financial terms such as "book value." These usually appear in a separate definitions section near the beginning of the document.

As declarations, definitions often use linking verbs. Although "is" is the most common linking verb, most standalone definition provisions will use "means" instead. Sometimes, a definition's core sentence will be supplemented by a phrase or additional sentence that makes use of "includes." If the drafter is concerned that the definition will be interpreted narrowly to exclude certain items, those items can be listed in a supplemental phrase or sentence that use "includes" rather than "means." Likewise, if the drafter wishes to rule out other things, a phrase or clause using "does not include" addresses that concern.

2. PURPOSES, POWERS, DISSOLUTION EVENTS, AND OTHER LISTS

Whenever you create or adapt a provision that includes a list, make sure that the items in the list share the same grammatical structure. For instance, "The Corporation is organized and operated exclusively for the purposes of financial assistance to low-income persons and combating community deterioration." can be improved by inserting "providing" before "financial."

You may need to construct a list that begins with items expressed in dissimilar grammatical forms. Take, for instance, the following list of events that might occasion the dissolution of a limited liability company:

- The Member elects to dissolve. [full sentence]
- the forfeiture of the charter for failure to file an annual business entity report with the Secretary of State [noun phrase]
- conducting unlawful business [gerund phrase]

You may with some difficulty revise each item to conform to a single grammatical form (e.g., all noun phrases or all gerund phrases) If however you elect not to make the items in a list grammatically parallel, then you may want to tabulate the items using the list format, as opposed to the sentence format, as the punctuation used to demarcate items in a list tabulation works better for items that are not parallel with one another.

3. CONDITIONS AND LIMITATIONS

When writing a standalone condition, you should use the verb "must." Such provisions are fairly rare in charter and governance documents. They are far more common in contracts governing the sale of complex assets such as real estate or businesses. Discretionary authority and rights provisions in organizational documents, however, frequently condition and/or limit the entitlements they confer. When they do so, these provisions often fold the limitation or condition into the same sentence that creates the power or right. For example, "[i]f the Member renders services to the Company, the Member shall be entitled to compensation commensurate with the value of such services." The right to payment created in a member by this provision is limited to situations in which the member has performed valuable work for the LLC. If there were a list of a half a dozen or more conditions that the member had to satisfy in order to receive payment, then it would be appropriate to use a list tabulation with each item containing a standalone condition using "must." But, with a single condition, a simple "if . . . then" construction works best. Note that the "then" in the example above is implied, as is frequently the case.

Limitations on discretionary authority can be imposed through the use of "only if" or simply "only." In everyday discourse, the word "only" is frequently misplaced. For instance, if you read: "[a]mendments to this Agreement may only be made with the consent of the Member.", then you would probably understand the writer to be communicating that consent of the member is required for an amendment to the agreement rather than that an amendment to the agreement is the only thing that can be made with consent of the member. But the placement in this example indicates that "only" modifies "be made" rather than "with the consent of the member." When drafting a legal document, you must be careful in where you place "only." In this case, the correct rendering would be: "Amendments to this Agreement may be made only with the consent of the Member." By placing "only" directly before "with the consent of the Member" the nature of the restriction is clear.

4. SETTING OUT TIMES, DATES, AMOUNTS, AND OTHER NUMERICAL ITEMS

Descriptions of time periods and deadlines produce instances of ambiguity among the easiest to overlook. If a fiscal year ends at "midnight on December 31st", it may seem apparent that the fiscal year includes all of the day on December 31st. But an argument can be made that "midnight" refers to the beginning of December 31st rather than to the end. One solution would be to use 11:59 pm or even 11:59:59 pm, rather than the inherently ambiguous "midnight." Another possibility is to specify whether "midnight" refers to the beginning or ending of a day in a definition provision.

When establishing time periods for notice:

<table>
<tr><th>Avoid:</th><th>Instead, Use:</th></tr>
<tr><td rowspan="3">"within ___ days of"</td><td>"no later than ___ days after"</td></tr>
<tr><td>"no later than ___ days before"</td></tr>
<tr><td>"no earlier than ___ days before"</td></tr>
<tr><td>"between"</td><td rowspan="2">"beginning . . . on (at) . . . and ending on (at) . . ."</td></tr>
<tr><td>"from . . . until"</td></tr>
<tr><td>"by"</td><td>"on or before"</td></tr>
</table>

<u>Numbers</u>: Here are some conventions to follow when drafting provisions that involve numerical references. For monetary amounts, always use Arabic numbers unless the use of words like "millions" and "billions" can be substituted for multiple "0"s. For other numerical expressions, write out the words for the whole numbers zero through ten, but use digits for any other number. For common fractions, such as one half, one fourth, one third, two thirds and three fourths, use words. For all other fractions, use Arabic numbers.

CHAPTER 5

ORGANIZING A LIMITED LIABILITY COMPANY

■ ■ ■

A. THE CHOICE BETWEEN LLC AND FOR-PROFIT CORPORATION

1. WHAT MAKES FOR-PROFIT ENTITIES DIFFERENT: OWNERSHIP AND DISTRIBUTION OF REVENUE

Unlike nonprofit corporations, for-profit entities are not forbidden from distributing excess revenue to the people who run them. In fact, that is typically their primary purpose. Nevertheless, all three main benefits discussed in Chapter 2 remain relevant. The importance of **limiting liability risk** stands unchanged. Likewise, the for-profit needs a **decision-making structure** that is **effective** and inspires confidence for those who invest as co-owners. Although for-profit entities cannot generally expect the income tax system to subsidize their efforts, **favorable tax treatment** is no less important for for-profit entities than it is for charities. But the presence of owners as the principals of for-principal entities introduces a fourth benefit of formal business entity that was unknown to nonprofits: **effective equity structure.** The charter and governance documents of for-profits frequently address issues of how profits and losses are allocated among co-owners as well as how and when distributions of excess revenue are made. This benefit also plays a crucial role in shaping the provisions that govern how and when ownership interests can be transferred, a subject that will be explored in the next chapter.

2. WHAT MAKES LLCs DIFFERENT: SIMPLICITY AND FLEXIBILITY

The vast majority of small businesses that seek liability limitation protection nowadays are formed as limited liability companies, also known as LLCs. Far more popular than the close corporation or the partnership forms, the LLC is easy to set up and extremely flexible, while offering the same **liability protection** as the corporation.

Decision making in an LLC is also very flexible and, thus, can be very simple if that is what the member or members wish. Every for-profit corporation has shareholders. In the case of most corporations, the shareholders elect a board of directors, which governs the corporation. Members of an LLC can designate a manager to run the company, but most small business LLCs elect to be member-managed. Where corporation bylaws have many provisions about directors' election and meeting procedures, there typically is very little written in an LLC operating agreement about if or how members are to confer with one another about business decisions.

The **equity structure** of LLCs and corporations can be simple or complex. Corporations call their owners shareholders, and the owners of LLC interests are members. But the fact that corporation interests are measured in numbers of shares and LLC membership is expressed in percentage interests makes very little difference. Nevertheless, a need for a complex equity structure is the leading reason why the LLC form is rejected in favor of the corporation. When sophisticated outside investors, such as angel investors or venture capitalists, buy into a new enterprise, they are often open to the founders continuing to run the organization in return for, among other things, a preferred claim on the business's revenue and assets. Even though the LLC form is flexible enough to accommodate these requirements, the corporation has tried-and-true approaches with which sophisticated investors (and their lawyers) are more familiar.

The LLC shows superior flexibility to the corporation in the area of **tax treatment.** By default, an LLC is taxed as either a sole proprietorship or a partnership, depending on whether it has multiple members. These options are unavailable to a corporation. Moreover, an LLC can elect to be taxed as a C Corp or, if it qualifies, as an S Corp. Founders of a typical small business do not have to choose between being an LLC and receiving S-Corp tax treatment. They can choose to be both an LLC and an S Corp at the same time, because the former is a type of entity form under state business organization law while the latter is a tax classification under federal income tax law (as well as that of most states). Two different bodies of law can look at the same business and classify it under different categories from one another (e.g., an LLC is not a corporation under state law, but can be a corporation (S-type or C-type) under federal income tax law.)

The S-Corp classification may be attractive to business owners whose profits are not strictly dependent on the services they provide to the company. For businesses that make money by marking up goods sold or services rendered by non-owner employees, their owners may have to hand over less in personal Social Security and Medicare contributions by electing S-Corp tax treatment. Also, LLCs with multiple members may find the more structured, less complicated tax accounting of subchapter S preferable to that of partnership tax.

But there are tradeoffs. Owners who work on behalf of entities classified as corporations do so as employees not sole proprietors or partners, so their reasonable salary income will be subject to all the withholding procedures that go with payroll. More importantly, any entity electing S-Corp status must meet the restrictions that define that classification. If it does not, the IRS will treat it as a C Corp and tax its owners twice. Because the IRS penalizes taxpayers who underpay taxes, a client may find it very costly to be mistaken about its tax status. As will be discussed briefly later in this chapter, the element of the S-Corp definition most relevant to LLC formation is the requirement that an S Corp have only one class of stock. An LLC operating agreement that gives differing economic rights to its members may disqualify the entity from S-Corp classification.

Finally, state income tax law can further complicate the question of seeking S-Corp classification, regardless of whether the entity formed as a corporation or an LLC. The discussion of favorable tax treatment to this point has assumed that every state in the U.S. will classify, for its income tax purposes, a venture, nonprofit or for-profit, in the same way that the IRS does. This assumption is true for a great many simple business forms, but not every state will confer S-Corp benefits on an entity just because the federal government does so. Thus, your client may enjoy pass-through taxation as an S Corp for federal income tax purposes but find itself subject to double taxation in its home state. So, unless the benefits of S-Corp status are clear, and its restrictions can be accommodated with certainty, a multi-member LLC may be better off sticking with its default classification as a partnership.

DISCUSSION QUESTION 5–A

For each of the following new for-profit ventures, consider the advantages and disadvantages to each of organizing as an LLC in its home jurisdiction as opposed to filing as a corporation either in the same state or in Delaware. What role does the LLC's relative lack of formality in decision making play in your recommendation? How does the availability to an LLC of any of the federal income tax classifications factor in?

1) A pair of recently certified personal trainers wish to start a fitness business at one location with the hopes of rapid expansion to many more sites throughout the region in the coming years.

2) Three women wish to start a neighborhood child-care business out of one of their homes. At first, it will be just for school-age children during after-school hours, but they plan to expand it to full-time care for toddlers in the second year and infants the following year.

3) An inventor has created a new household kitchen tool for which she has filed a provisional patent application. She has no desire to manufacture the product herself but instead wishes to license it to a major kitchen tool producer.

B. ARTICLES OF ORGANIZATION

Although the exercises in this chapter will encourage you to consult the LLC statutes for the jurisdictions in which you will practice, the discussion of drafting the LLC charter and governance documents will draw upon Indiana's LLC statute. Signed into law in the early mid-1990s, the Indiana Business Flexibility Act is representative of the four dozen other state LLC laws enacted in the same period.

IC 23–18–2–4 Formation; articles of organization; contents

(b) Articles of organization shall contain the following:

(1) The name of the limited liability company.

(2) The street address of the limited liability company's registered office in Indiana and the name of the limited liability company's registered agent at that office.

(3) The latest date upon which the limited liability company is to dissolve, or a statement that the duration of the limited liability company is perpetual until dissolution in accordance with this article.

(4) If the articles of organization provide for a manager or managers, a statement to that effect.

(5) Any other matters not inconsistent with this article that the members agree to include . . . . .

The standard articles of organization form for an LLC is even simpler than the one for a nonprofit corporation. Both have spaces for the organization's name and, if any, the principal office address, as well as for the names and addresses of the registered agent and the organizer(s). The typical LLC form has no purpose section as it assumes that the organization follows the default provision in the statute, which allows for any lawful purpose. The LLC articles form does require choices between limited and perpetual existence and between member management and manager management. But that's it.

The decision to select perpetual duration over limited life is an easy one. Very few LLCs pick a date certain (typically forty or sixty years hence) upon which the entity will cease to exist. The fact that many state LLC statutes still require an answer to this question is a vestige of the LLC's first decade as an entity form. Prior to 1997, LLCs needed to avoid taking on too many characteristics of corporations in order to avoid being classified as corporations for tax purposes. Limiting the duration of the LLC was a popular way of securing favorable tax treatment. At the end of 1996, the IRS abandoned this approach in favor of allowing LLCs to qualify for any of the classifications for which they would otherwise qualify. Since then, virtually all new LLCs are perpetual, just like corporations.

The decision between the member-managed and manager-managed types of LLC warrants more consideration. As noted above and discussed further in Chapter 7, large businesses or ventures that hope to grow large through capital raised by passive investors often choose the corporation form over the LLC. But, for those businesses with non-participating owners that nevertheless prefer the LLC form, the manager-managed LLC offers a workable alternative to business management by large committee. A manager of an LLC may be selected from one of the members; but, more typically, the members hire professional third parties to run the business on a day-to-day basis. Many small ventures start off at least as member-managed LLCs because they lack the finances to turn offer all management duties to a salaried professional.

When multiple people own a small company, third parties dealing with one of those owners may think that that one owner has the authority to speak for the company. Indeed, the LLC statute in Indiana encourages them to deal with that LLC member in that way unless they have knowledge that the member is not authorized to commit a member-managed LLC in the matter. The LLC statute allows that rule to be changed but not in the operating agreement. If an LLC does not want each and every member to have the power to bind the company, then the articles of organization need to provide a different rule such as only the member or, working jointly, members with a majority interest being able to bind the company.

Because apparent authority is a rule that affects third parties, the statute requires that any departure from its default approach (apparent authority for each member of the LLC) be contained in the articles, which are filed and publicly available for third parties to see. There may not be a great many other issues that need to appear in the articles as opposed to the operating agreement. If an issue does need to be addressed in the articles as opposed to the operating agreement, it is almost certainly because the articles are required to be on file with the state. Interestingly, most of the default rules described in the next section may NOT be varied by a contrary rule in the articles. If they are to be changed, that change must appear in a written operating agreement signed by the member(s).

If the checklist phase for creating the articles of organization is simpler than that of the one for nonprofit incorporation, the outlining and drafting is also easier than it was for the nonprofit corporation charter document. Below is a summary of the checklist items together with notes on how their form and content are impacted by the statute and the particular circumstances of the client.

Checklist Item	**LLC Statute Limits**	**Client Inquiry**
Entity Name	Distinct from other names; not misleading re: purpose; LLC identifier	Trademark concerns: name to promote goods/ services?
Reg. Agent & Address	In-state business office address of state resident	Does client know someone willing to provide address?
Organizer(s) Name(s) & Address(es)	Any individual or entity	Counseling as to role in org. process
Term of Existence or Perpetual?		Can generally assume perpetual
Member-Managed or Manager-Managed?		Depends on # and participation of members

The discussion of drafting provisions for nonprofit articles dealt with purposes, the dissolution clause and other possible provisions. The LLC articles of organization can usually be completed without the filing lawyer adding a single full sentence to the state-provided form.

Articles of Organization for an LLC

ARTICLES OF ORGANIZATION
DOMESTIC LIMITED LIABILITY COMPANY
State Form 49459 (R6 / 6-16)
Approved by State Board of Accounts, 2016

Indiana Code 23-18-2-4
23-18-12-3

FILING FEE: $100.00

ARTICLES OF ORGANIZATION

The undersigned, desiring to form a Limited Liability Company *(hereinafter referred to as "LLC")* pursuant to the provisions of the Indiana Business Flexibility Act, executes the following Articles of Organization.

ARTICLE I – NAME AND PRINCIPAL OFFICE

Name of LLC *(The name must include the words Limited Liability Company or an abbreviation thereof.)*			
Address of Principal Office *(number and street – **PO box not accepted**)*	City	State	ZIP code

ARTICLE II – REGISTERED OFFICE AND AGENT

Registered Agent: The name and street address of the LLC's Registered Agent and Registered Office for service of process are:

Name of Registered Agent *(Cannot be the LLC itself.)*			
Address of Registered Office *(number and street or building – **PO box not accepted**)*	City	State IN	ZIP code

Required:
☐ By checking the box, the Signator(s) represent(s) that the Registered Agent named in the application has consented to the appointment of Registered Agent.

ARTICLE III – DISSOLUTION

☐ The LLC is perpetual until dissolution.
OR
☐ The latest date upon which the LLC is to dissolve *(month, day, year)*: _____

ARTICLE IV – MANAGEMENT

The LLC will be managed by its manager or managers. ☐ Yes ☐ No

☐ The LLC will be a single member LLC *(optional)*.

In Witness Whereof, the undersigned executes these Articles of Organization and verifies, subject to penalties of perjury, that the statements contained herein are true, this _____ day of _____, _____.

Signature	Printed name
This instrument was prepared by *(name)*:	
Address *(number and street, city, state, and ZIP code)*	

C. OPERATING AGREEMENT

1. CREATING THE CHECKLIST

The differences between the governance document of the LLC and that of the corporation are even greater than those between the two kinds of charter documents. Because **decision making** in an LLC can be very simple and direct, the checklist related to the operating agreement will normally be much simpler than the one for nonprofit bylaws. The operating agreement for a single-member LLC can be very simple since making decisions in a single-owner business may not involve any "process" at all. The first benefit, maintaining **liability risk limitation,** however, requires a formal separation between the member/owner and the LLC entity. The member's signing of an agreement that is not signed by anyone else certainly highlights this formality involved in setting up an LLC. Like the nonprofit bylaws provisions that merely recite statutory default provisions, certain parts of the single-member LLC operating agreement can remind the member of the commitments to recordkeeping and other formalities that will demonstrate to anyone interested that the LLC is not just the owner operating under a "doing-business-as" (or d/b/a) name.

Due to the importance of **equity structure** in the for-profit entity, the multi-member LLC operating agreement needs to address a variety of accounting issues related to the tracking of capital contributions, operating profits and losses, and distributions to members. Many LLC statutes require that the LLC record in writing both the initial amounts of the member's capital contributions and the events which would bring about the dissolution of the LLC. Such a requirement usually does not mandate that either of these issues be addressed in the operating agreement, but drafters invariably include them. Frequently, the initial capital contributions to an LLC are listed on a schedule that is attached to the operating agreement. Below is an arrangement of a typical operating agreement articles grouped into five functional categories.

DISCUSSION QUESTION 5–B

Review the multi-member operating agreement short form at the end of this chapter and fill in the blanks in the list below with the missing article headings.

Formation (Provisions Restating & Expanding upon the Articles)

Preamble (Formation)

____

Term

____

Member Accounting Provisions

Capital Contributions

____

____

Distributions

Tax Matters

Members & Management

Members

Management

Changes in Ownership

Withdrawal of Member

____

____

General Provisions

Liability of Members

Exculpation of Member-Managers

____

____

DISCUSSION QUESTION 5–C

Which of these can be eliminated from the checklist for a single-member LLC? Look at the single-member operating agreement form and compare your new checklist to the section headings in the form at the end of this chapter.

---

2. ANSWERING THE CHECKLIST QUESTIONS: KNOWING THE LAW

As with nonprofit corporation bylaws, the law you will focus on in creating the LLC operating agreement is statutory. This is not to say that case law has no impact on the drafting of an LLC's operating agreement. Although the LLC statute seeks to be clear about the very limited nature of its default rules regarding a member's fiduciary duties to the LLC, cases regarding self-dealing in LLC governance disputes should be studied to understand what the complete state of the law is. Only then will you be able to see if and how an operating agreement should be written to reflect the mutual expectations of the founders.

The chart in this section provides a list of default rules that concern issues on the operating agreement checklist created in the prior section. Unlike the analogous chart for bylaws in Chapters 3 and 7, there is no column for mandatory rules in the LLC operating agreement chart below. That is because the LLC statute in Indiana, as well as in many other jurisdictions, only has two "non-negotiable" rules that impact the content of an operating agreement. One limits the ability of the LLC to distribute profits to its members. The other lists the records that an LLC must keep. Although the first rule contains a section that can varied by the operating agreement, neither of these issues has a separate related default rule in the statute. They are important (and brief) enough to reprint in their entirety.

IC 23–18–5–6 Distributions

Sec. 6.(a) A distribution may not be made if after giving effect to the distribution:

(1) the limited liability company would not be able to pay its debts as the debts become due in the usual course of business; or

(2) the limited liability company's total assets would be less than the sum of its total liabilities plus, unless the operating agreement permits otherwise, the amount that would be needed if the affairs of the limited liability company were to be wound up at the time of the distribution to satisfy any preferential rights that are superior to the rights of members receiving the distribution.

This rule protects the interests of creditors from company members looking to use the LLC's liability limitation to avoid paying the company's debts. Subsection (a)(1) requires that any distribution of profits or capital not deprive the LLC of the ability to get the cash it needs to pay its bills as they are due. Subsection (a)(2) essentially bars the distribution of profits or capital to members who have no equity in the company. If the liabilities of a company exceed the value of its assets, then no members have positive capital account values. If some members are entitled to priority in the distribution of assets, then those rights must figure into the calculation for distributions to the others, unless the operating agreement provides otherwise.

Although the rule against not handing out phantom profits to owners applies across the board to all formal for-profit business entities, you may not want to assume that the founders of your client know the rule. For that reason, you may want to reprint it word-for-word in the LLC operating agreement just to make it sure they can refer to it as needed.

IC 23–18–4–8 Records; inspection; full disclosure; omissions

Sec. 8.(a) A limited liability company must keep at its principal office the following records and information:

(1) A list with the full name and last known mailing address of each member and manager, if any, of the limited liability company from the date of organization.

(2) A copy of the articles of organization and all amendments.

(3) Copies of the limited liability company's federal, state, and local income tax returns and financial statements, if any, for the three (3) most recent years, or if the returns and statements were not prepared,

copies of the information and statements provided to or that should have been provided to the members to enable them to prepare their federal, state, and local tax returns for the same period.

(4) Copies of any written operating agreements and all amendments and copies of any written operating agreements no longer in effect.

(5) Unless otherwise set forth in a written operating agreement, a writing setting out the following:

(A) The amount of cash, if any, and a statement of the agreed value of other property or services contributed by each member and the times at which or events upon the happening of which any additional contributions agreed to be made by each member are to be made.

(B) The events, if any, upon the happening of which the limited liability company is to be dissolved and its affairs wound up.

In the provision above, a list of four strict requirements is followed by a default rule. The specific information given here should be recited word-for-word in the operating agreement to serve as a reference for the members seeking guidance on mandated formalities. A records provision that recited the first four subsections and ended without reference to the fifth might be interpreted as rejecting the default rule. If the members do not want to be obligated to keep both of these types of records, the safer drafting choice would be to negate the duty.

DISCUSSION QUESTION 5–D

Consult your state's LLC statute and see if the mandatory provisions relating to prohibited distributions and required records you find vary from the Indiana statute (if in Indiana, pick the state you will take the bar in or a neighboring state).

The chart below contains the Indiana statute's default rules. Those provisions can be overridden only by a contrary approach written in the articles of organization contain the phrase "unless articles." The other rules listed can be overridden <u>only</u> by a provision in the operating agreement. The LLC statutes differs significantly from corporation statutes in this regard. In the context of corporations, any default rule that could be changed in the bylaws could instead be changed in the articles of incorporation. But, with LLCs, the provisions of operating agreements are able to vary just about any of the statute's default rules. The table below lists the default rules provided by the Indiana statute. The truncated cites are to the specific sections of Title 23, Article 18 of the Indiana Code. As with the analogous chart in Chapter 3, those default rules that impose, unless overridden, a requirement or prohibition on the company and/or its members are listed in bold.

Op Agreement Checklist	Default Provision
Decision Making (4–3)	Majority in interest
Apparent Authority to Bind LLC (3–1.1)	Each member (or manager), unless articles
Capital Contributions (5–1)	No member commitment to make addt'l capital contributions
Withdrawal (6–6.1)	**No right to withdraw before dissolution**
Assignability of Membership (6–3.1)	Freely assignable, economic interest only; unanimous consent needed for membership admission
Member Transactions involving LLC business or information (4–2)	**Member that profits personally from conduct of LLC business or from using LLC information must give such profits to the LLC**
Allocation of profits/losses (5–3)	Per agreed relative value of capital contributions
Distributions (5–4, 5–8)	Per agreed relative value of capital contributions; no right/duty to take in-kind
Exculpation (4–2)	Member not liable to company unless willful or reckless
Indemnification (2–2(14))	Co. may indemnify unless willful or reckless
Expulsion (no provision)	**Member may not be expelled by vote of other members**
Amendment (4–3)	Unanimous consent of the member(s)

EXERCISE 5–1

Consult your state's LLC statute and see if the default provisions you find vary from the Indiana statute on the following four subjects (if in Indiana, pick the state you will take the bar in or a neighboring state):

a) Apparent Authority to Bind LLC

b) Withdrawal

c) Exculpation

d) Indemnification

Make your own table with just those default (and mandatory, if any) provisions and use it when adapting an operating agreement form for use in your state.

---

3. ANSWERING THE CHECKLIST QUESTIONS: KNOWING THE CLIENT'S NEEDS

When representing a nonprofit entity in formation, a lawyer has no guarantee that the entity's founders will all agree on the content of the charter and governance documents. A process for decision making and an understanding that some disagreements with made decisions may be deep enough to induce exit before the venture begins are important to both nonprofits and for-profit formations. But for-profit formation presents a unique challenge for the lawyer.

When members of an LLC pool their funds together and agree to share profits, they are, in effect, on opposite sides of a joint venture contract. No competent lawyer would quickly and carelessly agree to represent both parties to a contract. Your decision to represent the entity rather than its individual members and to clearly communicate that to them does make a difference as to whether there are conflicts between multiple current clients.

But the decision not to represent the individual owners means that you will not be giving each of them advice as to whether the operating agreement is a good deal for him or her personally. You should encourage them to get individual advice on the terms of the agreement and allow time for such consultation when your drafting timetable. Different levels of contribution and differing personal financial circumstances will frequently generate adverse interests and power imbalances. You cannot, nor should you try to, propose terms that even out these differences. As the lawyer working on behalf of the venture to formalize the venture, you should generate options and be transparent about the consequences of one choice over another.

For example, the decision to have all or most business decisions made by those with a majority in interest is a governance option that is embraced by a wide variety of small business founders with large, small, and medium stakes in their ventures. In the absence of some prior agreement to the contrary, no one is forcing a prospective member with a proposed minority investment to agree to that way of running the business. In the end, the parties must decide if and how to move forward. The goal is to create an equity structure that effectively allocates profits and losses and distributes funds. Likewise, an effective decision-making process needs to be fair and efficient. The first test of the relevant provisions in delivering those benefits is whether the language agreed upon inspires confidence in everyone who is investing.

4. ANSWERING THE CHECKLIST QUESTIONS: TAX CONSIDERATIONS

The beginning of the chapter highlighted the flexibility of the LLC regarding tax treatment as well as decision making and equity structure. Even though it is commonly believed that small business founders must choose between an LLC and an S Corp, the law does not impose that restriction. An LLC may elect to be treated as an S Corp *if it qualifies.*

Although the Internal Revenue Code imposes several prerequisites for Subchapter S tax treatment, it is the single-class-of-stock restriction that is most likely to concern the lawyer drafting the operating agreement. The IRS has stated: "Generally, a corporation is treated as having only one class of stock if all outstanding shares of the corporation's stock confer identical rights to distribution and liquidation proceeds."[1] Thus, some members can have different voting rights (or none at all). But the provisions in the operating agreement dealing with distributions of assets during or at the end of the LLC's existence cannot treat some members of the LLC/S Corp differently than others. If an entity that has elected S-Corp treatment fails to meet the requirements in Subchapter S, it will not revert to its default status. Instead, it will be subjected, retroactively, to double taxations as a C Corp.

Many operating agreement forms, particularly those written by lawyers not mindful of the S-Corp possibility, assume that the LLC will be taxed according to its default status. For single-member LLCs, the single class of stock rule does not present a problem. But many multiple-member LLC agreements not only state the LLC's intention to be treated as a partnership but also incorporate partnership tax rules in the distributions provisions. Such language often references Treas. Reg. 1.704–1 or distribution based on capital account balances. Because a distribution provision created for partnership tax treatment bases distribution on capital account balances rather than ownership percentages, the possibility that the proportional relationship between the former might differ from the ratio between the latter could lead the IRS to conclude that the distribution provision creates more than one class of stock and thereby disqualifies the LLC from S-Corp treatment. When working with an LLC electing S-Corp status, you should make sure the operating agreement form that you have chosen to work from is either designed for S-Corp tax treatment or adapted with that in mind. With the pitfalls presented by the

[1] Internal Revenue Service, Instructions for Form 2553. In addition to the provisions expressly dealing with distributions and liquidation, variety in buy-sell arrangements can also lead to an IRS finding that more than one class of stock has been created.

flexibility of the LLC, a client committed to taking advantage of S-Corp tax treatment may be better off forming as a for-profit corporation instead of an LLC.

D. WRITING OUT THE PROVISION LANGUAGE

A multi-member LLC operating agreement is both a foundational governance document and a contract between co-owners. Like other contracts, it begins with the classic phrase "the parties agree as follows." It ends with the signatures of all the founding members. Bylaws, on the other hand, have no prefatory language and end with the lone of signature of the corporation's secretary attesting to their proper adoption. The actual provisions of operating agreements and bylaws, however, have a great deal of structural similarity.

Just like bylaws, operating agreements make some use of the <u>declaration</u> and frequently recite <u>statements of legal fact</u>. When the operating agreement's introductory sections recite or merely reference provisions in the articles of organization, they are not creating the legal reality but attesting to it. These sentences when they are unique to the operating agreement call into being the legal relationships they delineate. Sometimes, this act of creation is emphasized by the inclusion of the jargon term "hereby." If used sparingly to distinguish declarations from restated legal facts, it is far from the worst use of legalese. As set out on the chart, the verb structures in these types of provisions involve the present tense of action or linking verbs.

Whether it be for the handling of net revenue or for the distribution of capital, operating agreements are replete with <u>mandatory</u> and <u>discretionary procedures</u>. Although experts in contract drafting rightly urge their readers to use the active voice instead of the passive voice, procedural provisions are correctly cast in the passive voice. Mandatory procedures use "shall"; discretionary ones use "may."

The active voice is essential when creating either a <u>duty</u> or <u>discretionary authority</u>. In the LLC operating agreement, the subject, who is the bearer of the obligation or the power, is usually either the members or the LLC. "Shall" creates a duty. "May" establishes discretionary authority.

Notice in the table below that the multi-member agreement expresses the Company's indemnification obligation to the members as a duty. The analogous single-member LLC provision often expresses it as a <u>right</u> of the sole member. Such a provision can easily be rewritten to follow the approach of the multi-member operating agreement example. But you might find it more difficult to recast, as a right of the members, a multi-member indemnification that is originally expressed as a duty of the company. Do you see why? If the members are entitled to indemnification, are they entitled as a group only or individually as well. Expressing the obligation as a duty makes the latter interpretation more apparent. When expressing a right, use the passive "is (or shall be) entitled to."

When negating a duty for just one person or entity, use the phrase "is not required to." When negating a duty for more than one person and/or entity, use a negative subject. If the members are not obligated, write "No member is required to" instead of "The members are not required to."

Op. Agreement Provision Examples	Provision Type	Standard Verb (Voice)	Op. Agreement Provision Example Language
Members	Self-Executing Declaration	"is", "are" or other present tense verb (linking verb or active or passive voice)	The names and the business, residence or mailing addresses of the members **are** as follows:
Name	Statement of Legal Fact		The name of the limited liability company **is** _____. (restating Articles)
Allocation of Profits and Losses	Mandatory Procedure	"shall" (passive voice)	The Company's profits and losses **shall be allocated** in proportion to the value of the capital contributions of the Members.
Admission of Addt'l Members	Permissive Procedure	"may" (passive voice)	One or more additional Members of the Company **may be admitted** to the Company with the vote or written consent of a majority in interest of the Members
Indemnification	Duty	"shall" (active voice)	The Company **shall indemnify** . . .
	Right	"is (or shall) be entitled to" (passive voice)	The Member . . . **shall be entitled to** indemnification . . .
Additional Capital Contribution	Negation of Duty (for group)	"No member is required" (passive voice)	**No** member **is required to** make any additional capital contribution to the Company.
	Negation of Duty (for single)	"The member is not required . . ." (passive voice)	The Member **is not required to** make any additional capital contribution to the Company.
Withdrawal	Prohibited Action	"shall not" (active or passive)	Unless all members consent, a Member **shall not withdraw** from the Company before the dissolution and winding up of the Company in accordance with the Act
Assignability	Permitted Action/ Discretionary Authority/ Power	"may" (active voice)	A Member **may assign** in whole or part his or her membership interest in the Company; except . . .

EXERCISE 5–2

Before using a legal form as is, you should review it to make sure it is **complete, correct** and **clear.** The multi-member operating agreement form below contains one instance of falling short of each of these core legal document qualities.

a) As part of your checklist review, find the provision below that has been erased and use process of elimination to guess what it was.

b) For your outline review, find the one provision below that runs afoul of the Indiana limited liability company statute. How did you know which two sections to read in order to find the conflict with the LLC statute?

c) Look over the verbs in each of the provisions. See if you can find the one sentence that has two instances of incorrect verb structures given the types of operating agreement provisions that are being expressed in that one sentence. Try to repair the provision.

Operating Agreement—Member-Managed—Short Form[2]

OPERATING AGREEMENT OF *[NAME OF LIMITED LIABILITY COMPANY]*

This Operating Agreement (this "Agreement") of *[name of limited liability company]*, a *[name of state]* limited liability company (the "Company"), is adopted and entered into on *[date of agreement]*, by and among *[name of first member]*, *[name of second member]* and *[name of third member]*, as members (the "Members," which term includes any other persons who may become members of the Company in accordance with the terms of this Agreement and the Act) and the Company pursuant to and in accordance with the *[name of limited liability company statute]* of *[name of state]*, as amended from time to time (the "Act"). Terms used in this Agreement which are not otherwise defined shall have the respective meanings given those terms in the Act.

In consideration of the matters described above, and of the mutual benefits and obligations set forth in this agreement, the parties agree as follows:

ARTICLE ONE.

NAME

The name of the limited liability company under which it was formed is *[name of limited liability company]*.

[2] Reprinted from *American Jurisprudence Legal Forms 2d,* § 167A:10 with permission of Thomson Reuters. This form has been altered for purposes of this academic exercise.

ARTICLE TWO.

TERM

The Company shall continue until dissolved in accordance with the Act.

ARTICLE THREE.

MANAGEMENT

Management of the Company is vested in its Members, who shall manage the Company in accordance with the Act. Any Member exercising management powers or responsibilities shall be deemed to be a manager for purposes of applying the provisions of the Act, unless the context otherwise requires, and that Member shall have and be subject to all of the duties and liabilities of a manager provided in the Act. The Members shall have the power to do any and all acts necessary or convenient to or for the furtherance of the purposes of the Company set forth in this Agreement, including all powers of Members under the Act.

ARTICLE FOUR.

PURPOSE

The purpose of the Company is to engage in any lawful act or activity for which limited liability companies may be formed under the Act and to engage in any and all activities necessary or incidental to these acts.

ARTICLE FIVE.

MEMBERS

The names and the business, residence or mailing addresses of the members are as follows:

Name	**Address**
[name of member 1]	*[address of member 1]*
[name of member 2]	*[address of member 2]*
[name of member 3]	*[address of member 3]*

ARTICLE SIX.

CAPITAL CONTRIBUTIONS

The Members have contributed to the Company the following amounts, in the form of cash, property or services rendered, or a promissory note or other obligation to contribute cash or property or to render services:

Member	Amount of Capital Contribution
[name of member 1]	*$[dollar amount contributed 1]*
[name of member 2]	*$[dollar amount contributed 2]*
[name of member 3]	*$[dollar amount contributed 3]*

ARTICLE SEVEN.

ADDITIONAL CONTRIBUTIONS

No member is required to make any additional capital contribution to the Company.

ARTICLE EIGHT.

ALLOCATION OF PROFITS AND LOSSES

The Company's profits and losses shall be allocated in proportion to the value of the capital contributions of the Members.

ARTICLE NINE.

DISTRIBUTIONS

The amount of the Company's debt notwithstanding, any member may demand and receive that member's proportionate share of the funds in the Company bank account(s) as long as each Company bank account is left with a balance of at least $100 after said distribution.

ARTICLE TEN.

WITHDRAWAL OF MEMBER

Unless all members consent, a Member may not withdraw from the Company before the dissolution and winding up of the Company in accordance with the Act.

ARTICLE ELEVEN.

ASSIGNMENTS

A Member must be free to assign in whole or part his or her membership interest in the Company; except, however, an assignee of a membership interest should not become a Member without the vote or written consent of at least a majority in interest of the Members, other than the Member who assigns or proposes to assign his or her membership interest.

ARTICLE TWELVE.

ADMISSION OF ADDITIONAL MEMBERS

One or more additional Members of the Company may be admitted to the Company with the vote or written consent of a majority in interest of the Members (as defined in the Act).

ARTICLE THIRTEEN.

ARTICLE FOURTEEN.

EXCULPATION OF MEMBER-MANAGERS

A Member exercising management powers or responsibilities for or on behalf of the Company shall not have personal liability to the Company or its members for damages for any breach of duty in that capacity, except that nothing in this Article shall eliminate or limit:

(i) the liability of any Member-Manager if a judgment or other final adjudication adverse to him or her establishes that his or her acts or omissions were in bad faith or involved intentional misconduct or a knowing violation of law, or that he or she personally gained in fact a financial profit or other advantage to which he or she was not legally entitled, or that, with respect to a distribution to Members, his or her acts were not performed in accordance with Section *[number of section]* of the Act; or

(ii) the liability of any Member-Manager for any act or omission prior to the date of first inclusion of this paragraph in this Agreement.

ARTICLE FIFTEEN.

GOVERNING LAW

This Agreement shall be governed by, and construed in accordance with, the laws of *[name of state]*, all rights and remedies being governed by those laws.

ARTICLE SIXTEEN.

INDEMNIFICATION

To the fullest extent permitted by law, the Company shall indemnify and hold harmless, and may advance expenses to, any Member, manager or other person, or any testator or intestate of such Member, manager or other person (collectively, the "Indemnitees"), from and against any and all claims and demands whatsoever; except, however, that no indemnification may be made to or on behalf of any Indemnitee if a judgment or other final adjudication adverse to such Indemnitee establishes:

(i) that his or her acts were committed in bad faith or were the result of active and deliberate dishonesty and were material to the cause of action so adjudicated; or

(ii) that he or she personally gained in fact a financial profit or other advantage to which he or she was not legally entitled.

The provisions of this paragraph shall continue to afford protection to each Indemnitee regardless of whether he or she remains a Member, manager, employee or agent of the Company.

ARTICLE SEVENTEEN.

TAX MATTERS

The Members of the Company and the Company are entitled to have the Company be treated as a partnership for all income tax purposes and may not file all necessary and appropriate forms in furtherance of that position.

ARTICLE EIGHTEEN.

BOOKS AND RECORDS

The Members shall cause the Company to keep at its principal place of business the following:

(a) A list of all the members and their current addresses.

(b) A copy of the Certificate of Formation and the Company Operating Agreement and all amendments.

(c) Copies of the Company's federal, state and local income tax returns and reports, if any, for the three most recent years

(d) Copies of any financial statements of the limited liability company for the three most recent years.

The parties have executed this agreement the day and year first above written.

____

[Name of first member]

____

[Name of second member]

____

[Name of third member]

____

[Name of limited liability company]

By:

____

[Name of officer of limited liability company]

____

[Title of officer of limited liability company]

Please note that the above form has been deliberately altered to conflict with guidelines offered in the book. Because these alterations may make it unsuitable as a precedent for practice, DO NOT USE the above form as altered in your practice of law.

Single-Member Operating Agreement

LIMITED LIABILITY COMPANY

OPERATING AGREEMENT

FOR

____

A Single Member-Managed Limited Liability Company

This Limited Liability Company Operating Agreement ("this Agreement") of ____________ ("the Company") is entered into by ____________ ("the Member"), the sole member of the Company as of ___________ ("Effective Date")

ARTICLE I

1.1 **FORMATION.** The Member hereby does form the Company subject to the provisions of the Indiana Business Flexibility Act ("the Act") as currently in effect as of this date. Articles of Organization have been or shall be filed with the Secretary of State of Indiana.

1.2 **NAME.** The name of the Company is set forth in the Articles of Organization.

1.3 **TERM.** The Company shall continue in perpetuity or until:

(a) the Member elects to dissolve the Company; or

(b) the Company is dissolved by operation of law in accordance with the Act.

Nothing in subsection (b) above shall be construed to prevent the Member from continuing the Company in accordance with the Act after an administrative or other dissolution by operation of law.

1.4 **PURPOSE.** The purpose of the Company is to engage in any lawful act or activity in accordance with the Act.

1.5 **PRINCIPAL PLACE OF BUSINESS.** The location of the principal place of business of the Company shall be:

____

____

____

The Member may change the principal place of business from time to time as the Member sees fit.

ARTICLE II

2.1 **INITIAL CONTRIBUTIONS.** The Member has contributed or shall promptly contribute to the Company $ __________ in capital, such contribution being cash, property, services rendered, or promise(s) to contribute one or more of the same.

2.2 **ADDITIONAL CONTRIBUTIONS.** The Member is not required to make any additional capital contributions.

2.3 **PROFITS/LOSSES.** The Company's profits and losses shall be allocated to the Member.

2.4 **DISTRIBUTIONS.** Distributions shall be made to the Member, or to the Member's assignee, at the times and in the amounts determined by the Member. But no distribution shall be made if after giving effect to the distribution:

(a) the Company would not be able to pay its debts as the debts become due in the usual course of business; or

(b) the Company's total assets would be less than the sum of:

(i) its total liabilities plus

(ii) the amount that would be needed if the affairs of the Company were to be wound up at the time of the distribution to satisfy any preferential rights that are superior to the rights of the Member, or of the Member's assignee, receiving the distribution.

2.5 **TAX MATTERS.** The Member and the Company intend that the Company be treated as a disregarded entity for federal and state tax purposes. Neither the Company nor the Member shall take any action inconsistent with such tax treatment. This Agreement is to be construed so as to preserve the Company's tax status as a disregarded entity.

2.6 **FISCAL YEAR, BOOKS AND REPORTS.** The Company's fiscal year ("Fiscal Year") is the calendar year. The Member shall maintain complete and accurate books of account of the Company's affairs at the Company's principal place of business. Such books shall be kept using the accounting method chosen by the Member. The Member shall close the books of account after the close of each Fiscal Year and shall prepare a statement of the Member's distributive share of income and expense for income tax reporting purposes.

ARTICLE III

3.1 **THE MEMBER.** The name and place of residence of the Member is

____

____

____

3.2 **MANAGEMENT OF THE BUSINESS.** The Company shall be managed by the Member. The Member may do any and all acts necessary or convenient to further the purposes of the Company and shall have all powers of members under the Act.

ARTICLE IV

4.1 **ASSIGNMENT.** If a creditor of the Member ("Creditor-Assignee") is granted a partial or total assignment of the Member's membership interest in the Company, the Creditor-Assignee shall take an assignment of only the Member's economic interest in the Company, not the transfer of the membership in the Company, which membership shall be retained by the Member. The Creditor-Assignee shall not have any rights of the Member nor shall be authorized to participate in the management of the Company or to dissolve the Company, except that the Creditor-Assignee shall have the rights to receive any distributions authorized by the Member in the Member's sole discretion and shall be allocated the profits and losses of the Company. The Member shall be entitled to redeem the Member's economic interest upon payment to the Creditor-Assignee of the judgment in accordance with the appropriate court. Upon redemption by the Member, the Creditor-Assignee shall cease to have any economic interest in the Company.

4.2 **ADMISSION OF ADDITIONAL MEMBERS.** The Company may admit one or more additional members upon written approval of the Member. In the event of an admission of an additional member(s), this Agreement shall be amended. No additional member shall be deemed to have been admitted to the Company prior to signing with the Member an amended operating agreement.

ARTICLE V

5.1 **LIABILITY OF THE MEMBER.** The liability of the Member shall be limited to the extent provided by applicable law.

5.2 **EXCULPATION.** Any act or omission of the Member, the effect of which may cause or result in loss or damage to the Company or the Member, shall not subject the Member to any liability to the Member or the Company if done in good faith to promote the best interests of the Company.

5.3 **INDEMNIFICATION.**

(a) The Company shall indemnify the Member for any and all claims and demands made by reason of the fact the Member was or is a member of, or otherwise associated with, the Company, except in case of action or failure to act by the Member which action or inaction constitutes willful misconduct or recklessness. Such payment shall include reimbursement of or advance payment of instant expenses (including attorney's fees), judgments, fines, and amounts paid in settlement actually and reasonably incurred in connection with such action, suit or proceeding if the Member determines that the Member acted in good faith and in a manner the Member reasonably believed to be in or not opposed to the best interest of the Company, and with respect to any criminal action proceeding, has no reasonable cause to believe the Member's conduct was unlawful.

(b) The Company may indemnify any manager, employee or other person (inclusively referred to as "Discretionary Indemnitee") for any and all claims and demands made by reason of the fact that he or she is or was associated with the Company, except in case of action or failure to act by the manager, employee or other person which action or inaction constitutes willful misconduct or recklessness. Such payments may include reimbursement of or advance payment of instant expenses (including attorney's fees), judgments, fines, and amounts paid in settlement actually and reasonably incurred in connection with such action, suit or proceeding if the Member determines that the Discretionary Indemnitee acted in good faith and in a manner the Discretionary Indemnitee reasonably believed to be in or not opposed to the best interest of the Company, and with respect to any criminal action proceeding, has no reasonable cause to believe the Discretionary Indemnitee's conduct was unlawful.

(c) With respect to the indemnification provided above in subsections (a) and (b), the termination of any action, suit, or proceeding by judgment, order, settlement, conviction, or upon a plea of "no lo Contendere" or its equivalent, shall not in itself create a presumption that the Member or the Discretionary Indemnitee did or did not act in good faith and in a manner which the Member or the Discretionary Indemnitee reasonably believed to be in the best interest of the Company, and, with respect to any criminal action or proceeding, had reasonable cause to believe that the conduct of the Member or the Discretionary Indemnitee was lawful.

5.4 **COMPENSATION AND REIMBURSEMENT.** If the Member renders services to the Company, the Member shall be entitled to reasonable compensation for such services. The Company shall reimburse the Member for any expenses incurred by the Member in managing the Company

5.5 **DISSOLUTION.** The Member may dissolve the Company at any time. The Member may NOT dissolve the Company for a loss of the Member's membership interest. Upon dissolution, the Company shall pay outstanding debts prior to distributing cash, assets, and/or initial capital to the Member or the Member's assignee. No Creditor-Assignee may order the dissolution of the Company or act to prevent the Member from continuing the Company upon administrative or other dissolution by operation of law.

5.6 **GOVERNING LAW.** This Agreement shall be governed by and construed in accordance with the Act and the laws of the State of Indiana.

5.7 **RECORDS.** The Member shall cause the Company to keep at its principal place of business the following:

(a) A copy of the articles of organization and all amendments.

(b) Copies of the limited liability company's federal, state, and local income tax returns and financial statements, if any, for the three (3) most recent years, or if the returns and statements were not prepared, copies of the information and statements provided to or that should have been provided to the members to enable them to prepare their federal, state, and local tax returns for the same period.

(c) Copies of this Agreement and all amendments and copies of any written operating agreements no longer in effect.

The Member and the Company have executed this agreement as of the Effective Date.

____

[Name of Member]

____

[Name of Company]

By:

____

[Name of Member]

Sole Member

CHAPTER 6

DRAFTING BUY-SELL ARRANGEMENTS

■ ■ ■

A. PROCEDURES GOVERNING TRANSFER OF OWNERSHIP INTERESTS

The Indiana LLC statute provides a default answer to the question of whether members can sell their ownership interests by saying "Yes, and no." According to Indiana Code § 23–18–6-3.1, members may sell their economic interests in the LLC but not their voting rights. Any transfer by a member would result in a new "co-owner" who can receive a share of the profits but not necessarily participate in the management of the LLC. The question of the new co-owner's authority to take part in the management of the LLC would be decided by its continuing members. The relevant section of the short-form multi-member LLC operating agreement, reprinted for Exercise 5–2, tracks the default rule provided by Indiana's LLC statute.

In large public corporations, stock is a commodity that can be easily bought or sold with no disruption to the business by any small single transfer. But with small businesses, any change in ownership can also mean a change in leadership. The statutory default approach described above separates the sale of economic interests from any change in management. Many potential buyers of an interest in a small business may decide against a purchase that does give them a proportionate role in management. As such, the price anyone may be willing to pay for that membership interest may be significantly reduced. This downward pressure on purchase price may be just as strong if not stronger in the context of the closely held corporation.

In the corporation form, stockholders are stockholders. Some kinds of stock come with full voting rights; other kinds come with little or no voting rights. But, generally, shares of stock with voting rights do not lose those voting rights upon transfer to a new owner. The only way that owners of a small corporation may be able to control who has a seat at the table is by restricting transfer of the shares altogether. Ultimately, the question of when and how ownership interests can be transferred must consider and balance the interests of remaining owners and those of the departing owner(s).

One way of satisfying both sides is to have a departing owner sell to one or more remaining owners or the company as a whole. The first step to setting up such a buy-sell arrangement is identifying the circumstances under which an owner's departure would be inevitable or even mutually desirable. The next step involves coming up with a pricing mechanism under those circumstances.

Once it is known that a member's interest may soon be transferred, it can be difficult to negotiate a fair pricing procedure for the insider purchase of that ownership interest. The best time to come up with a fair and effective method is at the time the LLC is created. Take note that in setting up buy-sell arrangements you and the client are not trying to determine now the actual price at which someone's interest will be sold years from now. Instead, the founders, with your help, are laying down the rules that will determine the method for setting the price at which an owner's interest is made available to the other owners—individually, as a group, or both.

The owners will want to have some control over who can join the company as a leader. Likewise, the owners will be concerned about how they or the company they own would come up with the cash to buy a departing owner's membership interest. On the other hand, each of the owners looks forward to ways of reaping financial rewards from his or her ownership interests, which may include selling them at some point. The details of how these competing concerns are balanced are better hammered out before anyone knows who will be cashed out first.

For the small business LLC, this chapter will look at two situations in which a member wishes to sell his or her interest to a third party. In the first, the member has an actual offer in hand; in the second, the member has a minimum price in mind at which he or she is confident of a sale. Apart from those potential voluntary transfers, both the small business LLC and the start-up corporation need to plan for the possibility that an owner may die or lose his or interest to a creditor. The third form presented in this chapter anticipates involuntary transfers such as a shareholder's loss of stock to a creditor, a shareholder's death, and a founding shareholder's departure from corporate leadership. The buy-sell arrangements that preempt voluntary transfers to third parties are called first rights. The corporation protects itself from involuntary transfer through a repurchase option in which the purchase price is based on a valuation of the stock.

B. FIRST RIGHTS

When a member receives an offer that he or she would like to accept, then the price in that offer can set the price for transfer to the other members through a structure known as a right of first refusal (RoFR). Under this approach, before an offering member can accept a third-party purchase offer, he or she must notify the other members of the offer price and give them a chance to match it within a set period of time, usually 30 days. The other members then notify the offering member of their decisions, if the other members accept more shares than are for sale, the total amount offered is divided according to their relative stakes in the company. Any shares not purchased are then available to the third party.

The right of first offer (RoFO) resembles a right of first refusal but is somewhat more attractive to third parties and, perhaps therefore, to a member wishing to sell. Instead of the offering member communicating to the other member an actual offer to purchase from a third party, the offering member simply declares his or her willingness to sell a certain amount of his or her membership in the LLC at a price he or she believes is low enough to attract third-party interest. What induces the offering member to set a reasonably low price? If shares remain unsold after the other members have had their chance to buy, the offering member can sell only at a price as low as the one originally communicated. From the perspective of the offering member who already knows what he or she can get from third parties, the RoFO works in a very similar way as the RoFR. But, without a legally binding commitment to purchase from a third-party, an offering member cannot take advantage of the RoFR process. Since an offering member might find it difficult to convince third parties to make legally binding commitments to purchase shares that can be bought out from under them, the RoFO approach offers a significantly higher chance of a transfer.

True family businesses may choose to restrict transfer altogether. For them, controlling who owns the business is just too important to be concerned about any one member being able to get a fair price for his or her interest. Even a blanket prohibition can be overridden with the consent of all the members. Ownership of a business is a property right, and the law generally looks at the enforceability of strong restraints on the alienability of private property with skepticism. Yet, for more than a century now, courts have regarded certain business relationships, such as co-ownership of a small business, as being worthy of protection through freely agreed to transfer constraints. Consent-based restrictions on the sale of company ownership stakes are the most likely to be upheld when challenged. [1] The level of co-owner agreement can be set at majority or at super-majority instead of at unanimity.

A wide variety of businesses may elect a structure that balances the desire to control who holds the ownership stakes with the ability of owners to realize the financial value of those ownership interests. Those types of businesses may be best served by the right of first offer or right of first refusal approaches to possible sales to third parties. But, in the context of

[1] As we will explore later in this chapter's discussion of planning for involuntary transfers, a requirement that any transfer of an ownership interest be approved by the other owners will not succeed in preventing an owner from losing, at least economic rights of, his or her stake in the business. The most that LLC members facing the prospect of sharing the company with a creditor of one of their number is to follow the statutory default approach to all transfers and restrict the creditor's gain to the economic interest only.

LLCs, the choice to use a first-rights approach requires consideration of both of the alternatives to it:

- staying with the statutory default of allowing free transfer of the economic interest but consent for the admission of a new member; and
- requiring voluntary transfer of any part of the ownership rights to be subject to the approval to the other members.

Choosing between first rights, also called preemptive rights, and the two other contenders listed above may seem difficult. How do your clients value the right to count on fellow owners remaining involved with the freedom to move on? But, even when a determination in favor of setting up a right for insiders to anticipate and preempt outsiders' attempts to buy in, the question remains as to whether the more appropriate mechanism if right of first offer or right of first refusal.

DISCUSSION QUESTION 6–A

Imagine that you have been assigned two different small business clients that are both interested in confronting the issue of transferability of ownership interests.

1) The first is a health and fitness business being formed by two friends who graduated college together three years ago. Neither are native to your city but both are happy there and look forward to growing the business into several locations in the region.

2) The second is a garage-door installation business that two brothers and a sister have recently purchased from their father, who is now retiring. All are in their mid-late forties and have almost twenty years each in the business. They are committed to keeping the enterprise successful and employing some of their own young adult children.

Do you offer a first rights arrangement to either client as an option? If so, which one(s) and why? If not, why not? What else would you to know about the businesses and their co-owners in preparing your counseling? If a first rights approach is preferred, which of the two types would you recommend? Why?

C. CHECKLIST AND OUTLINE: MAPPING OUT A PROCESS FOR FIRST RIGHTS

In drafting the governance documents of nonprofit corporations, the checklist and outline phases focused on the identification of the decision makers and the process for making decisions. The bylaws provisions so generated form the sturdy workings of a new institution. The option procedures described in this chapter are more linear and dynamic.

The questions of if and how certain ownership interests will be transferred are answered through a step-by-step process outlined below. In each case, an occurrence of some kind initiates the series of events. In most cases, the person bound by the option has a duty to notify the holder of the right to exercise it. The holder has the power to purchase the interests but must make a commitment within the stated period of time. The process then branches to deal with the option holder's purchase or declination. To illustrate how these multi-step processes are constructed, the table in the next section will compare the steps providing the relevant provision cites for the forms that follow.

Basic Process	Right of First Offer	Right of First Refusal
Triggering event	Offeror desires to sell shares—§2.01(a)	Offeror has third-party bona fide offer—§2.01(a)
Communication to option holder	Must include price and other terms for sale—§2.01(b)(i)	Must include price/ terms from third-party offer—§2.01(b)(i)
Option holder's time period to make a decision	Typically within 10 days—§2.01(b)(ii)	
Consequences of option holder's declination	Offeror free to sell at price at least as high—§2.01(d)	Offeror free to accept third-party offer—§2.01(d)
Procedure for option holder's purchase	Option Holder/ Buyer(s) must close per terms of offer notice —§2.01(c)	Option Holder/Buyer(s) must close per terms of offer notice, which must give at least 60 days—§2.01(c)
Procedure for offeror if declination	Offeror has 60–90 days to close or process starts over—§2.01(d)	

D. DRAFTING CONSIDERATIONS

In Chapter 4, you learned that long complicated sentences could be reduced by the use of defined terms as shorthand for complex conceptual elements. Buy-sell provisions provide excellent examples of this technique. Look at the following provision describing a mandated purchase of a deceased member's interests.

> On the death of any Member, his or her estate shall immediately be deemed to have offered to sell to the LLC the deceased member's LLC interests at the Agreement Price, and the LLC shall accept such offer and agree to buy the deceased member's LLC interests.
>
> The Agreement Price shall be the fair market value of the deceased member's LLC interests as determined by an independent certified public accountant ("CPA") selected by the LLC. This valuation shall be determined under the same methods as would be used for determining the estate tax value of the deceased member's LLC interests.

The core provision is a single compound sentence just over four-lines long. The key defined term requires an additional two sentences, one of which borrows the valuation method from estate tax law. The term "Agreement Price" appears only once in the core provision, yet if the drafter had attempted to present its full meaning in that core provision, then that single sentence would have doubled in length. Shorthand and incorporation by reference are important tools in drafting.

Each of the first rights forms below dedicate nearly half of its five pages to definitions. The definitions sections include seemingly simple words like "Person", "Independent Third Party" and "Transfer" that play crucial roles in establishing the triggering events that that set the option processes in motion. Also note that other terms, such as "Member" and "Affiliate" are presumed to be defined in the LLC's operating agreement. More specialized terms, such as "ROFO (ROFR) Notice Period" and "Pro Rata Portion" are used to define periods of time and fractions. The former is not defined in the first section but instead in the first provision in which it is put to work. This approach obviates the need for those reading the core of the document from having to refer back to the definitions section to understand the substantive meaning of the agreement.

In addition to its discussion of definitions, Chapter 4's summary of deadline and time period provisions also warrant revisiting. Deadlines for fulfilling duties or windows for exercising a power are usually set with reference to a date or to a period of time. If the deadline is a specified date (e.g., "December 31st," "the last business day of the month," or the "10 day after

___"), then use "on or before," not "by." If it is expressed as a period of time, then write "no later than ___ days after" instead of "within ___ days of."

The provision types discussed in previous chapters will be sufficient to create buy-sell arrangements. Normally, declarations are written in the present tense. But, options frequently declare rights or other legal facts subject to certain conditions through the use of "shall." (e.g., "In the event of any such default, the transferor shall be entitled to pursue such remedies . . . .").

EXERCISE 6–1

Using the chart above as your guide, locate in the Right of First Offer document below the specific provision in the cited subsection that creates the step described in the chart. For each of the six steps, write down the word(s) that make(s) up the verb in each of these key provisions and use that information to identify the type of each of the six provisions.

For instance, the first step, the triggering event, is addressed in § 2.01(a) by the provision ". . . each Member shall have a right of first offer if any other Member (the **"Offering Member"**), proposes to sell any Equity Securities." The verb phrase is "shall have a right", which makes the sentence a right-creating provision (or, alternatively, a declaration of legal fact).

Review the six core provisions again. Identify at least one example of a descriptive conceptual element and at least one instance of an evaluative conceptual element. Is the evaluative element problematic in terms of being **clear**? Is the descriptive so rigid that it risks not being "**correct**"? If need be, go ahead and review Section A of Ch. 4.

LLC Agreement: Right of First Offer[2]

Drafting Note: Read This Before Using Document

The right of first refusal is a standard clause in many LLC agreements. It requires a member who has received an offer from a third party to purchase any or all of its membership interests in a company to offer those membership interests to the other members before consummating the sale to the third party. If the other members choose not to buy all of the offered membership interests (or, in some agreements, if they choose to buy less than all the offered membership interests), the offering member can sell them (or the remainder of them) to the third party.

A right of first refusal is common in LLC agreements because the members want to control who can become a member in the company. With this right, a member can prevent a third party from becoming an investor in the company and simultaneously increase its ownership interest.

This Standard Clause is a sample of a right of first refusal. The specific terms of the right of first refusal, like the rest of the LLC agreement, may differ depending on the nature of the transaction and the negotiating strength of the parties (see *Practice Note, LLC Agreement Commentary*).

If your client indicates that it wants a right of first offer, do not include a right of first refusal. Although there are no legal constraints against including both provisions, because the procedures that must be followed in both cases can be lengthy and ultimately achieve the same goal, the inclusion of both provisions is not practical.

Other Transfer Restrictions

In addition to the right of first refusal, LLC agreements typically include other transfer restrictions (such as a tag-along right and a drag-along right). Depending on the percentage interest being sold and the tag-along conditions, any member who does not wish to participate in the right of first refusal transaction can exercise its tag-along right and sell all or a percentage of its interest in the company to the third party (see *Standard Clause, LLC Agreement: Tag-along Rights*).

If the LLC agreement includes a tag-along right, it will usually include its corollary, a drag-along right. A drag-along right gives a majority member who is selling all or a significant percentage of its interest to a third party the right to force the other members to also sell all or a percentage of their interests to such third party as well. Depending on the majority member's percentage interest, the wishes of the third party and the drag-along

---

[2] The Standard Clause was first published by Practical Law on its Practical Law Corporate and M&A web service at http://us.practicallaw.tr.com/1-383-8859. It is reprinted with the permission of Thomson Reuters. The parenthetical and other references in the Drafting Notes instructing the reader to "see" related materials are to documents also available through Practical Law.

conditions, the majority member may force any member who is not participating in the right of first refusal to also sell its interests (see *Standard Clause, LLC Agreement: Drag-along Rights*).

END DRAFTING NOTE

ARTICLE I

DEFINITIONS

Capitalized terms used herein shall have the meanings set forth in this Article [1].

"Business Day" means a day other than a Saturday, Sunday or other day on which commercial banks in the City of New York are authorized or required to close.

Drafting Note: Business Day: Definition

This definition is typically used in domestic transactions. However, if any of the members are located outside of the US (such as London or Tokyo), these cities may also be included in addition to the City of New York.

END DRAFTING NOTE

"Equity Securities" means any and all Units of the Company and any securities of the Company convertible into, or exchangeable or exercisable for, such Units, and warrants or other rights to acquire such Units.

Drafting Note: Equity Securities: Definition

This definition may require modification depending on the capital structure of the company and whether it has (or is able to issue) profits interests or other types of securities.

END DRAFTING NOTE

"Government Approval" means any authorization, consent, approval, waiver, exception, variance, order, exemption, publication, filing, declaration, concession, grant, franchise, agreement, permission, permit, or license of, from or with any Government Authority, the giving of notice to or registration with any Government Authority or any other action in respect of any Government Authority.

"Government Authority" means any federal, state, local or foreign government or political subdivision thereof, or any agency or instrumentality of such government or political subdivision, or any self-regulated organization or other non-governmental regulatory authority or quasi-governmental authority (to the extent that the rules, regulations or orders of such organization or authority have the force of law), or any arbitrator, court or tribunal of competent jurisdiction.

"Independent Third Party" means, with respect to any Member, any Person who is not an Affiliate of such Member.

[**"Initial Public Offering"** means any underwritten public offering pursuant to a registration statement filed in accordance with the Securities Act.]

Drafting Note: Initial Public Offering: Definition

For the purposes of this Standard Clause, include either this defined term or Qualified Public Offering (see Drafting Note, Qualified Public Offering: Definition).

END DRAFTING NOTE

"Lien" means any mortgage, pledge, security interest, option, right of first offer, encumbrance or other restriction or limitation of any nature whatsoever.

[**"Offer Price"** has the meaning set forth in Section [2.01(c)].]

Drafting Note: Offer Price: Definition

The inclusion of the defined term Offer Price depends on whether the LLC agreement provides for the Offering Member to include a price for the Offered Units in its notice to the other members. See Drafting Notes, Consideration and Exercise of Right of First Offer for further information.

END DRAFTING NOTE

"Offered Units" has the meaning set forth in Section [2.01(a)].

"Offering Member" has the meaning set forth in Section [2.01(a)].

"Offering Member Notice" has the meaning set forth in Section [2.01(b)].

"Person" means any individual, corporation, limited liability company, limited or general partnership, joint venture, association, joint-stock company, trust, unincorporated organization, government or any agency or political subdivisions thereof.

"Pro Rata Portion" means, with respect to any Purchasing Member, on the date of the Offering Member Notice, the number of Equity Securities equal to the product of (i) the total number of Offered Units and (ii) a fraction determined by dividing (x) the number of Units owned by such Purchasing Member by (y) the total number of Units owned by all of the Purchasing Members.

Drafting Note: Pro Rata Portion: Definition

The definition of Pro Rata Portion dictates the apportionment of the Offered Units among those members who have chosen to exercise their right of first offer if more than one member offers to purchase all the Offered Units. In this Standard Clause, although the members will ultimately purchase a portion of fully diluted Equity Securities, their percentage participation in the sale is calculated on the basis of their ownership of outstanding Units. This way, primacy is given to ownership of outstanding Units for purposes of determining each member's pro rata participation, while the ownership of convertible securities is set aside. The definition can be adjusted to calculate each member's Pro Rata Portion on the basis of their ownership of Equity Securities (for example, see Standard Document, LLC Agreement (Multi-Member, Manager-Managed): Common Pro Rata Portion).

If the LLC agreement in question contemplates more than two members and refers to a pro rata concept in different contexts, be sure to clarify that for purposes of the right of first offer, clause (y) above refers to the Purchasing Members' Units, not all the members' Units.

END DRAFTING NOTE

"Purchasing Member" has the meaning set forth in Section [2.01(c)].

[**"Qualified Public Offering"** means the sale, in a firm commitment underwritten public offering led by a nationally recognized underwriting firm pursuant to an effective registration statement under the Securities Act, of Units (or common stock of the Company upon conversion of such Units) having an aggregate offering value (net of underwriters' discounts and selling commissions) of at least $[AMOUNT], following which at least [PERCENTAGE]% of the total Units (or common stock of the Company upon conversion of such Units) on a fully diluted basis shall have been sold to the public and shall be listed on any national securities exchange or quoted on the Nasdaq Stock Market System.]

Drafting Note: Qualified Public Offering: Definition

This is a sample definition of Qualified Public Offering. The purpose of adding the dollar and percentage thresholds is to test whether the company's value has increased as anticipated and the members are able to realize that value. This term may be defined a number of different ways, but is generally an offering that satisfies certain specific requirements (such as the net proceeds received by the company, the per unit value of the company's membership interests, the return received by the members from the offering or the sale of their units, or the percentage of the company's units (or common stock on the conversion of the units) involved in the offering).

END DRAFTING NOTE

"ROFO Notice Period" has the meaning set forth in Section [2.01(b)(ii)].

"ROFO Offer Notice" has the meaning set forth in Section [2.01(c)].

"Securities Act" means the Securities Act of 1933, as amended, or any successor federal statute, and the rules and regulations thereunder which shall be in effect at the time.

"Transfer" means to, directly or indirectly, sell, transfer, assign, pledge, encumber, hypothecate or similarly dispose of, either voluntarily or involuntarily, or to enter into any contract, option or other arrangement or understanding with respect to the sale, transfer, assignment, pledge, encumbrance, hypothecation or similar disposition of, any Equity Securities owned by a Person or any interest (including but not limited to a beneficial interest) in any Equity Securities owned by a Person.

"Waived ROFO Transfer Period" has the meaning set forth in Section [2.01(d)].

Drafting Note: Other Defined Terms

Certain terms are capitalized but not defined in this Standard Clause because they will be defined elsewhere in the LLC agreement (for example, terms such as Agreement, Affiliate, Company and Member). These defined terms should conform to the LLC agreement being used.

Membership interests are the equity interest that members hold in the limited liability company. A unit represents a piece of a membership interest in the same way that a "share" represents a piece of stock ownership. The definition of this term depends on how the membership interests are divided among the members (for example, in units, by percentage and class). In this Standard Clause, membership interests are expressed in units.

END DRAFTING NOTE

ARTICLE II

RIGHT OF FIRST OFFER

Section 2.01 Right of First Offer.

(a) **Right of First Offer.** [At any time/At any time prior to the consummation of [an Initial Public Offering/a Qualified Public Offering]], and subject to the terms and conditions specified in this Section [2.01], each Member shall have a right of first offer if any other Member (the **"Offering Member"**), proposes to sell any Equity Securities (the **"Offered Units"**) owned by it to any Independent Third Party. Each time the Offering Member proposes to Transfer any Offered Units (other than Transfers permitted pursuant to Section [PERMITTED-TRANSFERS SECTION] [and Transfers made pursuant to Section [DRAG-ALONG RIGHTS SECTION]]), the Offering Member shall first make an offering of the Offered Units to the other Members in accordance with the following provisions of this Section [2.01].

Drafting Note: Timing of ROFO

If the LLC agreement includes a lock-up period (a period of time after the execution of the agreement during which no party can transfer its units other than to an affiliate), make the following changes:

- Add a defined term "Lock-up Period," which may be defined as, "[NUMBER OF YEARS] after the date of this Agreement."
- Replace the phrase "At any time" with the phrase "At any time following the expiration of the Lock-up Period."
- Replace the phrase "At any time prior to the consummation of [an Initial Public Offering/a Qualified Public Offering]" with the phrase "After the expiration of the Lock-up Period but prior to the consummation of [an Initial Public Offering/a Qualified Public Offering]."

The right of first offer does not usually apply to transfers that are conducted after an Initial Public Offering or a Qualified Public Offering (as the case may be). If the LLC agreement contemplates an IPO or QIPO as an exit strategy or a liquidity event, the second bracketed phrase should be used.

Availability of ROFO

This Standard Clause assumes that all members have a right of first offer. However, this is not always the case. Depending on the nature of the transaction and the parties involved, this right may be limited to:

- **Certain key members.** In private equity transactions this right is often limited to the sponsor, its affiliates and co-investment vehicles.
- **Non-management members.** Members who receive their units as part of an employee bonus or compensation plan often do not have a right of first offer.

Some LLC agreements provide that the right of first offer may not be exercised by the minority members if the majority member exercises its drag-along right. The argument against including this limitation is that so long as the majority member is able to sell its units and achieve liquidity, it should be indifferent to the identity of the buyer (be it the other members or an independent third party).

Company ROFO

Some LLC agreements also provide that the company has the first right to redeem any or all of the units before they are offered to the members. A member that does not expect to want, or to be able to afford, to exercise its right of first offer might favor this provision, since it has the effect of maintaining the members' existing equity ratios without forcing the members to make any further investment in the company.

END DRAFTING NOTE

(b) **Offer Notice.**

(i) The Offering Member shall give written notice (the **"Offering Member Notice"**) to the Company and the other Members stating its bona fide intention to Transfer the Offered Units and specifying the number of Offered Units and the material terms and conditions, including the price, pursuant to which the Offering Member proposes to Transfer the Offered Units.

Drafting Note: Consideration

As drafted, the Offering Member must provide the price at which it would be selling its membership interest to the other members. In this scenario, the other members do not alter the price or bid against each other, but simply choose whether to accept or decline the offer.

In some agreements, the Offering Member provides all the material terms of the offer except for the price, leaving it to the other members to bid against each other. This may result in the Offering Member receiving a higher price for the Offered Units than if it were to specify a purchase price in the Offering Member Notice. However, this approach can only work if there is a large enough group of members to create a competitive bidding environment. If there are only one or two other members, the Offering Member should specify the price. In any event, the more common approach is to include the price in the Offering Member Notice.

END DRAFTING NOTE

(ii) The Offering Member Notice shall constitute the Offering Member's offer to Transfer the Offered Units to the other Members, which offer shall be irrevocable for a period of [ten (10)] [Business Days/days] (the **"ROFO Notice Period"**).

(iii) By delivering the Offering Member Notice, the Offering Member represents and warrants to the Company and each other Member that: (x) the Offering Member has full right, title and interest in and to the Offered Units; (y) the Offering Member has all the necessary power and authority and has taken all necessary action to sell such Offered Units as contemplated by this Section [2.01]; and (z) the Offered Units are free and clear of any and all Liens other than those arising as a result of or under the terms of this Agreement.

(c) **Exercise of Right of First Offer.**

(i) Upon receipt of the Offering Member Notice, each Member shall have until the end of the ROFO Notice Period to offer to purchase all (but not less than all) of the Offered Units by delivering a written notice (a **"ROFO Offer Notice"**) to the Offering Member and the Company stating that it offers to purchase such Offered Units on the terms specified in the Offering Member Notice. Any ROFO Offer Notice so delivered shall be binding upon delivery and irrevocable by the applicable Member. If more than one Member delivers a ROFO Offer Notice, each such Member (the **"Purchasing Member"**) shall be allocated its Pro Rata Portion of the Offered Units, unless otherwise agreed by such Members.

Drafting Note: Exercise of Right of First Offer

This Standard Clause contemplates that each non-offering Member must offer to purchase all of the Offered Units. In contrast to the right of first refusal, however, there is more of a rationale to allow the other members to purchase less than all the Offered Units, since the Offering Member does not already have a third-party buyer who is prepared to buy a certain-sized stake in the company. As alternatives, therefore, the parties can agree that the other members:

- **Can offer to purchase any portion of the Offered Units.** In this case, the Offering Member agrees to sell the number offered to be purchased and may then sell any remaining portion to the Independent Third Party.
- **Must offer to purchase its entire pro rata portion of the Offered Units, or none at all.** In this case, if any member elects not to buy its pro rata share, the Offering Member can either sell such member's pro rata share to the third party or reallocate such units pro rata to the other members in accordance with their ownership interests.

Both of these alternative formulations give the other members more flexibility because they are not forced to purchase all or nothing. The formulation that is used is a matter of negotiation among the members.

Competitive Bidding

If the Offering Member wishes to generate a bidding process for the Offered Units and does not include a price in the Offering Member Notice, replace the entire clause (i) above with the following:

"(i) Upon receipt of the Offering Member Notice, each Member shall have until the end of the ROFO Notice Period to offer to purchase all (but not less than all) of the Offered Units by delivering a written notice (a **"ROFO Offer Notice"**) to the Offering Member and the Company stating that it offers to purchase such Offered Units on the terms specified in the Offering Member Notice and specifying the price it is offering to pay for such Offered Units (the **"Offer Price"**). Any ROFO Offer Notice shall be binding upon delivery and irrevocable by the applicable Member. If the Offer Price set forth in any ROFO Offer Notice is less than the Offer Price set forth in any other ROFO Offer Notice, the Offering Member shall, within [five (5)] [Business Days/days] after the expiration of the ROFO Notice Period, deliver written notice to the Members and the Company specifying the highest Offer Price set forth in any ROFO Notice, whereupon each other ROFO Offer Notice shall be deemed automatically revoked[; *provided*, that any Member whose ROFO Offer Notice has been revoked shall have the right, exercisable within [ten (10)] [Business Days/days] after the expiration of the ROFO Notice Period, to match the highest Offer Price initially offered by delivering a revised ROFO Offer Notice to the Offering Member, the Company and the other Members]. In the event that more than one Member delivers a ROFO Offer Notice offering the same, highest price [(including pursuant to the matching right set forth in the proviso in the preceding sentence)], each such Member (the **"Purchasing Members"**) shall be allocated its Pro Rata Portion of the Offered Units, unless otherwise agreed by such Members."

This version of the right of first offer requires a participating member to specify the price at which it wishes to purchase the Offered Units. The member is at a disadvantage in this situation because when it submits its irrevocable offer it may not know whether there are any other parties (whether another member or a third party) who are interested in purchasing the units. A member who wishes to exercise its right of first offer assumes the risk of overpaying for the Offered Units or offering too low a price and losing the opportunity to buy the Offered Units.

To account for the risk of underpricing the Offered Units, this version also contains bracketed language that contemplates a matching right for each member to match the highest price offered for the Offered Units and participate pro rata in the sale.

Financing Condition

Some LLC agreements allow a member who cannot secure the necessary financing to revoke its offer to buy the units. However, this is rare and not usually included. Include this revocation right if your client is unlikely to have the cash on hand and may have to secure financing either from a third party, or in the case of a private equity transaction, from its investors. However, do not add this provision without first discussing it with your client. If this provision is to be included, the following language should be inserted at the end of the second sentence of either version of clause (i) above:

"; *provided*, that any Member may revoke its ROFO Offer Notice at any time within [20] [Business Days/days] following delivery thereof if such Member is unable to secure financing on terms and conditions reasonably acceptable to such Member."

END DRAFTING NOTE

(ii) Each Member that does not deliver a ROFO Offer Notice during the ROFO Notice Period shall be deemed to have waived all of such Member's rights to purchase the Offered Units under this Section [2.01], and the Offering Member shall thereafter, subject to the rights of any Purchasing Member, be free to Transfer the Offered Units to any Independent Third Party without any further obligation to such Member pursuant to this Section [2.01].

(iii) Each Member who delivers a ROFO Offer Notice shall be deemed to have waived any rights that such Member may have pursuant to Section [TAG-ALONG RIGHTS SECTION] of this Agreement.

(d) **Consummation of Sale.** If no Member delivers a ROFO Offer Notice in accordance with Section [2.01](c), the Offering Member may, during the [sixty (60)] [Business Day/day] period following the expiration of the ROFO Notice Period (which period may be extended for a reasonable time not to exceed [90] [Business Days/days] to the extent reasonably necessary to obtain any Government Approvals) (the **"Waived ROFO Transfer Period"**), and subject to the provisions of Section [TAG-ALONG RIGHTS SECTION] with respect to those Members who have not delivered ROFO Offer Notices, Transfer all of the Offered Units to an Independent Third Party on terms and conditions no more favorable to the Independent Third Party than those specified in the Offering Member Notice. If the Offering Member does not Transfer the Offered Units, or if such Transfer is not consummated, within the Waived ROFO Transfer Period, the right provided hereunder shall be deemed to be revived and the Offered Units shall not be offered to any Person unless first re-offered to the Members in accordance with this Section [2.01].

(e) **Cooperation.** Each Member shall take all actions as may be reasonably necessary to consummate the sale contemplated by this Section [2.01] including, without limitation, entering into agreements and delivering certificates and instruments and consents as may be deemed necessary or appropriate.

(f) **Closing.** At the closing of any sale and purchase pursuant to this Section [2.01], the Offering Member shall deliver to the Purchasing Member(s) certificate or certificates representing the Offered Units to be sold (if any), accompanied by evidence of transfer and all necessary transfer taxes paid and stamps affixed, if necessary, against receipt of the purchase price therefor from such Purchasing Member(s) by certified or official bank check or by wire transfer of immediately available funds.

LLC Agreement: Right of First Refusal[3]

Drafting Note: Read This Before Using Document

The right of first refusal is a standard clause in many LLC agreements. It requires a member who has received an offer from a third party to purchase any or all of its membership interests in a company to offer those membership interests to the other members before consummating the sale to the third party. If the other members choose not to buy all of the offered membership interests (or, in some agreements, if they choose to buy less than all the offered membership interests), the offering member can sell them (or the remainder of them) to the third party.

A right of first refusal is common in LLC agreements because the members want to control who can become a member in the company. With this right, a member can prevent a third party from becoming an investor in the company and simultaneously increase its ownership interest.

This Standard Clause is a sample of a right of first refusal. The specific terms of the right of first refusal, like the rest of the LLC agreement, may differ depending on the nature of the transaction and the negotiating strength of the parties (see *Practice Note, LLC Agreement Commentary*).

If your client indicates that it wants a right of first offer, do not include a right of first refusal. Although there are no legal constraints against including both provisions, because the procedures that must be followed in both cases can be lengthy and ultimately achieve the same goal, the inclusion of both provisions is not practical.

Other Transfer Restrictions

In addition to the right of first refusal, LLC agreements typically include other transfer restrictions (such as a tag-along right and a drag-along right). Depending on the percentage interest being sold and the tag-along conditions, any member who does not wish to participate in the right of first refusal transaction can exercise its tag-along right and sell all or a percentage of its interest in the company to the third party (see *Standard Clause, LLC Agreement: Tag-along Rights*).

If the LLC agreement includes a tag-along right, it will usually include its corollary, a drag-along right. A drag-along right gives a majority member who is selling all or a significant percentage of its interest to a third party the right to force the other members to also sell all or a percentage of their interests to such third party as well. Depending on the majority member's percentage interest, the wishes of the third party and the drag-along

[3] The Standard Clause was first published by Practical Law on its Practical Law Corporate and M&A web service at http://us.practicallaw.tr.com/2-383-9900. It is reprinted with the permission of Thomson Reuters. The parenthetical and other references in the Drafting Notes instructing the reader to "see" related materials are to documents also available through Practical Law.

conditions, the majority member may force any member who is not participating in the right of first refusal to also sell its interests (see *Standard Clause, LLC Agreement: Drag-along Rights*).

END DRAFTING NOTE

ARTICLE I

DEFINITIONS

Capitalized terms used herein shall have the meanings set forth in this Article [1].

"Business Day" means a day other than a Saturday, Sunday or other day on which commercial banks in the City of New York are authorized or required to close.

Drafting Note: Business Day: Definition

This definition is typically used in domestic transactions. However, if any of the members are located outside of the US (such as London or Tokyo), these cities may also be included in addition to the City of New York.

END DRAFTING NOTE

"Equity Securities" means any and all Units of the Company and any securities of the Company convertible into, or exchangeable or exercisable for, such Units, and warrants or other rights to acquire such Units.

Drafting Note: Equity Securities: Definition

You may need to modify this definition depending on the capital structure of the company and whether it has (or is able to issue) profits interests or other types of securities.

END DRAFTING NOTE

"Government Approval" means any authorization, consent, approval, waiver, exception, variance, order, exemption, publication, filing, declaration, concession, grant, franchise, agreement, permission, permit, or license of, from or with any Government Authority, the giving of notice to or registration with any Government Authority or any other action in respect of any Government Authority.

"Government Authority" means any federal, state, local or foreign government or political subdivision thereof, or any agency or instrumentality of such government or political subdivision, or any self-regulated organization or other non-governmental regulatory authority or quasi-governmental authority (to the extent that the rules, regulations or orders of such organization or authority have the force of law), or any arbitrator, court or tribunal of competent jurisdiction.

"Independent Third Party" means, with respect to any Member, any Person who is not an Affiliate of such Member.

[**"Initial Public Offering"** means any offering of Units (or common stock of the Company upon conversion of such Units) pursuant to a registration statement filed in accordance with the Securities Act.]

Drafting Note: Initial Public Offering: Definition

For the purposes of this Standard Clause, you should include this defined term or Qualified Public Offering (see Drafting Note, Qualified Public Offering: Definition).

END DRAFTING NOTE

"Lien" means any mortgage, pledge, security interest, option, right of first offer, encumbrance or other restriction or limitation of any nature whatsoever.

"Offer Price" has the meaning set forth in Section [2.01(c)].

"Offered Units" has the meaning set forth in Section [2.01(a)].

"Offering Member" has the meaning set forth in Section [2.01(a)].

"Offering Member Notice" has the meaning set forth in Section [2.01(b)].

"Person" means any individual, corporation, limited liability company, limited or general partnership, joint venture, association, joint-stock company, trust, unincorporated organization, government or any agency or political subdivisions thereof.

"Pro Rata Portion" means, with respect to any Purchasing Member, on the date of the Offering Member Notice, the number of Equity Securities equal to the product of (i) the total number of Offered Units and (ii) a fraction determined by dividing (x) the number of Equity Securities owned by such Purchasing Member by (y) the total number of Equity Securities owned by all of the Purchasing Members.

Drafting Note: Pro Rata Portion: Definition

The definition of Pro Rata Portion dictates the apportionment of the Offered Units among those members who have chosen to exercise their right of first refusal if more than one member offers to purchase all the Offered Units. In this Standard Clause, the term is defined by reference to each member's ownership of fully diluted ownership of Equity Securities. In other agreements, however, Pro Rata Portion is calculated on the basis of each member's ownership of outstanding units.

If your LLC agreement has more than two members and refers to a pro rata concept in different contexts, be sure to clarify that for purposes of the right of first refusal, clause (y) above refers to the Purchasing Members' Equity Securities, not all the members' Equity Securities.

END DRAFTING NOTE

"Purchasing Member" Has the meaning set forth in Section [2.01(c)].

[**"Qualified Public Offering"** means the sale, in a firm commitment underwritten public offering led by a nationally recognized underwriting firm pursuant to an effective registration statement under the Securities Act, of Units (or common stock of the Company upon conversion of such Units) having an aggregate offering value (net of underwriters' discounts and selling commissions) of at least $[AMOUNT], following which at least [PERCENTAGE]% of the total Units (or common stock of the Company upon conversion of such Units) on a fully diluted basis shall have been sold to the public and shall be listed on any national securities exchange or quoted on the Nasdaq Stock Market System.]

Drafting Note: Qualified Public Offering: Definition

This is a sample definition of Qualified Public Offering. The purpose of using this term, as opposed to any other offering, is to test whether the company's value has increased as anticipated and the members are able to realize that value. This term may be defined a number of different ways, but is generally defined as an offering that satisfies certain specific requirements (such as the net proceeds received by the company, the per unit value of the company's membership interests, the return received by the members from the offering or the sale of their units, or the percentage of the company's units (or common stock on the conversion of the units) involved in the offering).

END DRAFTING NOTE

"ROFR Notice Period" has the meaning set forth in Section [2.01(c)].

"ROFR Offer Notice" has the meaning set forth in Section [2.01(c)].

"Securities Act" means the Securities Act of 1933, as amended, or any successor federal statute, and the rules and regulations thereunder which shall be in effect at the time.

"Transfer" means to, directly or indirectly, sell, transfer, assign, pledge, encumber, hypothecate or similarly dispose of, either voluntarily or involuntarily, or to enter into any contract, option or other arrangement or understanding with respect to the sale, transfer, assignment, pledge, encumbrance, hypothecation or similar disposition of, any Equity Securities owned by a Person or any interest (including but not limited to a beneficial interest) in any Equity Securities owned by a Person.

"Waived ROFR Transfer Period" has the meaning set forth in Section [2.01(d)].

Drafting Note: Other Defined Terms

Certain terms are capitalized but not defined in this Standard Clause because they will be defined elsewhere in the LLC agreement (for example, Agreement, Affiliate, Company, Member and Units). You need to tailor these defined terms for your LLC agreement.

Membership interests are the equity interest that members hold in the limited liability company. A unit represents a piece of a membership interest in the same way that a "share" represents a piece of stock ownership. The definition of this term depends on how the membership interests are divided among the members (for example, in units, by percentage and class). In this Standard Clause, membership interests are expressed in units.

END DRAFTING NOTE

ARTICLE II

RIGHT OF FIRST REFUSAL

Section 2.01 Right of First Refusal.

(a) **Right of First Refusal.** [At any time/At any time prior to the consummation of [an Initial Public Offering/a Qualified Public Offering]], and subject to the terms and conditions specified in this Section [2.01], each Member shall have a right of first refusal if any other Member (the **"Offering Member"**), receives an offer from an Independent Third Party that the Offering Member desires to accept to purchase all or any portion of the Equity Securities owned by the Offering Member (the **"Offered Units"**). Each time the Offering Member receives an offer for any of its Equity Securities, the Offering Member shall first make an offering of the Offered Units to the other Members in accordance with the following provisions of this Section [2.01] prior to Transferring such Offered Units to the Independent Third Party (other than Transfers that are permitted by Section [PERMITTED-TRANSFERS SECTION] [or Transfers made pursuant to Section [DRAG-ALONG RIGHTS SECTION]]).

Drafting Note: Timing of ROFR

If your LLC agreement includes a lock-up period (a period of time after the execution of the agreement during which no party can transfer its units other than to an affiliate), make the following changes:

- Add the term "Lock-up Period", which may be defined as "[NUMBER OF YEARS] after the date of this Agreement".
- Replace the phrase "At any time" with the phrase "At any time following the expiration of the Lock-up Period".

- Replace the phrase "At any time prior to the consummation of [an Initial Public Offering/a Qualified Public Offering]" with the phrase "After the expiration of the Lock-up Period but prior to the consummation of [an Initial Public Offering/a Qualified Public Offering]".

The right of first refusal does not usually apply to transfers that are conducted after an Initial Public Offering or a Qualified Public Offering (as the case may be). If your LLC agreement contemplates an IPO or QIPO as an exit strategy or a liquidity event, the second bracketed phrase should be used.

Availability of ROFR

This Standard Clause assumes that all members have a right of first refusal. However, this is not always the case. Depending on the nature of the transaction and the parties involved, this right may be limited to:

- **Certain key members.** In private equity transactions this right is often limited to the sponsor, its affiliates and co-investment vehicles.
- **Non-management members.** Members who receive their units as part of an employee bonus or compensation plan often do not have a right of first refusal.

Some LLC agreements provide that the right of first refusal is unavailable to members who are forced to sell if the drag-along right is exercised by the majority member. The argument against including this limitation is that so long as the majority member is able to sell its units and achieve liquidity, it should be indifferent to the identity of the buyer (be it the other members or an independent third party).

If the parties agree to not include this limitation, remove the bracketed language at the end of Section 2.01(a) above.

Company ROFR

Some LLC agreements also provide that the company has the first right to redeem any or all of the units before they are offered to the members. A member that does not expect to want, or to be able to afford, to exercise its right of first refusal might favor this provision, since it has the effect of maintaining the members' existing equity ratios without forcing the members to make any further investment in the company.

END DRAFTING NOTE

(b) **Offer Notice.**

(i) The Offering Member shall, no later than [five] [Business Days/days] after receipt of the offer from the Independent Third Party, give written notice (the **"Offering Member Notice"**) to the

Company and the other Members stating that it has received a bona fide offer from an Independent Third Party and specifying: (w) the number of Offered Units to be sold by the Offering Member; (x) the name of the person or entity who has offered to purchase such Offered Units; (y) the per Unit purchase price and the other material terms and conditions of the Transfer, including a description of any non-cash consideration in sufficient detail to permit the valuation thereof; and (z) the proposed date, time and location of the closing of the Transfer, which shall not be less than [60] [Business Days/days] from the date of the Offering Member Notice.

Drafting Note: Consideration

As drafted, the Offering Member is entitled to sell its interest in the company for non-cash consideration. Many agreements limit the sale of any Equity Securities subject to a right of first refusal to cash to eliminate the time and effort it takes to determine the fair market value of any non-cash consideration. If you wish to include this limitation, subclause (y) above may be modified as follows:

> "(y) the per Unit purchase price (which for the avoidance of doubt shall be cash) and the other material terms and conditions of the sale; and"

END DRAFTING NOTE

(ii) The Offering Member Notice shall constitute the Offering Member's offer to Transfer the Offered Units to the other Members, which offer shall be irrevocable until the end of the ROFR Notice Period.

(iii) By delivering the Offering Member Notice, the Offering Member represents and warrants to the Company and each other Member that: (x) the Offering Member has full right, title and interest in and to the Offered Units; (y) the Offering Member has all the necessary power and authority and has taken all necessary action to sell such Offered Units as contemplated by this Section [2.01]; and (z) the Offered Units are free and clear of any and all Liens other than those arising as a result of or under the terms of this Agreement.

(c) **Exercise of Right of First Refusal.**

(i) Upon receipt of the Offering Member Notice, each Member shall have [10] [Business Days/days] (the **"ROFR Notice Period"**) to elect to purchase all (and not less than all) of the Offered Units by delivering a written notice (a **"ROFR Offer Notice"**) to the Offering Member and the Company stating that it offers to purchase such Offered Units on the terms specified in the Offering Member Notice. Any ROFR Offer Notice shall be binding upon delivery and irrevocable by the applicable Member. If more than one Member delivers a ROFR Offer Notice, each such Member (the **"Purchasing Member"**) shall be allocated its Pro Rata Portion of the Offered Units, unless otherwise agreed by such Members.

Drafting Note: Exercise of Right of First Refusal

This provision contemplates that each other member must elect to purchase all of the Offered Units. If more than one member is interested in purchasing the Offered Units, each member has the right to purchase its pro rata portion (in accordance with its ownership interest).

Other agreements allow the members to commit to purchase their respective pro rata portion of the Offered Units. These agreements often include a reallocation mechanism that allows those members who have offered to purchase their entire allotment to also buy their pro rata portion of the unclaimed units. These agreements usually include a caveat that if less than all the Offered Units are claimed through this mechanism, the members lose their right of first refusal entirely and the Offering Member can sell all the Offered Units to the Independent Third Party.

Regardless of which mechanism is employed, LLC agreements do not usually allow the members to ultimately purchase less than all of the Offered Units, because:

- The Offering Member should be in the same position whether its interests are purchased by the third party or the other members.
- If the other members are able to purchase only a portion of the offered units, the Offering Member may end up selling less than the Offered Units because the third party may not be interested in the remaining portion.

END DRAFTING NOTE

(ii) Each Member that does not deliver a ROFR Offer Notice during the ROFR Notice Period shall be deemed to have waived all of such Member's rights to purchase the Offered Units under this Section [2.01], and the Offering Member shall thereafter, subject to the rights of any Purchasing Member, be free to sell the Offered Units to the Independent Third Party specified in the Offer Notice without any further obligation to such Member pursuant to this Section [2.01].

(iii) Each Member who delivers a ROFR Offer Notice shall be deemed to have waived any rights that such Member may have pursuant to Section [TAG-ALONG RIGHTS SECTION].

(d) **Consummation of Sale.** If no Member delivers a ROFR Notice in accordance with Section [2.01](c), the Offering Member may, during the [60] [Business Day/day] period immediately following the expiration of the

ROFR Notice Period (which period may be extended for a reasonable time not to exceed [90] [Business Days/days] to the extent reasonably necessary to obtain any Government Approvals) (the **"Waived ROFR Transfer Period"**), and subject to the provisions of Section [TAG-ALONG RIGHTS SECTION] with respect to those Members who have not delivered ROFR Offer Notices, Transfer all of the Offered Units to the Independent Third Party on terms and conditions no more favorable to the Independent Third Party than those set forth in the Offering Member Notice. If the Offering Member does not Transfer the Offered Units within such period or, if such Transfer is not consummated within the Waived ROFR Transfer Period, the rights provided hereunder shall be deemed to be revived and the Offered Units shall not be Transferred to the Independent Third Party unless the Offering Member sends a new Offering Member Notice in accordance with, and otherwise complies with, this Section [2.01].

(e) **Cooperation.** Each Member shall take all actions as may be reasonably necessary to consummate the sale contemplated by this Section [2.01] including, without limitation, entering into agreements and delivering certificates and instruments and consents as may be deemed necessary or appropriate.

(f) **Closing.** At the closing of any sale and purchase pursuant to this Section [2.01], the Offering Member shall deliver to the Purchasing Member(s) certificate or certificates representing the Offered Units to be sold (if any), accompanied by evidence of transfer and all necessary transfer taxes paid and stamps affixed, if necessary, against receipt of the purchase price therefore from such Purchasing Member(s) by certified or official bank check or by wire transfer of immediately available funds.

E. PLANNING FOR INVOLUNTARY TRANSFERS

To this point in the chapter, we have considered the possibility of first rights, often called preemptive rights, as an alternative to total prohibition of transfer. By planning for involuntary transfers, the drafting attorney completes the work of anticipating upheavals in the equity structure of his or her client. A thoughtful approach to buy-sell arrangements in a closely held corporation will anticipate the possibility of stockholders' shares being taken from them against their will. Even if they do not or cannot pledge their stock as collateral on personal loans, the stockholder could still have their ownership stakes attached by courts enforcing judgments against them or transferred to former spouses in divorce proceedings. In these cases, a redemption provision that takes the stock back at par value may seem tempting, but a competent drafting attorney will caution founders about establishing a mechanism that is blatantly unfair to the would-be new stockholder. It may be successfully challenged as a fraudulent attempt to hinder a creditor, leaving the founders with no protection at all. Rather than rely on pegging the redemption price to book value, an objective but low-ball valuation of the company, a prudent valuation approach will call for an appraiser to be hired. Appraisers will find it impossible to judge the market value of something as unique as a small business in the same way they would price a single-family home (by looking at recent comparable sales). Instead, the appraiser is much more likely to calculate the value of the business using its net income data. The appraiser divides the annual net earnings of the business by a capitalization rate, essentially an interest rate appropriate to the risk profile of that small business considered as an investment opportunity. This capitalized net earnings value should yield a price that the typical investor would pay to own the business as a whole. The Shareholder Agreement form reprinted below requires the hiring of an appraiser without specifying a particular valuation method. In the competition between rules and standards, between descriptive and evaluative conceptual elements early in Chapter 4, the direction to hire an appraiser is an example of a procedural mechanism used to avoid the pitfalls of a rule-based valuation method that is too rigid to be reliably **correct** and a standard for value that cannot be sufficiently **clear** in meaning to resolve decisively disagreements between the parties.

The death of a stockholder is similarly planned for as a form of involuntary transfer. Section 6(b) of the form below, however, creates an alternative to the appraised-value option mechanism. The corporation can plan ahead for the need to cash out a deceased shareholder by purchasing life insurance, the proceeds of which can be used to fund that redemption. The corporation is authorized to purchase life insurance policies for each shareholder. Rather than have the amount of the death benefit tied to the ever-fluctuating market value of that shareholder's share of the corporation, the provision calls for the shareholder and the corporation to agree on an amount of coverage. In the event of the shareholder's death, the shareholder's designated beneficiary(ies) receive(s) the insurance proceeds in lieu of the decedent's stock, and the stock shares are cancelled.

LLCs also may benefit by planning for involuntary transfer of interests, and corporations may wish to establish cross-purchase arrangements to preempt sale of stock to third parties. The shareholder's agreement below shows how a corporation can integrate first rights with valuation-based mechanisms designed for involuntary transfers. Converting its comprehensive provisions for use by an LLC would not be too difficult, but a drafter looking to work as efficiently as possible may prefer to find an LLC buy-sell form just as complete in its approach.

DISCUSSION QUESTION 6–B

For each of the signing shareholder life events listed immediately below, locate the provision(s) that address the question of transferability of shares raised by that occurrence. If the provision uses a first-right mechanism, identify which type. If the provision creates an option tied to a valuation or a fixed value, identify who hold(s) the option and how is the compensation determined.

1) Departure of the shareholder from work for the corporation two years prior to the completion of his or her five-year work agreement

2) The receipt, one year into his five-year work agreement, by the shareholder of a financially favorable offer to purchase all his or her vested shares

3) The death of the shareholder one year after completing his or her five-year work agreement

Shareholder Agreement[4]

This Agreement is made and entered as of the ___ day of ________, 20___, by and among * * * * * *, Inc., a __________ corporation, and the undersigned shareholders of the corporation (the "Shareholders").

RECITALS

WHEREAS, the Shareholders currently are the owners of 100% of the issued and outstanding shares of the capital stock of the corporation and are Active in the Business (as defined below) of the corporation;

WHEREAS, there is no ready market for the purchase or sale of the capital stock of the corporation;

WHEREAS, the Shareholders wish to protect the management and control of the corporation against intrusion by persons not Active in the Business of the corporation or not acceptable to the Shareholders as co-owners of the corporation's business, and to provide a ready market for their shares of capital stock of the corporation (the "Shares") under certain circumstances;

WHEREAS, one of the Shareholders is paying a portion of the purchase price for his Shares in the form of consulting services to be performed for the corporation; and

WHEREAS, the Shareholders thus deem it to be in their best interests to provide for certain restrictions on their transfer of the Shares and to create certain options and obligations for their purchase and sale of the Shares, and the voting of the Shares, all as provided below;

NOW, THEREFORE, in consideration of the premises and the mutual covenants herein contained, it is hereby agreed as follows:

---

[4] Reprinted from Jean L. Batman, Advising the Small Business with permission of ABA Publications. ©2012 by the American Bar Association. Reproduced with permission. All rights reserved. This information or any portion thereof may not be copied or disseminated in any form or by any means or stored in an electronic database or retrieval system without the express written consent of the American Bar Association.

1. PURPOSES OF AGREEMENT; DEFINITIONS.

(a) Protective Purpose. It is the purpose of this Agreement to protect the management and control of the corporation against intrusion by persons not Active in the Business of the Corporation or not acceptable to the Shareholders as co-owners or managers of the corporation's business.

(b) Market Purpose of Agreement. It is also the purpose of this Agreement to provide for and/or limit the disposition of the Shares held by the Shareholders under certain circumstances.

(c) "Shareholder" Defined. The term "Shareholder," as used in this Agreement, shall be deemed to mean the signatories to this Agreement and any other person who hereafter becomes a holder of Shares.

(d) "Active in the Business" Defined. The term "Active in the Business", as used in this Agreement, shall mean involved in the day-to-day business of the corporation as an officer, independent contractor, or employee of the corporation, or involved in the policy and direction of the corporation as a member of the Board of Directors.

(e) Shares Subject to Vesting. In consideration of the fact that %%% is paying the purchase price for his (her) Shares in the form of consulting services to be performed for the corporation, his Shares shall be subject to vesting as follows: one-sixtieth (1/60th) of the One Hundred Eleven Thousand (111,000) Shares to be issued to him (her) shall vest at the end of each month of service to the corporation he (she) completes pursuant to that certain Software Maintenance and Support Agreement between the corporation and __________, Inc. dated of even date herewith (the "Consulting Agreement"), beginning on the date first set forth above. The unvested portion of the Shares held by Mr. %%% may be voted by him (her) but is not subject to transfer, sale, assignment, hypothecation, encumbrance or alienation and will return to the status of authorized but unissued Shares in the event of such Shareholder's resignation, death, disability, retirement, termination from WinX Enterprises Solutions, Inc., or in the event of the termination of the Consulting Agreement. In the event Company is acquired or merges with another entity which is not majority owned by the Shareholders, Mr. %%%'s shares shall become fully vested immediately prior to the closing of such sale or merger.

2. ENFORCEMENT PROVISIONS.

(a) General Restriction on Transfer. Except as hereinafter set forth, neither the Shares nor any interest therein, including without limitation the right to vote the Shares, shall be validly sold, exchanged, assigned, pledged or encumbered or otherwise transferred, for consideration or by way of gift, bequest, or otherwise, either voluntarily, involuntarily, or by operation of law, and no purported transferee shall be recognized as a shareholder of the corporation for any purpose whatsoever unless and until said Shares shall have been released from the restrictions upon transfer as hereinafter provided; and in any such case the purported transferee shall sign a counterpart of this Agreement.

(b) Occurrence of Transfer. A transfer or attempt to transfer subject to the provisions of this Agreement shall be deemed to occur whenever any interest in any of the Shares is transferred or attempted to be transferred, irrespective of whether any change in the record ownership thereof occurs.

(c) Agreement Available For Inspection. An original copy of this Agreement duly executed by the corporation and by the Shareholders shall be delivered to the corporation's Secretary and shall be made available at the principal office of the corporation for inspection by any person requesting it.

(d) Legend. Each certificate evidencing the Shares issued after the effective date of this Agreement shall have conspicuously printed on it the following legend:

> THE TRANSFER, SALE, ASSIGNMENT, HYPOTHECATION, ENCUMBRANCE OR ALIENATION OF THE SHARES REPRESENTED BY THIS CERTIFICATE IS RESTRICTED BY A SHAREHOLDER AGREEMENT AMONG ALL OF THE SHAREHOLDERS OF THIS CORPORATION AND THIS CORPORATION DATED ______, 20___. A COPY OF THE SHAREHOLDER AGREEMENT IS AVAILABLE FOR INSPECTION DURING NORMAL BUSINESS HOURS AT THE PRINCIPAL OFFICE OF THE CORPORATION. ALL OF THE TERMS AND PROVISIONS OF THE SHAREHOLDER AGREEMENT ARE HEREBY INCORPORATED BY REFERENCE AND MADE A PART OF THIS CERTIFICATE.

(e) Printing Legend on Existing Certificates. Each Shareholder shall immediately upon execution of this Agreement, present the certificate representing his or her Shares to the Secretary and cause the Secretary to print on the certificate, in a prominent manner, the legend set forth in paragraph 2(d) of this Agreement, if such certificates have already been issued.

(f) Restrictions on After-Acquired and After-Issued Shares. The terms of this Agreement shall apply to all of the Shares in existence at the time this Agreement is executed, to any Shares transferred in any manner by a Shareholder, and to any additional Shares the corporation may issue to a holder of Shares as a recapitalization, reorganization, stock dividend, stock split or reverse stock split. The corporation may require that a transferee, as a condition of transfer, execute an agreement similar to this Agreement. Any new shares issued by the corporation shall be subject to the legend condition set forth in paragraph 2(d) of this Agreement.

(g) Deposit with Corporation. Concurrently with the execution of this Agreement, each Shareholder shall endorse a stock assignment separate from the certificate representing his or her Shares and shall deposit the assignment and the certificate representing his or her Shares with the Secretary. Despite the endorsement and deposit, each Shareholder shall have the right to vote his or her Shares and receive dividends paid on them until his or her Shares are sold or transferred as provided in this Agreement.

(h) Remedies. The rights and remedies provided by this Agreement are cumulative and the use of any one right or remedy by any party shall not preclude or waive its right to use any or all other remedies. Said rights and remedies are given in addition to any other rights the parties may have at law or in equity. Without limiting the foregoing, the parties hereto agree that irreparable harm would occur in the event that any of the terms of this Agreement were not performed fully by the parties hereto or were otherwise breached, and that money damages are an inadequate remedy for breach of the Agreement because of the difficulty of ascertaining and quantifying the amount of resulting damage. Therefore, it is agreed that the parties hereto shall be entitled to an injunction or injunctions to restrain, enjoin and prevent breaches of this Agreement by the other parties and to enforce specifically the terms and provisions of this Agreement, and that no bond or other security shall be required in obtaining such equitable relief and the undersigned hereby consent to the issuance of such injunction and to the ordering of specific performance.

(i) Delays. Except where a time period is specified, no delay on the part of any party in the exercise of any right, power, privilege or remedy hereunder shall operate as a waiver thereof, nor shall any exercise or partial exercise of any such right, power, privilege or remedy preclude any further exercise thereof or the exercise of any right, power, privilege or remedy.

3. TRANSFERS DURING LIFETIME.

(a) Notice of Offer. In the event any Shareholder (the "Offering Shareholder") desires to sell or otherwise transfer any or all of his Shares to the other Shareholders (the "Remaining Shareholders"), subject to the limitations set forth in subparagraph 3(e) below, or to a third party or parties other than a Shareholder's individual retirement account or a trust created for estate planning purposes, then, in any such event, the Offering Shareholder shall give written notice to the Secretary of the corporation (the "Offer Notice") and shall specify in the Offer Notice the following:

(i) the name, address and occupation of the proposed transferee(s) and the number of Shares proposed to be transferred to the proposed transferee(s) (the "Offered Shares");

(ii) the price per share and terms of sale set by the Offering Shareholder for the Offered Shares or that the transfer is by way of gift or otherwise for no consideration.

The price specified pursuant to (ii) above or, if applicable, the price specified pursuant to subparagraphs 3(e) and 3(f) below, shall constitute, and shall hereinafter be referred to as, the "Offered Price." Delivery of the Offer Notice to the Secretary shall be deemed to be an offer by the Offering Shareholder to sell the Offered Shares to the corporation and the Remaining Shareholders at the Offered Price. Such offer may be accepted in the "Offer Period," which shall be the forty-five (45) day period commencing on the date the Offer Notice is delivered to the Secretary (the "Offer Date"), and may not be withdrawn by the Offering Shareholder during the Offer Period.

(b) Right of Corporation To Purchase Offered Shares. If the corporation is then in a position under applicable laws of the State of California to acquire shares issued by it, the corporation shall have the right to acquire all or, subject to the last sentence of subparagraph 3(d), a portion of the Offered Shares at the Offered Price. Said right shall be exercised no later than ten (10) days after the Offer Date by notice in writing transmitted to all shareholders stating the corporation's intent to acquire the Offered Shares.

(c) Right of Remaining Shareholders To Purchase Offered Shares. If the corporation cannot then legally acquire the Offered Shares or if the corporation does not exercise its right to do so within the period specified in subparagraph 3(b), the Secretary shall, no later than five (5) days after the expiration of such period, deliver a copy of the Offer Notice to the Remaining Shareholders. Subject to the provisions of subparagraph 3(d) below, the Remaining Shareholders shall have the right, but shall be under no obligation, to acquire all or part of the Offered Shares at the Offered Price.

(d) Purchase of Offered Shares By Remaining Shareholders. Prior to the expiration of the Offer Period, the Remaining Shareholders, or any of them, if they desire to acquire the Offered Shares, shall deliver by mail or otherwise to the Secretary a written notice (the "Acceptance Notice") of their acceptance of the Offering Shareholder's offer, stating the number of said shares each of them desires to purchase at the Offered Price. No later than five (5) days after its receipt, the Secretary shall deliver to the Offering Shareholder a copy of the Acceptance Notice(s). Delivery of a copy of the Acceptance Notice(s) to the Offering Shareholder shall create a binding contract between the Remaining Shareholders signing the Acceptance Notice and the Offering Shareholder. Notwithstanding anything herein contained to the contrary, in the event the corporation and the Remaining Shareholders have elected to purchase only a portion of the

Offered Shares on or before the last day of the Offer Period, then each contract for the purchase and sale of only a portion of the Offered Shares shall become null and void at the option of the Offering Shareholder, exercised in a written notice given to the corporation and/or the Remaining Shareholders on or before the fifth (5th) business day following the end of the Offering Period. In the event more than one of the Remaining Shareholders wishes to purchase some or all of the Offered Shares, each Remaining Shareholder shall have the right to purchase a pro rata number of the Offered Shares based on such Shareholder's ownership interest in the corporation prior to the purchase of the Offered Shares.

(e) Offer For Non-Cash Consideration. In the event the Offered Shares are proposed to be transferred, either in whole or in part, for a consideration other than cash, then each of the Remaining Shareholders and the corporation shall have the right to acquire the Offered Shares in the manner and upon the terms and conditions herein set forth at a price per share in cash determined as set forth in paragraph 6.

(f) Offer For No Consideration. In the event that the Offered Shares are proposed to be transferred for no consideration, then each of the Remaining Shareholder and the corporation shall have the right to acquire the Offered Shares upon the terms and conditions herein set forth at the purchase price per share determined in the manner set forth in paragraph 6.

(g) Notice of Offers to Acquire All or Portion of Offered Shares. In the event the Offering Shareholder receives no offers or offers for only a portion of the Offered Shares from the corporation and the Remaining Shareholders, and the Offering Shareholder exercises his option specified in subparagraph 3(d) hereof, the Offering Shareholder may transfer the Offered Shares at any time no later than sixty (60) days after the expiration of the Offering Period to the proposed transferee for the Offered Price as specified in the Offer Notice; provided, however, that the prospective transferee shall receive and hold the Offered Shares subject to all of the provisions and restrictions of this Agreement.

(h) Payment of Purchase Price. In the absence of a separate agreement between the Offering Shareholder and the Remaining Shareholders and/or the corporation regarding the terms of payment for the Offered Shares, the transfer of the Offered Shares to the Remaining Shareholders and/or the corporation, shall be consummated in the following manner: the Secretary shall set a closing date which shall be no later than thirty (30) days after receipt by the Offering Shareholder of the notice specified in paragraph 3(b) or the Acceptance Notice specified in paragraph 3(d) (the "Closing Date"). At least ten (10) days prior to the Closing Date, the Secretary shall notify the Remaining Shareholders and/or the corporation in writing as to the number of such shares which he or it is obligated to acquire, the purchase price per share, and the Closing Date (the "Closing Notice"), and shall also send a copy of the Closing Notice to the other party or parties to the transaction. On or before the Closing Date, each purchaser of shares shall deliver to the Secretary the purchase price of the Offered Shares to be acquired by him or it in cash or by certified check made out to the Offering Shareholder. Subject to receipt of the cash or checks for the purchase price, on the Closing Date the Secretary shall transfer said shares of stock on the books of the corporation by registering such Shares in the name of the transferee or transferees who have delivered to him the purchase price for the Offered Shares; and the Secretary shall, at the same time, transmit the purchase price to the Offering Shareholder.

(i) Default. If the corporation or Remaining Shareholders fail to deliver to the Secretary on or prior to the Closing Date the aggregate purchase price of the Shares to be acquired by such transferee(s), the Secretary shall immediately notify in writing the other party or parties of such default, and shall, unless and until instructed to the contrary by said transferee(s), hold in trust for said transferee(s) the certificate or certificates representing the number of Offered Shares as to which such default has occurred. In the event of any such default, the transferor shall be entitled to pursue such remedies at law or in equity to which he may be entitled for the transferee's breach of the obligation to acquire said Shares.

4. DEATH OF A SHAREHOLDER.

(a) Purchase by Corporation. Each Shareholder agrees that the corporation shall redeem the vested portion of any Shares standing of record in the name of a deceased Shareholder or in the name of an entity in which a deceased Shareholder is a majority owner (the "Deceased Shareholder") at the time of his death (the "Redemption"). Consummation of such Redemption shall occur in the manner specified in subparagraph 3(h) on the date set by the Secretary, which date shall be no later than sixty (60) days following the qualification of the executor or other representative of the Deceased Shareholder or no later than ninety (90) days after the death of the Deceased Shareholder, whichever is earlier. Upon Redemption, the corporation shall pay the estate of the Deceased Shareholder for such Deceased Shareholder's Shares a price determined according to paragraph 6 of this Agreement.

(b) Purchase by Surviving Shareholders. If the corporation, for any reason, cannot legally perform the provisions of subparagraph 4(a) of this Agreement, in whole or in part, the surviving Shareholders shall purchase on the terms and conditions and at the price specified in paragraph 6 from the estate of the Deceased Shareholder all of the Shares owned by the Deceased Shareholder that the corporation is unable to purchase.

(c) Transfer of Deceased Owner's Shares to Shareholder Spouse. Notwithstanding anything herein to the contrary, in the event the spouse of the Deceased Shareholder is a shareholder of record, either alone or jointly with the Deceased Shareholder, immediately prior to the Deceased Shareholder's death, at the option of such spouse the Shares of the Deceased Shareholder may be transferred to such spouse, either by operation of law or by purchase of such Shares at the purchase price and in the manner specified in subparagraph 4(a) hereinabove.

(d) Costs. The estate of the Deceased Shareholder shall bear, and hold the corporation harmless from, all costs and expenses required for securing court orders, court decrees, court approvals and tax clearances required to enable the estate of the Deceased Shareholder to transfer to the corporation and/or the surviving Shareholders full legal and equitable title to the Deceased Shareholder's Shares.

(e) Estate of Deceased Shareholder Defined. The term "estate of the Deceased Shareholder" as used in this Agreement shall mean and include as those terms are defined by the law of the State of California:

(i) the duly appointed and qualified executor or administrator of the Deceased Shareholder;

(ii) the surviving joint tenant of the Deceased Shareholder where Shares are owned by the Deceased Shareholder and a person who is not Active in the Business of the corporation; and,

(iii) any other person who may, because of the community property or other law of any jurisdiction, acquire without formal probate proceedings any right, title or interest in or to the Deceased Shareholder's Shares.

5. OTHER EVENTS CONSTITUTING AN OFFER TO SELL.

(a) In the event any Shareholder Active in the Business of the corporation (the "Offering Shareholder"):

(i) terminates his employment with the corporation (whether as an employee or independent contractor);

(ii) resigns from the Board of Directors;

(iii) is terminated by the corporation from employment with the corporation;

(iv) is adjudicated a bankrupt, voluntary or involuntary, or makes an assignment for the benefit of creditors;

(v) files a complaint for involuntary dissolution of the corporation pursuant to Section 1800(a) of the California Corporations Code or similar provision then in effect; or

(vi) elects to wind up and dissolve the corporation pursuant to Section 1900(a) of the California Corporations Code or similar provision then in effect; or any other event should occur which, were it not for the provisions of this Agreement, would cause a Shareholder's Shares, or any part thereof, to be transferred, assigned, canceled, or sold to any person, voluntarily or involuntarily, under circumstances which would not bring such transfer within paragraphs 3 or 4 of this Agreement, then such event shall be deemed to constitute an offer to sell the Shares so being transferred, assigned or sold and shall give rise to the same rights to purchase as are set forth in paragraph 3 of this Agreement for an Offer Notice, on the terms set forth therein.

(b) Notwithstanding the foregoing, if the transfer described in paragraph 5(a) arises out of a decree of dissolution or separate maintenance or property settlement or separation agreement, or out of a disposition by the spouse of a Shareholder to a person other than said Shareholder, then such Shareholder shall have the exclusive right, for a period of thirty (30) days, to purchase such Shares (to be exercised by giving written notice to the Secretary and to the spouse or personal representative, heirs, or assigns of the spouse), at the purchase price per Share determined in the manner set forth in paragraph 6.

(c) Upon the occurrence of any event which shall be deemed an offer to sell under this paragraph 5, the Offering Shareholder shall immediately notify the Secretary of the occurrence of such event in the manner set forth in subparagraph 3(a).

(d) Fifth Year Option. Upon the fifth (5th) anniversary of this Agreement, Shareholder %%%% shall be deemed to have offered to sell his Shares under this paragraph 5 and the same rights to purchase shall arise as are set forth in paragraph 3 of this Agreement for an Offer Notice, on the terms set forth therein.

6. PURCHASE PRICE.

(a) Appraised Value. Except as otherwise specifically provided herein, the purchase price per share at which Offered Shares shall be bought and sold in any calendar year shall be determined by appraisal. No later than thirty (30) days after the occurrence of the event requiring the determination of the price for the Shares under this Agreement, the corporation shall employ an appraiser to appraise the Shares and determine their value. The cost of the appraisal shall be paid by the corporation. Notwithstanding anything herein to the contrary, the corporation shall not be required to obtain an appraisal more than once in any twelve (12) month period.

(b) Life Insurance. The corporation may purchase and maintain life insurance policies insuring the lives of the Shareholders wherein the beneficiary of the policy shall be designated by each Shareholder so insured in an amount mutually determined by the corporation and the Shareholder. The existence of such coverage shall relieve the corporation of any obligation to purchase Offered Shares pursuant to the redemption provisions in paragraph 4 of this Agreement, and the payment of such death benefit to the Shareholder's designated beneficiary shall be deemed a full and complete satisfaction and discharge of all such deceased Shareholder's rights, claims, ownership and interests, and those of his estate, hereunder against the corporation, other than any claim or obligation based upon a debt for money lent to or borrowed from the corporation, and the Deceased Shareholder's Shares shall be canceled.

7. VOTING AND GOVERNANCE COVENANTS.

(a) Board Members. The Shareholders shall vote their Shares as necessary to elect XXXX and $$$$$ to the Board of Directors. In the event XXXX or $$$$$ cease to serve as a member of the Board, the resulting vacancy shall be filled by the Director ceasing to serve, or if she is unable to make such designation, by the remaining member(s) of the Board. The corporation shall reimburse the reasonable expenses of Directors for costs incurred in attending meetings of the Board of Directors; and

(b) Board Powers. The Board of Directors shall meet periodically to conduct the regular business of the Board, including the review of the corporation's financial condition and the approval of its operating budget. Expenditures not accurately reflected in the current operating budget approved by the Board shall be approved by the Board of Directors in advance. All compensation to be paid to officers of the corporation, including the reimbursement of expenses shall be approved by the Board of Directors in advance. No additional Shares shall be issued, no options for Shares granted, and no instruments executed by the corporation which are convertible into Shares without the approval of the Board of Directors in advance.

(c) Limitation on Shareholder Dilution. As of the date first set forth above, the relative ownership of the Shareholders, on a fully diluted basis, is as follows:

XXXX	80.0%
$$$$$	10.0%
%%%%	10.0%

Unless the Shareholders unanimously agree otherwise in writing, the undersigned shall vote their Shares and exercise their powers as members of the Board of Directors of the corporation as required to ensure that the corporation does not issue additional Shares in any transaction that disproportionately dilutes any of the Shareholders (i.e., Shares may be issued pro rata to the Shareholders, such as in a stock split, or may be issued to third parties in such transactions as the Board of Directors may deem advisable to advance the interests of the corporation).

8. NOTICES. All notices required by this Agreement shall be written, and either personally delivered or sent by registered U.S. mail, postage prepaid. Notice to be given to the corporation shall be delivered or addressed to the corporation at its principal place of business. Notices to be given to the Shareholders shall be delivered or addressed to them at their respective addresses given to the Secretary for the purpose of notice or, if no such address is given, in care of the corporation at its principal place of business.

9. ADDITIONAL SHARES. This Agreement shall apply to any shares hereinafter issued to a party hereto and to any stock dividend, stock split, or other distribution of shares of the corporation made upon or in exchange for the Shares.

10. TERMINATION OF AGREEMENT. This Agreement shall terminate on:

(a) The written agreement of all the parties;

(b) The dissolution or bankruptcy of the corporation;

(c) The death of all of the Shareholders within a period of sixty (60) days, such termination to be deemed to have occurred on the day preceding the date of death of the first Shareholder;

(d) At such time as only one Shareholder remains, the Shares of the other Shareholders having been transferred or redeemed in full; or

(e) The effectiveness of a registration of the securities of the corporation under the Securities Act of 1933 in connection with an initial public offering by the corporation.

11. AGREEMENT TO PERFORM NECESSARY ACTS. Each party agrees to perform any further acts and execute and deliver any documents which may be reasonably necessary to carry out the provisions of this Agreement.

12. AMENDMENT OF AGREEMENT. The provisions of this Agreement may be waived, altered, amended, or repealed, in whole or in part, only upon the written consent of the parties hereto.

13. SUCCESSORS AND ASSIGNS. This Agreement shall bind and inure to the benefit of the successors, assigns, personal representatives, heirs and legatees of the respective parties.

14. VALIDITY CLAUSE. It is intended that each section of this Agreement shall be viewed as separate and divisible, and in the event that

any such section shall be held to be invalid, the remaining sections shall continue to be in full force and effect.

15. COPY OF AGREEMENT. Immediately after execution of this Agreement by the parties hereto, an original counterpart hereof shall be delivered to the Secretary and shall be shown by him to any person making inquiry concerning it.

16. PRONOUNS. All personal pronouns used in this Agreement, whether used in the masculine, feminine or neuter gender, shall include all other genders.

17. COUNSEL FOR THE CORPORATION. Each Shareholder acknowledges that counsel for the corporation, [_____ Legal Venture Counsel, Inc.] drafted this Shareholder Agreement on behalf of the corporation. Each Shareholder acknowledges that such Shareholder:

(a) has been advised that his or her interests in the Agreement may conflict with those of the corporation and the other Shareholders;

(b) has been advised that this Agreement may have tax consequences; and

(c) has been advised to seek independent counsel regarding this Agreement.

18. ATTORNEYS FEES. In the event that any suit or action is instituted to enforce any provision in this Agreement, the prevailing party in such dispute shall be entitled to recover from the losing party all fees, costs and expenses of enforcing any right of such prevailing party under or with respect to this Agreement, including without limitation, such reasonable fees and expenses of attorneys and accountants, which shall include, without limitation, all fees, costs and expenses of appeals.

19. GOVERNING LAW AND CONSENT TO PERSONAL JURISDICTION. This Agreement shall be governed by and construed under the laws of the State of California without giving effect to the principles of conflicts of laws. The parties hereby irrevocably and unconditionally submit to the jurisdiction of the Courts of the State of California and of the United States of America for the Northern District of California and agree that any legal action or proceeding relating to this Agreement may be brought in such courts. The parties hereby waive to the fullest extent permitted by law in connection with any such action or proceeding any objections they may now or hereafter have to the venue of any such action or proceeding in any such court or that such action or proceeding was brought in an inconvenient court and agrees not to plead or claim the same.

20. WAIVER OF RIGHT TO JURY TRIAL. The parties hereby irrevocably and knowingly waive to the fullest extent permitted by law any right to a

trial by jury in any action or proceeding, including, without limitation, any counterclaim, arising out of this Agreement, or any other agreements or transactions related hereto or thereto. The parties agree that any such action or proceeding shall be tried before a court and not a jury. In the event the parties' waiver of a trial by jury is deemed invalid, the parties hereby agree that any action or proceeding, including, without limitation, any counterclaim, arising out of this Agreement, or any other agreements or transactions related hereto or thereto, shall be determined by judicial reference.

21. COUNTERPARTS. This Agreement may be executed in counterparts, each of which shall be deemed an original, but all of which together shall constitute one and the same instrument.

22. NO AGREEMENT REGARDING EMPLOYMENT. The undersigned acknowledge and agree that nothing in this Agreement shall confer any right with respect to continuation of employment by the corporation or interfere in any way with the rights of the parties to terminate the employment of any of the undersigned at any time, with or without cause.

IN WITNESS WHEREOF, the undersigned have executed this Agreement effective as of the day and year first above written.

SHAREHOLDERS * * * *, INC.

__________________________ By: __________________________

$$$$$ XXXX, President

____

XXXX

____

F. TETHERING FOUNDERS TO THEIR START-UPS

Founders of a start-up venture formed with the hope of growing rapidly over three to seven years may have a specific timetable in mind: one that involves strong commitment to remain in ownership and work toward shared goals but anticipates a time when the founders have greater ability to realize the value they have built. For these, reverse vesting, often just called "vesting," arrangements allow fellow founders and passive investors to have confidence that these indispensable entrepreneurs are incentivized to stick with the growth plan and see it through to success. Start-up founders choose to form Delaware corporations to make their ventures attractive to outside investors. They formalize their commitment to the business through reverse vesting arrangements for the same reason.

Non-founder employees of the corporation may be signed up with the promise of stock options as part of their compensation. As the options vest, the employees are increasingly incentivized to continue to build the value of the company. Founders typically get all the voting rights of their stock up front but only realize its full financial value after they have stayed with the company throughout the agreed-upon vesting period. Instead of the stock being transferred to them in the form of options, the stock is transferred at the outset with most of it subject to a redemption option that is triggered when they elect to leave. Thus the stock reverse vests over time in the founders as the corporation's call option on the founders' stock disappears. The option price is not set at market value but at a much, much lower price, sometimes par value.

The mechanics of such a stock restriction agreement are relatively simple when compared with the multiple steps associated with first rights and the valuation procedures needed in cases of involuntary transfer. The events that trigger the corporation's right to repurchase are described in the agreement. The price to be paid by the corporation is set in the agreement. What changes over time is the amount of the founder's stock that is subject to the restriction. Some agreements are structured to unlock the full value of the owner's stock at a constant rate at a monthly basis. Others take a "cliff" approach and reduce the scope of the redemption annually or semi-annually. Another type of agreement will tie vesting to certain productivity milestones.

The form below is designed for a corporation that, after several years of operation, is receiving significant equity investment from passive stockholders. It provides for restricting some or all those shares that were already fully vested in the founder. The redemption price is set not at par value but at the price the founder originally acquired the stock. Since the founder's original capital contribution may have been nominal, the difference between the two may not be that great. Per § 1(b), the founder will have a certain percentage of his or her stock released from the repurchase restriction in a cliff a specified number of months after signing the agreement. Thereafter, the lapse of the repurchase right will be monthly and constant. The lapse will accelerate if the corporation is acquired or merges and will accelerate again if the founder is ousted less than a year later. This protects the founder from being dismissed without realizing the value he or she created.

Stock Restriction Agreement[5]

THIS STOCK RESTRICTION AGREEMENT is entered into as of _____ _____, 20__, by *[name of corporation]*, a Delaware corporation (the "Company"), and _____ (the "Purchaser").

RECITALS

WHEREAS, the parties entered into a Stock Purchase Agreement dated as of _____ _____, 20__ (the "Stock Purchase Agreement"), pursuant to which the Purchaser acquired _____ Shares of the Company's Common Stock (the "Purchased Shares") for $________ per Share (the "Purchase Price"); and

WHEREAS, pursuant to the Stock Purchase Agreement, the Purchased Shares were fully vested and not subject to repurchase by the Company; and

WHEREAS, in order to induce the Company to enter into a sale of shares of its Series _____ Preferred Stock to certain investors, the Purchaser hereby agrees to the imposition of contractual restrictions with respect to the Purchased Shares, and the Purchaser and the Company hereby agree that this Agreement shall govern the right of the Company to repurchase the Purchased Shares in certain circumstances; and

WHEREAS, capitalized terms not defined above are defined in Section 9 of this Agreement.

NOW, THEREFORE, in consideration of the mutual promises and covenants set forth herein, the parties hereby agree as follows:

SECTION 1. RIGHT OF REPURCHASE.

(a) Scope of Repurchase Right.

Until they vest in accordance with Subsection (b) below, the Purchased Shares shall be Restricted Shares and shall be subject to the Company's Right of Repurchase. The Company, however, may decline to exercise its Right of Repurchase or may exercise its Right of Repurchase only with respect to a portion of the Restricted Shares. The Company may exercise its Right of Repurchase only during the Repurchase Period following the termination of the Purchaser's Service. The Right of Repurchase may be exercised automatically under Subsection (d) below. If the Right of Repurchase is exercised, the Company shall pay the Purchaser an amount equal to the Purchase Price for each of the Restricted Shares being repurchased.

(b) Lapse of Repurchase Right.

The Right of Repurchase shall lapse with respect to the first ____% of the Purchased Shares when the Purchaser completes _____ months of

[5] Reprinted from P. Garth Gartrell, et al., Executive Compensation for Emerging Growth Companies 3d (Emerging Growth Companies Series) with permission of Thomson Reuters.

continuous Service after the Vesting Commencement Date. The Right of Repurchase shall lapse with respect to an additional ____% of the Purchased Shares when the Purchaser completes each month of continuous Service thereafter. [In addition, the following rules shall apply if the Company is subject to a Change in Control before the Purchaser's Service terminates:

> (i) At all times after the Change in Control, the vested portion of the Restricted Shares shall be determined by adding 12 months to the Purchaser's actual Service.
>
> (ii) If the Purchaser is subject to an Involuntary Termination within 12 months after the Change in Control, then the vested portion of the Restricted Shares shall be determined by adding an additional 12 months to the Purchaser's actual Service (for a total of 24 months).]

(c) Escrow.

Upon execution of this Agreement, the certificate(s) for Restricted Shares shall be deposited in escrow with the Company to be held in accordance with the provisions of this Agreement. Any additional or exchanged securities or other property described in Subsection (f) below shall immediately be delivered to the Company to be held in escrow. All ordinary cash dividends on Restricted Shares (or on other securities held in escrow) shall be paid directly to the Purchaser and shall not be held in escrow. Restricted Shares, together with any other assets held in escrow under this Agreement, shall be (i) surrendered to the Company for repurchase upon exercise of the Right of Repurchase or the Right of First Refusal or (ii) released to the Purchaser upon his or her request to the extent that the Shares have ceased to be Restricted Shares (but not more frequently than once every six months). In any event, all Purchased Shares that have ceased to be Restricted Shares, together with any other vested assets held in escrow under this Agreement, shall be released within 90 days after the earlier of (i) the termination of the Purchaser's Service or (ii) the lapse of the Right of First Refusal.

(d) Exercise of Repurchase Right.

The Company shall be deemed to have exercised its Right of Repurchase automatically for all Restricted Shares as of the commencement of the Repurchase Period, unless the Company during the Repurchase Period notifies the holder of the Restricted Shares pursuant to Section 6 that it will not exercise its Right of Repurchase for some or all of the Restricted Shares. During the Repurchase Period, the Company shall pay to the holder of the Restricted Shares the purchase price determined under Subsection (a) above for the Restricted Shares being repurchased. Payment shall be made in cash or cash equivalents and/or by canceling indebtedness to the Company incurred by the Purchaser in the purchase of the Restricted

Shares. The certificate(s) representing the Restricted Shares being repurchased shall be delivered to the Company.

(e) Termination of Rights as Stockholder.

If the Right of Repurchase is exercised in accordance with this Section 1 and the Company makes available the consideration for the Restricted Shares being repurchased, then the person from whom the Restricted Shares are repurchased shall no longer have any rights as a holder of the Restricted Shares (other than the right to receive payment of such consideration). Such Restricted Shares shall be deemed to have been repurchased pursuant to this Section 1, whether or not the certificate(s) for such Restricted Shares have been delivered to the Company or the consideration for such Restricted Shares has been accepted.

(f) Additional or Exchanged Securities and Property.

In the event of a merger or consolidation of the Company with or into another entity, any other corporate reorganization, a stock split, the declaration of a stock dividend, the declaration of an extraordinary dividend payable in a form other than stock, a spin-off, an adjustment in conversion ratio, a recapitalization or a similar transaction affecting the Company's outstanding securities, any securities or other property (including cash or cash equivalents) that are by reason of such transaction exchanged for, or distributed with respect to, any Restricted Shares shall immediately be subject to the Right of Repurchase. Appropriate adjustments to reflect the exchange or distribution of such securities or property shall be made to the number and/or class of the Restricted Shares. Appropriate adjustments shall also be made to the price per share to be paid upon the exercise of the Right of Repurchase, provided that the aggregate purchase price payable for the Restricted Shares shall remain the same. In the event of a merger or consolidation of the Company with or into another entity or any other corporate reorganization, the Right of Repurchase may be exercised by the Company's successor.

(g) Transfer of Restricted Shares.

The Purchaser shall not transfer, assign, encumber or otherwise dispose of any Restricted Shares without the Company's written consent, except as provided in the following sentence. The Purchaser may transfer Restricted Shares to one or more members of the Purchaser's Immediate Family or to a trust established by the Purchaser for the benefit of the Purchaser and/or one or more members of the Purchaser's Immediate Family, provided in either case that the Transferee agrees in writing on a form prescribed by the Company to be bound by all provisions of this Agreement. If the Purchaser transfers any Restricted Shares, then this Agreement shall apply to the Transferee to the same extent as to the Purchaser.

(h) Assignment of Repurchase Right.

The Board of Directors may freely assign the Company's Right of Repurchase, in whole or in part. Any person who accepts an assignment of the Right of Repurchase from the Company shall assume all of the Company's rights and obligations under this Section 1.

(i) Part-Time Employment and Leaves of Absence.

If the Purchaser commences working on a part-time basis, then the Company may adjust the vesting schedule set forth in Subsection (b) above in accordance with the Company's part-time work policy or the terms of an agreement between the Purchaser and the Company pertaining to his or her part-time schedule. If the Purchaser goes on a leave of absence, then the Company may adjust the vesting schedule set forth in Subsection (b) above in accordance with the Company's leave of absence policy or the terms of such leave. Except as provided in the preceding sentence, Service shall be deemed to continue while the Purchaser is on a *bona fide* leave of absence, if (i) such leave was approved by the Company in writing and (ii) continued crediting of Service is expressly required by the terms of such leave or by applicable law (as determined by the Company). Service shall be deemed to terminate when such leave ends, unless the Purchaser immediately returns to active work.

SECTION 2. SUCCESSORS AND ASSIGNS.

Except as otherwise expressly provided to the contrary, the provisions of this Agreement shall inure to the benefit of, and be binding upon, the Company and its successors and assigns and be binding upon the Purchaser and the Purchaser's legal representatives, heirs, legatees, distributees, assigns and transferees by operation of law, whether or not any such person has become a party to this Agreement or has agreed in writing to join herein and to be bound by the terms, conditions and restrictions hereof.

SECTION 3. NO RETENTION RIGHTS.

Nothing in this Agreement shall confer upon the Purchaser any right to continue in Service for any period of specific duration or interfere with or otherwise restrict in any way the rights of the Company (or any Parent or Subsidiary employing or retaining the Purchaser) or of the Purchaser, which rights are hereby expressly reserved by each, to terminate his or her Service at any time and for any reason, with or without cause.

SECTION 4. TAX ELECTION.

The imposition of the Right of Repurchase under this Agreement may result in adverse tax consequences that may be avoided or mitigated by filing an election under Code Section 83(b). Such election may be filed only within 30 days after the date of this Agreement. The form for making the

Code Section 83(b) election is attached to this Agreement as Exhibit A. **The Purchaser should consult with his or her tax advisor to determine the tax consequences of executing this Agreement and the advantages and disadvantages of filing the Code Section 83(b) election. The Purchaser acknowledges that it is his or her sole responsibility, and not the Company's, to file a timely election under Code Section 83(b), even if the Purchaser requests the Company or its representatives to make this filing on his or her behalf.**

SECTION 5. LEGEND.

All certificates evidencing Purchased Shares shall bear the following legend (in addition to any legend(s) required by the Stock Purchase Agreement or applicable law):

THE SHARES REPRESENTED HEREBY MAY NOT BE SOLD, ASSIGNED, TRANSFERRED, ENCUMBERED OR IN ANY MANNER DISPOSED OF, EXCEPT IN COMPLIANCE WITH THE TERMS OF A WRITTEN AGREEMENT BETWEEN THE COMPANY AND THE REGISTERED HOLDER OF THE SHARES (OR THE PREDECESSOR IN INTEREST TO THE SHARES). SUCH AGREEMENT GRANTS TO THE COMPANY CERTAIN REPURCHASE RIGHTS UPON TERMINATION OF SERVICE WITH THE COMPANY. THE SECRETARY OF THE COMPANY WILL UPON WRITTEN REQUEST FURNISH A COPY OF SUCH AGREEMENT TO THE HOLDER HEREOF WITHOUT CHARGE.

SECTION 6. NOTICE.

Any notice required by the terms of this Agreement shall be given in writing. It shall be deemed effective upon (i) personal delivery, (ii) deposit with the United States Postal Service, by registered or certified mail, with postage and fees prepaid or (iii) deposit with Federal Express Corporation, with shipping charges prepaid. Notice shall be addressed to the Company at its principal executive office and to the Purchaser at the address that he or she most recently provided to the Company in accordance with this Section 6.

SECTION 7. ENTIRE AGREEMENT.

This Agreement constitutes the entire contract between the parties hereto with regard to the subject matter hereof. It supersedes any other agreements, representations or understandings (whether oral or written and whether express or implied) which relate to the subject matter hereof.

SECTION 8. CHOICE OF LAW.

This Agreement shall be governed by, and construed in accordance with, the laws of the State of Delaware, as such laws are applied to contracts entered into and performed in such State.

SECTION 9. DEFINITIONS.

(a) "**Agreement**" shall mean this Stock Restriction Agreement.

(b) "**Board of Directors**" shall mean the Board of Directors of the Company, as constituted from time to time.

(c) "**Cause**" shall mean:

(i) An unauthorized use or disclosure by the Purchaser of the Company's confidential information or trade secrets, which use or disclosure causes material harm to the Company;

(ii) A material breach by the Purchaser of any agreement between the Purchaser and the Company;

(iii) A material failure by the Purchaser to comply with the Company's written policies or rules;

(iv) The Purchaser's conviction of, or plea of "guilty" or "no contest" to, a felony under the laws of the United States or any state thereof;

(v) The Purchaser's gross negligence or willful misconduct;

(vi) A continuing failure by the Purchaser to perform assigned duties after receiving written notification of such failure from the Board of Directors; or

(vii) A failure by the Purchaser to cooperate in good faith with a governmental or internal investigation of the Company or its directors, officers or employees, if the Company has requested the Purchaser's cooperation.

(d) "**Change in Control**" shall mean (i) the consummation of a merger or consolidation of the Company with or into another entity or (ii) the dissolution, liquidation or winding up of the Company. The foregoing notwithstanding, a merger or consolidation of the Company shall not constitute a "Change in Control" if immediately after such merger or consolidation a majority of the voting power of the capital stock of the continuing or surviving entity, or any direct or indirect parent corporation of such continuing or surviving entity, will be owned by the persons who were the Company's stockholders immediately prior to such merger or consolidation in substantially the same proportions as their ownership of the voting power of the Company's capital stock immediately prior to such merger or consolidation.

(e) "**Code**" shall mean the Internal Revenue Code of 1986, as amended.

(f) "**Consultant**" shall mean a person who performs bona fide services for the Company, a Parent or a Subsidiary as a consultant or advisor, excluding Employees and Outside Directors.

(g) "**Employee**" shall mean any individual who is a common-law employee of the Company, a Parent or a Subsidiary.

(h) "**Immediate Family**" shall mean any child, stepchild, grandchild, parent, stepparent, grandparent, spouse, sibling, mother-in-law, father-in-law, son-in-law, daughter-in- law, brother-in-law or sister-in-law and shall include adoptive relationships.

(i) "**Involuntary Termination**" shall mean the termination of the Purchaser's Service by reason of:

> (i) The involuntary discharge of the Purchaser by the Company (or the Parent or Subsidiary employing him or her) for reasons other than Cause; or
>
> (ii) The voluntary resignation of the Purchaser following (A) a change in the Purchaser's position with the Company (or the Parent or Subsidiary employing him or her) that materially reduces his or her level of authority or responsibility, (B) a reduction in the Purchaser's base salary by more than 10% or (C) receipt of notice that the Purchaser's principal workplace will be relocated more than 30 miles.

(j) "**Outside Director**" shall mean a member of the Board of Directors who is not an Employee.

(k) "**Parent**" shall mean any corporation (other than the Company) in an unbroken chain of corporations ending with the Company, if each of the corporations other than the Company owns stock possessing 50% or more of the total combined voting power of all classes of stock in one of the other corporations in such chain.

(*l*) "**Repurchase Period**" shall mean a period of 180 consecutive days commencing on the date when the Purchaser's Service terminates for any reason, including (without limitation) death or disability.

(m) "**Restricted Share**" shall mean a Purchased Share that is subject to the Right of Repurchase.

(n) "**Right of First Refusal**" shall mean the Company's right of first refusal described in the Stock Purchase Agreement.

(*o*) "**Right of Repurchase**" shall mean the Company's right of repurchase described in Section 1.

(p) "**Service**" shall mean service as an Employee, Outside Director or Consultant.

[Comment: Consider deleting all references to "Outside Director," so that service as Outside Director does not count for vesting. _____]

(q) "**Share**" shall mean one share of Stock.

(r) "**Stock**" shall mean the Common Stock of the Company, with a par value of $________ per Share.

(s) "**Subsidiary**" shall mean any corporation (other than the Company) in an If unbroken chain of corporations beginning with the Company, if each of the corporations other than the last corporation in the unbroken chain owns stock possessing 50% or more of the total combined voting power of all classes of stock in one of the other corporations in such chain.

(t) "**Transferee**" shall mean any person to whom the Purchaser has directly or indirectly transferred a Purchased Share.

(u) "**Vesting Commencement Date**" shall mean _____, _____, 20__.

IN WITNESS WHEREOF, each of the parties has executed this Agreement, in the case of the Company by its duly authorized officer, as of the day and year first above written.

Purchaser:	*[name of corporation]*
__________	By: __________
	Title: __________

Exhibit A

Section 83(b) Election

The undersigned taxpayer hereby elects, pursuant to Section 83(b) of the Internal Revenue Code of 1986, as amended, to include in gross income as compensation for services the excess (if any) of the fair market value of the shares described below over the amount paid for those shares.

1. The name, taxpayer identification number, address of the undersigned, and the taxable year for which this election is being made are:

TAXPAYER'S NAME: __________

TAXPAYER'S SOCIAL SECURITY NUMBER: __________

ADDRESS:

TAXABLE YEAR: Calendar Year 20__

2. The property with respect to which the election is made is _____ shares of the common stock of *[name of corporation]*.

3. The property was transferred on ___________.

4. The property is subject to a repurchase right pursuant to which the issuer has the right to acquire the property at the original purchase price if for any reason taxpayer's service with the issuer is terminated. The issuer's repurchase right lapses in a series of installments over a _____-year period ending on ___________, 20__.

5. The fair market value of the property at the time of transfer (determined without regard to any restriction other than a nonlapse restriction as defined in Section 1.83-3(h) of the Income Tax Regulations) is: $________ per share times _____ shares = $________.

6. The amount paid for such property is $________ per share times _____ shares = $________.

7. The amount to include in gross income is $________. [the result of the amount reported in Item 5 minus the amount reported in Item 6]

The undersigned taxpayer will file this election with the Internal Revenue Service office with which taxpayer files his or her annual income tax return not later than 30 days after the date of transfer of the property. A copy of the election also will be furnished to the person for whom the services were performed. Additionally, the undersigned will include a copy of the election with his or her income tax return for the taxable year in which the property is transferred. The undersigned is the person performing the services in connection with which the property was transferred.

Dated: ___________ ___________

Taxpayer

CHAPTER 7

CREATING A DELAWARE FOR-PROFIT CORPORATION

■ ■ ■

A. CHOOSING AND FORMING THE FOR-PROFIT CORPORATION OVER OTHER OPTIONS

Your analysis of a client's choice of form options is driven by the general benefits conferred by a formal entity structure. As you learned in Chapter 5, a for-profit entity has four: **liability risk limitation, effective decision-making structure, effective equity structure,** and **favorable tax treatment.** Both the LLC organized in the business's home state and the Delaware corporation offer a strikingly similar approach to limiting liability, especially as to third parties. As you may have already seen in reading Chapters 3 and 5, corporate governance is more formal and less flexible than the decision-making structure available to the LLC. At first blush, this off-the-rack approach of corporation statutes may seem a clear disadvantage. But, when it comes to decision making, the Delaware corporation is a known quantity as compared to the LLC of any state, including Delaware. Lawyers for angel investors and venture capital firms will feel more comfortable structuring investment in a Delaware corporation than building an LLC from scratch. Although the LLC also offers flexibility as to tax treatment, the inclusion of outside investors often relegates rapidly growing businesses to C-Corp tax status anyway.

Although LLC formation and maintenance costs vary greatly from state to state, many jurisdictions will allow small business owners to form and maintain an LLC at a substantially lower cost than the amounts expected of a similarly sized Delaware corporation. The initial certificate filing cost in Delaware is competitive, but Delaware also has an annual franchise tax, which is largely dependent on the number of shares authorized in the certificate of incorporation. Authorizing 5000 shares or less will cost the entity $175 per year. Even though companies with 5000 or fewer shares can have millions of dollars invested in them by dozens of people, many founders want to start with a pool of millions of shares. The cachet that comes with this will cost them at least $350 per year, but as long as they pick a nominal par value for all stock, do not have more than $500,000 in assets, and have issued the majority of the authorized stock, then they should not be paying more than the $350 per year for the franchise tax.

DISCUSSION QUESTION 7–A

For each of the following new for-profit ventures, consider the benefits and costs to each of choosing to incorporate in Delaware as opposed to organizing as an LLC in its home jurisdiction. If the prospects for the kind of outside investment that usually makes the Delaware corporation a necessity are still several years off, what else would you want to know about the business before recommending against the LLC even as an initial organizational form?

1) A pair of recently certified personal trainers wish to start a fitness business at one location with the hopes of rapid expansion to many more sites throughout the region in the coming years.

2) Four young entrepreneurs have come together to develop a social media platform focused on pet owners. The first five years of the business plan call for steep scaling up of outreach and cloud computing resources without little or no move to monetize participation.

3) An inventor has created a new household kitchen tool for which she has filed a provisional patent application. She has no desire to manufacture the product herself but instead wishes to license it to a major kitchen tool producer.

B. DELAWARE CERTIFICATE OF INCORPORATION

No charter document can compete with the LLC articles of organization for its pure simplicity. Nonetheless, a Delaware for-profit corporation on its way to millions of dollars in capitalization in a few years can be formed with a single-page certificate of incorporation. The certificate has the standard blanks for entity name, registered agent and address, as well as the name(s) and address(es) of the incorporator(s). But the statute also requires the specification of the number of authorized shares and the par value, if any. This chapter will assume that the corporation will begin with only one class of stock. The Delaware General Corporation Law provides for the establishment of classes of stock but requires that it be done through the certificate of incorporation

Specifying par value is not required by Delaware state law, but the assumed par value method of calculating the franchise tax is not available to corporations that do not have a set par value. If the incorporator(s) want to have more than 30,000 shares, it is better to set a par value in the certificate of incorporation. Otherwise, the corporation will be paying more in franchise tax than it has to.

A good rule of thumb is to set par value at an amount that, when multiplied by the number of authorized shares, will be equal to or less than $1000. If the total initial investment by founding owners is to be less than $2000, reduce that $1000 cap to half the value of the total capital initially invested in the corporation. Thus, if the total par value you picked is $100 (because the initial capital invested was $200) and the number of authorized shares is 10,000,000, then the per-share par value would be $0.00001, and you would set that fractional amount as the par value in the certificate of incorporation.

To accommodate more sophisticated forms of investment, a certificate may need to be amended at the time investors who want preferred stock arrangement are brought on board. It may seem odd to choose the Delaware form and not set up the different classes of stock at the outset. But the details of stock classification may be important points in the negotiations by which outside investment is brought in. If these investor-accommodating changes can wait until the outside investors are joining, it may seem that incorporating in Delaware can also be put off. But choosing the Delaware corporate form now over that of the LLC or of a home state corporation will avoid the need for a subsequent conversion or reincorporation in Delaware and the transfer of bank accounts and other assets that come with that.

The chart on the next page includes one substantively significant provision that is not an issue that must be addressed in a certificate of incorporation. The ability of the bylaws to be amended by the board of directors, as opposed to by the stockholders only, can be established but only by an express provision in the certificate of incorporation.

Checklist Item	Delaware limits	Client Inquiry
Entity Name	Distinct from other names; not misleading re: purpose; corporate identifier	Trademark concerns: name to promote goods/services?
Reg. Agent & Address	In-state business office address of state resident	Does client know someone willing to serve?
Total Authorized # of Shares		Franchise tax is $175, if $\leq$ 5000; otherwise, probably at least $350
Par Value	Par value not required	If no par value, franchise tax set by auth. shares method; see discussion of par value above
Incorporator(s) name(s) & address(es)	Any individual or entity	Counseling as to role in incorporation process
Board authority to adopt and amend bylaws	Board has authority only if in certificate of incorp; otherwise stockholders	Small corp. client may not want to have to call stockholders' meeting to amend bylaws

Certificate of Incorporation—Delaware[1]

OF

[NAME OF CORPORATION]

The undersigned Incorporator, who is a natural person, desiring to form a corporation under the General Corporation Law of the State of Delaware, hereby certifies as follows:

FIRST: The name of the corporation is *[name of corporation].*

SECOND: The address of the registered office of the corporation in the state of Delaware is *[street address, including county]*, and the name of the initial registered agent of the corporation at that office upon whom process against this corporation may be served is *[name of agent].*

THIRD: The purpose of the corporation is to engage in any lawful act or activity for which corporations may be organized under the General Corporation Law of Delaware.

---

[1] Reprinted from West's Legal Forms, Business Organizations § 125:14 with permission of Thomson Reuters.

FOURTH: The total number of shares that the corporation shall have authority to issue is *[number of shares]* shares of common stock with a par value of $*[amount of par value]* per share.

FIFTH: The name and address of the incorporator of the corporation are: *[name of incorporator]*, *[address of incorporator]*.

SIXTH: The board of directors of the corporation is expressly authorized to adopt, amend, and repeal the bylaws of the corporation, subject to the power of the stockholders of the corporation to adopt, amend, and repeal the bylaws regardless of whether they were adopted or amended by the board of directors or shareholders.

DATED: *[date]*

C. DELAWARE CORPORATION BYLAWS

1. GETTING THE ORDER RIGHT

To outline the bylaws for a readable draft, the checklist items[2] must be arranged in a sensible order and the provisions must be organized into appropriate sections (or articles) and subsections. As with contracts, bylaws should start with the fundamentals and end with the boilerplate. Looking at who among the decision makers will select whom can give a chronological order to the bylaws:

- Preliminaries
- Meetings of Stockholders
- Directors
- Meetings of Directors
- Officers
- Committees
- Books and Records
- Corporate Policies
- General Provisions

Subsections—As you sketch out the provisions, you will get a sense of when subjects should be broken into different sections just as you see the need to break a prose discussion into several paragraphs. When certain provisions clearly belong together, you can create a hierarchy of sections and subsections.

---

[2] For a discussion of how to create a checklist for corporate bylaws, see Ch. 3, Section A.

The biggest difference between the Delaware for-profit corporation and the non-membership nonprofit corporation examined in Chapters 2 and 3 is the presence of stockholders. As with the directors' meetings, the provisions related to stockholders' meetings will deal with:

- Annual Meeting
- Special Meeting
- Quorum
- Voting

But there will also need to be separate provisions related to stockholder meetings for:

- Place of Meeting
- Notice of Meeting
- Record Date (for determining stockholder list)
- Proxies

The subsections of the other bylaws sections (or articles), such as board meetings, officers, committees, etc. correspond in a general manner to the nonprofit bylaws. The books and records provisions will include a provision for the issuances of stock certificates. The various equity structure provisions found in the LLC operating agreement relating to distributions and allocations of profits and losses are largely reduced in the basic Delaware bylaws form below to sections on transfers and dividends.

2. ANSWERING THE CHECKLIST QUESTIONS: KNOWING THE LAW

The next step, then, is to transform your comprehensive checklist into an **outline** that will lead to a **readable** draft that is **correct** in that it both complies with relevant law and meets the client's substantive goal of having an effective governance structure. Knowledge of state law is crucial to completing the outline. The drafter cannot know the substantive answers to the checklist questions without understanding the parameters set out in the statute. In sketching out the substance of your bylaws provisions, you will want to make sure that they will not be invalid under Delaware law. The table below lists relevant mandatory provisions in the Delaware General Corporation Law. These provisions apply to all nonprofits incorporated in the state regardless of what the articles or bylaws might provide. When drafting bylaws provisions, you do not want to insert a provision that contradicts a mandatory provision of the corporation statute. The table's third column lists provisions that create rules for Delaware corporations "unless the articles or bylaws provide otherwise." These are called default rules because they apply when the corporation's documents are silent on the issue.

Notice that some of the mandatory rules actually contain the verb "may" in them. These provisions in the center column are all mandatory in the sense that they cannot be changed by the bylaws, but the some of the rules, such as the ones dealing with resignation, provide for what may be done as opposed to what must or must not be done. Similarly, some of the default rules, such as those dealing with board meeting quorum and notice of special meetings, impose requirements on the corporation, but only if the governing documents do not override them. These mandating default rules are listed **in bold** because you may want to give particular attention to the requirements that you can change. Each topic is accompanied by a reference to the appropriate section or subsection of the Delaware General Corporation Law.

Checklist	Mandatory Provisions	Default Provisions
Stockholders Meetings		
Annual—§ 211	Bylaws shall determine date and time unless . . .	. . . stockholders elect directors by written consent
Call of Special—§ 211	Meetings may be called by board of directors	**Board alone may call special meeting**
Notice—§ 222	Must state place and time as well as any means of remote communication; not < 10 & not > 60 days before mtg.; electronic by revocable consent	
Quorum—§ 216	Must be ≥ 1/3 of shares entitled to vote	**Majority of shares entitled to vote**
Voting—§ 212	Proxies allowed; safe harbor process described	1 vote per share by (unless certificate); directors elected by plurality of shares present; by written ballot (unless certificate); all others, majority of shares present
Record Date—§ 213	DGCL § 213 provides Board's parameters for setting record date for determining who are shareholders entitled to notice & vote, entitled to notice & written consent	
Directors		
Number & Qualifications—§ 141(b)	Must have ≥ 1; must be natural person(s)	Range permitted w/ # set by board; need not be stockholders

Removal—§ 141(k)	Shareholders may w/o cause	
Resignation—§ 141(b)	May w/ written notice	
Officers		
Which req'd?—§ 142(a)	Secretary	
Removal—§ 142(b)		May w/o cause
Resignation—§ 142(b)	May w/ notice	
Committees—§ 141(c)(2)	Must include ≥ 1 director; may not approve dissolution or fill vacancies; may be created only by board of directors	
Directors Meetings		
Action w/o Meeting—§ 141(f)		Any action if approved in writing by all dirs.
Quorum—§ 141(c)(4)	Must be $\geq \frac{1}{3}$ of directors in office	**Majority of directors in office** (less by cert. only)
Waiver of Notice—§ 229	Written waiver = notice; actual attendance at mtg. w/o objection = waiver	
Share Certificates—§ 158	Any certificate to be signed by 2 officers; no bearer certificates	**Stock shares must be certificated unless board resolution.**
Records—§ 224, et al.	Various provisions about where and what to keep	
D&O payments—§ 141 (h)		Board may fix compensation.
Indemnification—§ 145	May indemnify if acted in good faith & reas. believed conduct was in org's best interests; may not if found liable; shall indemnify director successful on merits in defending lawsuit.	
Conflicts of Interest—§ 144	*No required process but safe harbor protecting validity of action if standard C of I procedure is followed*	
Amendment—§ 109	**Power to amend in the board if certificate gives power or names directors; otherwise, in shareholders**	

Since most default provision cans be overridden by a bylaws provision addressing the same issue, it may not seem worthwhile knowing any default provision's content once you have decided to address that issue in your bylaws. But knowing the default provision can offer you an initial option for your outline. Ultimately, you may reject it in favor of one or more alternatives that you think will better meet your client's needs. But the default provision is worth consulting as a middle-of-the-road norm.

Looking at it from the other side, discovering a default provision that works well for your client may lead you to the conclusion that you should not address the issue in your bylaws. After all, the default provision will still apply even if you do not recite it in your bylaws. Keep in mind, however, that you chose to include that issue, be it quorum or the number of directors on the board, in your checklist because you felt it a vital part of the governance structure. If that is so, you may not want to leave the question unaddressed in the bylaws nor to simply refer your client's leadership to the statute, which may not be easy for them to find.

3. ANSWERING THE CHECKLIST QUESTIONS: KNOWING THE CLIENT'S NEEDS

Once we understand the limits that the Delaware General Corporation Law places on the governance provisions in the bylaws, we are free to explore the various permissible options that might best suit the client's approach to decision making. By recalling the elements of effective decision making listed at the beginning of the chapter, we have a sense of the governance concerns common to most clients:

- fairness
- accountability
- timeliness
- risk protection
- resiliency in times of strong conflict
- inclusivity
- commitment to excellence
- transparency
- confidentiality
- resistance to corruption
- accurate identification of issues
- access to relevant information
- communication among decision makers

DISCUSSION QUESTION 7–B

Some of these aspects of good corporate decision making are so fundamental that they are relevant to nearly every core bylaws provision. Others, while still important, are promoted by just one or two provisions in the typical set of corporate bylaws. Upon review of the list above, you may even able to identify one or two items that are not addressed at all by bylaws. In preparation for classroom discussion, sort the list above into each of these three categories: fundamental, specific, and unaddressed.

DISCUSSION QUESTION 7–C

Now consider if any of the identified aspects of good decision making listed above are in tension with other qualities listed. See if you can find at least one item that could be promoted only to the detriment of some other item. How would you go about balancing them in outlining a set of bylaws? How, if at all, would you bring the client constituents into the discussion of balancing the two qualities?

Beyond those characteristics that you believe every corporation would seek out as part of its quest for good governance, there may be bylaws choices that a new corporation will make based on its particular limits or traits. Every benefit has its costs, and effective decision making is no different. Good governance, even when optimally structured, requires time, communication and information gathering. Counseling your client on the content of the bylaws means helping them compare the costs and benefits of certain provisions. This comparison of alternate approaches to a specific section of the bylaws is best handled at the outline stage of the drafting. The different options you provide a for-profit corporation with regard to certain provisions may be shaped by what you have learned about the client's resources and the way its leaders communicate with one another.

DISCUSSION QUESTION 7–D

Review the following connections made between facts learned about the client and sections of the bylaws that may be impacted by those realities. In class, discuss how the former might shape the provisions listed.

> Founders' differing skill sets, the availability of mentors and advisors ⟶ # of directors, officer roles, committees
>
> The founders' preferred modes of and times for communicating ⟶ meetings, action without meetings
>
> The business plan for capital growth, income/expenses ⟶ treasurer, budget/annual report, bank account, conflicts of interest

D. WRITING OUT THE PROVISION LANGUAGE

Whether you are writing out the full legal language of your provisions from scratch or revising a form, your focus at this final stage must be clarity. When learning prose writing, you were certainly taught to be clear and economical in your use of language, but you were also encouraged to keep your reader's interest by, among other things, varying your word choice. As already noted in the Chapters 1 and 4, ambiguity in a document intended to have legal effect must be avoided at all costs. A basic rule of drafting is: <u>If you mean the same thing, say it the same way</u>. This precept encourages not only consistency within and among documents but also standardization across related types of legal drafting.

For now, let's focus on the most important word choice any legal drafter makes in creating a sentence: which verb to use. To understand the proper verbs for bylaws provisions, you need to understand what kind of legal effect each type of provision has. Like statutes and the organization's articles of incorporation, the bylaws, for the most part, make legal <u>declarations</u> and outline <u>procedures</u>, both <u>mandatory</u> and <u>discretionary</u>, for valid action. The former are the kind of statements that might have been preceded in ages past with the clause "It is hereby declared that . . .". The plain language movement has succeeding in eliminating this preamble. When making a legal declaration, the drafter simply states the declaration in the present tense: "The name of the Corporation is . . . ."

Far more commonly, bylaws set out what is and what is not a valid way of making decisions, including which people should serve as decision makers. These provisions either mandate a particular way of proceeding by using the word "shall" or permit, without requiring, a procedure by using the word "may." Because these types of provision focus on how something should be done rather than who should be obligated to act in a particular way, these procedure provisions are generally written in the passive voice.

Sometimes though, bylaws do identify a particular person or persons and give them a responsibility. When a bylaws provision imposes a responsibility and/or a <u>duty</u> to act in a certain way, the provision's verb structure will use "shall" but be cast in the active voice. The subject of the sentence will be the person who has the responsibility or duty. Likewise, if a specific person or role is given some power or <u>discretionary authority</u>, then the verb used is "may", but again in active voice with the empowered person as the subject.

When a mandated procedure is ignored in the process of making a decision or taking an official action, the result may be that the decision or action lacks legal validity. When a corporate official disregards a duty he or she has under the bylaws, it is possible that he or she may have some liability to the corporation as a result. You should write personal obligation provisions in the active voice to be absolutely **clear** about who is obligated. On the other hand, the passive voice is used for procedures because those provisions are not concerned with imposing duties on certain people but instead with setting out how valid decisions are to be made. When expressing a right, use the passive "is (or shall be) entitled to."

The table on the next page sets out the various types of bylaws provisions along with the verb structure particular to each.

Bylaws Provision Examples	Provision Type	Standard Verb (Voice)	Bylaws Provision Example Language
Classes of Directors	Self-Executing Declaration	"is", "are" or other present tense verb (linking verb or active or passive voice)	There **is** only one class of Directors.
Classes of Stock	Statement of Legal Fact		The Corporation **shall have** one class of stock. (restating Articles)
Nomination & Election of Directors, Regular Meetings, many others	Mandatory Procedure	"shall" (passive voice)	Regularly meetings of the Board **shall be held** at least quarterly.
Removal	Permissive Procedure	"may" (passive voice)	An officer **may be removed,** with or without cause, as determined by a two-thirds vote of the Board present at any meeting at which there is a quorum.
Officers	Imposed Duty/ Responsibility	"shall" (active voice)	The Secretary **shall keep** accurate records and minutes of all meetings of the Corporation.
Stockholder Voting	Right	"is (or shall be) entitled to" (passive voice)	. . . each outstanding share entitled to vote **shall be entitled** to one vote on each matter submitted to a vote at a meeting of stockholders
Conflict of Interest, Indemnification Limit	Prohibited Action	"shall not" (active or passive voice)	Such person **shall not be counted** in determining the existence of a quorum at any meeting where the contract, transaction, or determination is under discussion or is being voted upon.
Committees, Discretionary Indemnification	Permitted Action/ Discretionary Authority/ Power	"may" (active voice)	The Board of Directors **may create** such committees with such power as it deems wise to have.
Resignation	Limit on Permitted Action/Discr. Authority/ Power	"may . . . only if" (active or passive voice)	A Director **may resign only** by submitting a written resignation to the President, the Secretary or to the other Directors.

EXERCISE 7–1

Before using a legal form as is, you should review it to make sure it is **complete, correct** and **clear.** The bylaws form below contains one instance each of falling short of these core legal document qualities. *None of these alterations appear after Article III.*

a) As part of your checklist review, find the provision below that has been erased and use process of elimination to guess what it was.

b) For your outline review, find one provision below that runs afoul of the Delaware corporation statute.

c) Look over the verbs in each of the provisions. See if you can find the one sentence that has two instances of incorrect verb structures given the types of bylaws provisions that are being expressed in that one sentence.

Bylaws—Delaware[3]

BYLAWS

OF

****, INC.

ARTICLE I—MEETINGS OF STOCKHOLDERS

1.1 Place of Meetings.

Meetings of the stockholders shall be held at such place within or without the State of Delaware as designated by the Board of Directors or the person or persons calling the meeting.

1.2 Annual Meetings.

The annual meeting of the stockholders for the election of directors and the transaction of such other business as may properly come before the meeting shall be held after the close of the Corporation's fiscal year on such date and at such time as shall be designated by the Board of Directors.

1.3 Special Meetings.

Special meetings may be called at any time by the President or by a majority of the Board of Directors.

[3] Reprinted from Jean L. Batman, Advising the Small Business with permission of ABA Publications. ©2012 by the American Bar Association. Reproduced with permission. All rights reserved. This information or any portion thereof may not be copied or disseminated in any form or by any means or stored in an electronic database or retrieval system without the express written consent of the American Bar Association. This form has been altered for the purposes of this exercise.

1.4 Notice of Meetings.

1.5 Quorum.

The holders of a majority of the stock issued and outstanding and entitled to vote thereat, present in person or represented by proxy, shall constitute a quorum at all meetings of the stockholders for the transaction of business except as otherwise provided by statute or by the Certificate of Incorporation. If, however, such quorum shall not be present or represented at any meeting of the stockholders, the stockholders entitled to vote thereat, present in person or represented by proxy, shall have power to adjourn the meeting from time to time, without notice other than announcement at the meeting, until a quorum shall be present or represented. At such adjourned meeting at which a quorum shall be present or represented any business may be transacted which might have been transacted at the meeting as originally notified. If the adjournment is for more than thirty (30) days, or if after the adjournment a new record date is fixed for the adjourned meeting, a notice of the adjourned meeting shall be given to each stockholder of record entitled to vote at the meeting.

When a quorum is present at any meeting, the vote of the holders of a majority of the stock having voting power present in person or represented by proxy shall decide any question brought before such meeting, unless the question is one upon which by express provision of the statutes or of the certificate of incorporation, a different vote is required in which case such express provision shall govern and control the decision of such question.

1.6 Voting.

Unless otherwise provided in the certificate of incorporation each stockholder shall at every meeting of the stockholders be entitled to one vote in person or by proxy for each share of the capital stock having voting power held by such stockholder, but no proxy shall be voted on after three years from its date, unless the proxy provides for a longer period.

ARTICLE II—DIRECTORS

2.1 Number, Election, and Term of Office.

The Board of Directors shall consist of not less than two nor more than nine members as fixed from time to time by the Board of Directors. The directors shall be elected at the annual meeting of the stockholders, except as provided in Section 2.2 of this Article, and each director elected shall hold office until his successor is elected and qualified. Directors need not be stockholders.

2.2 Vacancies.

Vacancies and newly created directorships resulting from any increase in the authorized number of directors may be filled by a majority vote of the directors then in office, although less than a quorum, or by a sole remaining director. The occurrence of a vacancy which is not filled by action of the Board of Directors shall constitute a determination by the Board of Directors that the number of directors is reduced so as to eliminate such vacancy, unless the Board of Directors shall specify otherwise. When one or more directors shall resign from the Board, effective at a future date, a majority of the directors then in office, including those who have so resigned, shall have power to fill such vacancy or vacancies, the vote thereon to take effect when such resignation or resignations shall become effective.

2.3 Meetings of Directors.

Meetings of the Board of Directors shall be held at such times and at such places within or without the State of Delaware as the Board of Directors shall determine from time to time; and no notice shall be required to be given of any such regular meeting. The Chairman or any director may call a special meeting of the Board of Directors by giving one (1) day's notice to each director by letter, telegram, electronic mail, telephone or other oral message. Attendance at any meeting without protest shall constitute a waiver of notice of such meeting. Except as otherwise provided by these Bylaws, a total number of one director shall constitute a quorum for the transaction of business, and the vote of a majority of the directors present at any meeting at which a quorum is present shall be the act of the Board of Directors. Attendance by a director at any meeting shall constitute consent to all actions taken at such meeting unless such director enters his dissent in the minutes of the meeting, or files such dissent with the secretary of the meeting prior to the adjournment of the meeting, or with the Secretary of the Corporation immediately following adjournment of the meeting.

2.4 Action Without a Meeting.

Any action required or permitted to be taken by the Board of Directors or any committee of the Board of Directors may be taken without a meeting, if all members of the Board of Directors, or such committee, shall individually or collectively consent in writing to such action. Such written consent or consents shall be filed with the minutes of the proceedings of the Board of Directors or committee of the Board of Directors, as appropriate.

Such action by written consent shall have the same force and effect as a unanimous vote of such directors.

2.5 Power of Directors.

The Board of Directors shall have all the powers normally conferred on a board of directors of a Delaware corporation, including, without limitation, (a) to charge, mortgage, hypothecate or pledge all or any of the assets of the Corporation, real or personal, movable or immovable, including book debts, rights, powers, franchises and undertakings, to secure the debt obligations or any money borrowed or other debt or liability of the Corporation and (b) to delegate to such one or more of the directors and officers of the Corporation, as allowed by law, the powers conferred on a board of directors to such extent and in such manner as the Board of Directors shall determine at the time of such delegation.

2.6 Committees of Directors.

(a) The board of directors may, by resolution passed by a majority of the whole board, designate one or more committees, each committee to consist of one or more of the directors of the corporation. The board may designate one or more directors as alternate members of any committee, who may replace any absent or disqualified member at any meeting of the committee.

(b) In the absence or disqualification of a member of a committee, the member or members thereof present at any meeting and not disqualified from voting, whether or not he or they constitute a quorum, may unanimously appoint another member of the board of directors to act at the meeting in the place of any such absent or disqualified member.

(c) Any such committee, to the extent provided in the resolution of the board of directors, shall have and may exercise all the powers and authority of the board of directors in the management of the business and affairs of the corporation, and may authorize the seal of the corporation to be affixed to all papers which may require it; any committee shall have the power and authority in to amend the certificate of incorporation, (except that a committee may, to the extent authorized in the resolution or resolutions providing for the issuance of shares of stock adopted by the board of directors as provided in Section 151(a) of the General Corporation Law of Delaware fix any of the preferences or rights of such shares relating to dividends, redemption, dissolution, any distribution of assets of the corporation or the conversion into, or the exchange of such shares for, shares of any other class or classes or any other series of the same or any other class or classes of stock of the corporation) adopting an agreement of merger or consolidation, recommending to the stockholders the sale, lease or exchange of all or substantially all of the corporation's property and assets, recommending to the stockholders a dissolution of the corporation or a revocation of a dissolution, or amending the bylaws of the corporation; and, unless the resolution or the certificate of incorporation expressly so provides, no such committee shall have the power or authority to declare a dividend or to authorize the issuance of stock or to adopt a certificate of ownership and merger. Such committee or committees shall have such name or names as may be determined from time to time by resolution adopted by the board of directors.

(d) Each committee shall keep regular minutes of its meetings and report the same to the board of directors when required.

2.7 Compensation of Directors.

Unless otherwise restricted by the certificate of incorporation or these Bylaws, the board of directors shall have the authority to fix the compensation of directors. The directors may be paid their expenses, if any, of attendance at each meeting of the board of directors and may be paid a fixed sum for attendance at each meeting of the board of directors or a stated salary as director. No such payment shall preclude any director from serving the corporation in any other capacity and receiving compensation therefor. Members of special or standing committees may be allowed like compensation for attending committee meetings.

2.8 Removal of Directors.

No director may be removed unless convicted of a crime of moral turpitude or adjudicated to have defrauded the Corporation.

ARTICLE III—OFFICERS

3.1 Enumeration.

The Board of Directors from time to time shall elect officers, to serve at the pleasure of the Board. Each officer shall hold office until his or her successor is elected and qualified, or until his or her earlier resignation or removal. Any officer may resign at any time upon written notice to the Corporation. The compensation of all officers shall be fixed by, or pursuant to authority delegated by, the Board of Directors from time to time. The officers of the Corporation must be elected by the Board of Directors and may not consist of a Chairman of the Board, a Chief Executive Officer, a Chief Operating Officer, a President, such number of Vice Presidents (if any) and Assistant Vice-Presidents (if any) as the Board shall from time to time elect, a Secretary, such number of Assistant Secretaries (if any) as the Board shall from time to time elect, a Treasurer, such number of Assistant Treasurers (if any) as the Board shall from time to time elect, a Chief

Financial Officer and such other officers (if any) as the Board shall from time to time elect. The Chairman of the Board shall be a member of the Board of Directors. The same person may hold any two or more offices.

3.2 Chairman of the Board.

The Chairman of the Board shall preside at meetings of the Board of Directors. The Chairman of the Board shall have such powers and perform such duties as shall from time to time be specified by the Board of Directors.

3.3 Chief Executive Officer.

Subject to such supervisory powers, if any, as may be given by the Board of Directors to the Chairman of the Board, if there be such an officer, the Chief Executive Officer of the Corporation shall, subject to the control of the Board of Directors, have general supervision, direction and control of the business and the officers of the Corporation. The Chief Executive Officer shall preside at all meetings of the stockholders and, in the absence or nonexistence of a Chairman of the Board, at all meetings of the Board of Directors. The Chief Executive Officer shall have the general powers and duties of management usually vested in the Chief Executive Officer of a corporation and shall have such other powers and duties as may be prescribed by the Board of Directors or these Bylaws.

3.4 President and Chief Operating Officer.

The President shall be the Chief Operating Officer and shall have such powers and perform such duties as shall from time to time be specified by the Board of Directors or delegated to the President by the Board of Directors. The President shall sign all certificates for shares of the capital stock of the Corporation and may, together with the Secretary, execute on behalf of the Corporation any contract that has been approved by the Board of Directors.

3.5 Vice President.

The Vice President or, if there shall be more than one, the Vice Presidents, in the order of their seniority unless otherwise specified by the Board of Directors, shall have all of the powers and perform all of the duties of the President during the absence or inability to act of the President. Each Vice President shall also have such other powers and perform such other duties as shall from time to time be prescribed by the Board of Directors or the President.

3.6 Secretary.

The Secretary shall record the proceedings of the meetings of the stockholders and directors in a book to be kept for that purpose, and shall give notice as required by statute or these Bylaws of all such meetings. The Secretary shall have custody of the seal of the Corporation and of all books, records, and papers of the Corporation, except such as shall be in the charge of the Treasurer or of some other person authorized to have custody and possession thereof by resolution of the Board of Directors. The Secretary may, together with the President, execute on behalf of the Corporation any contract that has been approved by the Board of Directors. The Secretary shall also have such other powers and perform such other duties as are incident to the office of the secretary of a corporation or as shall from time to time be prescribed by, or pursuant to authority delegated by, the Board of Directors.

3.7 Treasurer and Chief Financial Officer.

The Treasurer shall be the Chief Financial Officer and shall keep full and accurate accounts of the receipts and disbursements of the Corporation in books belonging to the Corporation, shall deposit all moneys and other valuable effects of the Corporation in the name and to the credit of the Corporation in such depositories as may be designated by the Board of Directors, may execute, or witness the execution of, on behalf of the Corporation any contract that has been approved by the Board of Directors, and shall also have such other powers and perform such other duties as are incident to the office of the treasurer of a corporation or as shall from time to time be prescribed by, or pursuant to authority delegated by, the Board of Directors.

3.8 Other Officers.

The powers and duties of each other officer who may from time to time be chosen by the Board of Directors shall be as specified by, or pursuant to authority delegated by, the Board of Directors at the time of the appointment of such other officer or from time to time thereafter. In addition, each officer designated as an assistant officer shall assist in the performance of the duties of the officer to which he or she is assistant, and shall have the powers and perform the duties of such officer during the absence or inability to act of such officer.

3.9 Additional Powers and Duties.

The Board of Directors may from time to time by resolution increase or add to the powers and duties of any of the officers of the Corporation. Except in cases in which the signing and execution shall have been expressly delegated by the Board of Directors to some other officer, employee or agent of the Corporation, the Chairman of the Board of Directors or the President or a Vice-President may sign and execute in the name of the Corporation all authorized deeds, mortgages, bonds, contracts or other instruments; provided, however, that a Vice-President may delegate to any other officer or manager reporting to such officer authority to sign and execute in the name of the Corporation all authorized contracts and similar instruments pursuant to a policy approved by the Board of Directors.

ARTICLE IV—INDEMNIFICATION

4.1 Directors and Officers.

The Corporation shall indemnify, to the fullest extent now or hereafter permitted by law, each director or officer (including each former director or officer) of the Corporation who was, is or becomes a party to, or a witness in, or is threatened to be made a party to, or otherwise becomes involved in as a witness or otherwise in any threatened, pending or completed action, suit or proceeding, whether civil, criminal, administrative or investigative, by reason of the fact that he or she is or was an authorized representative of the Corporation (as defined in Section 4.8 herein), against all expenses (including attorneys' fees and disbursements), judgments, fines (including excise taxes, interest and penalties) and amounts paid in settlement actually and reasonably incurred by him or her in connection with such action, suit or proceeding.

4.2 Timing of Indemnification.

The Corporation shall pay expenses (including attorneys' fees and disbursements) incurred by a director or officer of the Corporation referred to in Section 4.1 hereof in defending, prosecuting where the action was brought with the consent of the Board of Directors, or appearing as a witness in any civil or criminal action, suit or proceeding described in Section 4.1 hereof in advance of the final disposition of such action, suit or proceeding. The expenses incurred by such director or officer in his or her capacity as a director or officer of the Corporation shall be paid by the Corporation in advance of the final disposition of such action, suit or proceeding only upon receipt of an undertaking by or on behalf of such director or officer to repay all amounts advanced if it shall ultimately be determined that he or she is not entitled to be indemnified by the Corporation because he or she has not met the standard of conduct set forth in Section 4.5 hereof.

4.3 Authorized Representatives.

The Corporation may, as determined by the Board of Directors from time to time, indemnify to the fullest extent now or hereafter permitted by law, any person who was or is a party to or a witness in or is threatened to be made a party to or a witness in, or is otherwise involved in, any threatened, pending or completed action, suit or proceeding, whether civil, criminal, administrative or investigative, by reason of the fact that he or she is or was an authorized representative of the Corporation (as defined in Section 4.8 herein), against all expenses (including attorneys' fees and disbursements), judgments, fines (including excise taxes, interest and penalties), and amounts paid in settlement actually and reasonably incurred by him or her in connection with such action, suit or proceeding. Subject to Section 4.2 hereof, the Corporation may, as determined by the Board of Directors from time to time, pay expenses, including attorneys fees, incurred by any such person by reason of his or her participation in an action, suit or proceeding referred to in this Section 4.3 in advance of the final disposition of such action, suit or proceeding.

4.4 Nonexclusivity.

Each director and officer of the Corporation shall be deemed to act in such capacity in reliance upon such rights of indemnification and advancement of expenses as are provided in this Article. The rights of indemnification and advancement of expenses provided by this Article shall not be deemed exclusive of any other rights to which any person seeking indemnification or advancement of expenses may be entitled under any agreement, vote of stockholders or disinterested directors, decision of independent counsel, statute or otherwise, both as to action in such person's official capacity and as to action in another capacity while holding such office or position, and shall continue as to a person who has ceased to be an authorized representative of the Corporation and shall inure to the benefit of the heirs, executors, assigns and administrators of such person.

4.5 Standard for Indemnification.

Any indemnification under this Article shall be made by the Corporation only as authorized in the specific case upon a determination that indemnification of the authorized representative is proper in the circumstances because such person has acted in good faith and in a manner he or she reasonably believed to be in or not opposed to the best interests of the Corporation, and, with respect to any criminal action or proceeding had no reasonable cause to believe his or her conduct was unlawful. Such determination shall be made (1) by the Board of Directors by a majority vote of a quorum consisting of Directors who were not parties to such action, suit or proceeding, or (2) if such quorum is not obtainable, or, even if obtainable, a quorum of disinterested Directors so directs, by independent legal counsel in a written opinion, or (3) by the stockholders. The termination of any action, suit or proceeding by judgment, order, settlement, conviction, or upon a plea of nolo contendere or its equivalent, shall not, of itself, create a presumption that the officer or director did not act in good faith and in a manner which such officer or director reasonably believed to be in or not opposed to the best interests of the Corporation, and, with respect to any criminal action or proceeding, had reasonable cause to believe that such person's conduct was unlawful.

4.6 Insurance.

The Corporation shall purchase and maintain insurance on behalf of each director and officer against any liability asserted against or incurred by such director or officer in any capacity, or arising out of such director's or officer's status as such, whether or not the Corporation would have the power to indemnify such director or officer against such liability under the provisions of this Article. The Corporation shall not be required to maintain such insurance if it is not available on terms satisfactory to the Board of Directors or if, in the business judgment of the Board of Directors, either (i) the premium cost for such insurance is substantially disproportionate to the amount of coverage, or (ii) the coverage provided by such insurance is so limited by exclusions that there is insufficient benefit from such insurance. The Corporation may purchase and maintain insurance on behalf of any person referred to in Section 4.3 hereof against any liability asserted against or incurred by such person in any capacity, whether or not the Corporation would have the power to indemnify such person against such liability under the provisions of this Article.

4.7 Constituent Corporations.

For purposes of this Article, references to "the Corporation" shall include, in addition to the resulting corporation, any constituent corporation (including any constituent of a constituent) absorbed in a consolidation or merger which, if its separate existence had continued, would have had power and authority to indemnify its authorized representatives so that any person who is or was an authorized representative of such constituent corporation shall stand in the same position under this Article with respect to the resulting or surviving corporation as he or she would have with respect to such constituent corporation if its separate existence had continued.

4.8 Eligibility.

For the purposes of this Article, the term "authorized representative" shall mean a director, officer, employee or agent of the Corporation or of any subsidiary of the Corporation, or a trustee, custodian, administrator, or fiduciary of any employee benefit plan established and maintained by the Corporation or by any subsidiary of the Corporation, or a person serving another corporation, partnership, joint venture, trust or other enterprise in any of the foregoing capacities at the request of the Corporation.

ARTICLE V—SHARES OF CAPITAL STOCK

5.1 Issuance of Stock.

Shares of capital stock of any class now or hereafter authorized, securities convertible into or exchangeable for such stock, or options or other rights to purchase such stock or securities may be issued or granted in accordance with authority granted by resolution of the Board of Directors.

5.2 Stock Certificates.

Certificates for shares of the capital stock of the Corporation shall be in the form adopted by the Board of Directors, may be signed by the Chairman of the Board of Directors, or the President or Vice President and the Treasurer or the Assistant Treasurer or the Secretary or the Assistant Secretary of the Corporation, and may be sealed with the seal of the Corporation. All such certificates shall be numbered consecutively, and the name of the person owning the shares represented thereby, with the number of such shares and the date of issue, shall be entered on the books of the Corporation.

5.3 Transfer of Stock.

Shares of capital stock of the Corporation shall be transferred only on the books of the Corporation, by the holder of record in person or by the holder's duly authorized representative, upon surrender to the Corporation of the certificate for such shares duly endorsed for transfer, together with such other documents (if any) as may be required to effect such transfer.

5.4 Lost, Stolen, Destroyed, or Mutilated Certificates.

New stock certificates may be issued to replace certificates alleged to have been lost, stolen, destroyed, or mutilated, upon such terms and conditions, including proof of loss or destruction, and the giving of a satisfactory bond of indemnity, as the Board of Directors from time to time may determine.

5.5 Regulations.

The Board of Directors shall have power and authority to make all such rules and regulations not inconsistent with these Bylaws as it may deem expedient concerning the issue, transfer, and registration of shares of capital stock of the Corporation.

5.6 Record Date for Stock.

In order that the Corporation may determine the stockholders entitled to notice of or to vote at any meeting of stockholders or any adjournment thereof, or to express consent to corporate action in writing without a meeting, or entitled to receive payment of any dividend or other distribution or allotment of any rights, or entitled to exercise any rights in respect of any change, conversion or exchange of stock or for the purpose of any other lawful action, the board of directors may fix, in advance, a record date, which shall not be more than sixty (60) nor less than ten (10) days before the date of such meeting, nor more than sixty (60) days prior to any other action. A determination of stockholders of record entitled to notice of or to vote at a meeting of stockholders shall apply to any adjournment of the meeting: provided, however, that the board of directors may fix a new record date for the adjourned meeting.

ARTICLE VI—GENERAL PROVISIONS

6.1 Corporate Seal.

The Corporation may adopt a seal in such form as the Board of Directors shall from time to time determine.

6.2 Fiscal Year.

The fiscal year of the Corporation shall be as designated by the Board of Directors from time to time.

6.3 Authorization.

All checks, notes, vouchers, warrants, drafts, acceptances, and other orders for the payment of moneys of the Corporation shall be signed by such officer or officers or such other person or persons as the Board of Directors may from time to time designate.

6.4 Financial Reports.

Financial statements or reports shall not be required to be sent to the stockholders of the Corporation, but may be so sent in the discretion of the

Board of Directors, in which event the scope of such statements or reports shall be within the discretion of the Board of Directors, and such statements or reports shall not be required to have been examined by or to be accompanied by an opinion of an accountant or firm of accountants.

6.5 Effect of Bylaws.

No provision in these Bylaws shall vest any property right in any stockholder.

ARTICLE VII—AMENDMENTS

The authority to adopt, amend or repeal Bylaws of the Corporation is expressly conferred upon the Board of Directors, which may take such action by the affirmative vote of a majority of the whole Board of Directors at any regular or special meeting duly convened after notice of that purpose, subject always to the power of the stockholders to adopt, amend or repeal Bylaws.

I, ____________, do hereby certify:

1. That I am the duly elected Secretary of ****, Inc., a Delaware Corporation.

2. That the foregoing Bylaws, comprising fifteen (15) pages, including this page, constitute the Bylaws of the Corporation as of the ____ day of _________, 20___.

IN WITNESS WHEREOF, I have executed this certificate as of the ____ day of _________, 20___.

____

____

Secretary

Please note that the above form has been altered to conform to guidelines offered in the book but also to conflict with those guidelines for the purposes of the chapter's final exercise. Because the alterations of the latter kind may make it unsuitable as a precedent for practice, DO NOT USE the above form as altered in your practice of law.

CHAPTER 8

CREATING THE BENEFIT CORPORATION

■ ■ ■

A. HOW THE BENEFIT CORPORATION DIFFERS FROM THE OTHER ENTITY FORMS

The last decade has seen a flurry of legislative activity in the area of hybrid business organizations. The tremendous interest in social entrepreneurship has sparked innovation in corporate law. Nonprofits receive tax benefits for their single-minded dedication to socially valued activities, but they cannot scale up their contributions to the common good as quickly as for-profit entities that have access to equity markets. Social entrepreneurs who opt to form a Delaware corporation or some other for-profit entity may have a revenue model strong enough to minimize the loss of tax-deductible donations. But some are concerned that fiduciary duties to further economic interests of shareholders may imperil the commitment to the social mission.

Many social entrepreneurs wish to take advantage of the opportunities for rapid expansion but also want to set their businesses apart from large corporations that merely profess to pursue the common good for public relations reasons. The nonprofit form provides such strong legal constraints by focusing all assets on exempt purposes but does not allow for equity investment.

A benefit corporation is an entity that incorporates under a special corporation statute that facilitates the entity's pursuit of profit and public (sometimes called social) benefit simultaneously. The statutory provisions regarding duties of all the directors make it clear that the directors are not liable for failure to maximize profit in their pursuit of the corporation's benefit purposes.

Business entities of various forms have pursued an effective and reliable way of signaling their value commitments through an accreditation process. Just as certain nonprofits, such as universities, rely on quasi-independent certification nonprofits to judge the substantive quality of their institutions, social entrepreneurs have looked to B Lab, a certification provider that fights "greenwashing." B Lab's "B Corp" seal of approval is frequently confused with the benefit corporation form. You may wish to discuss the difference with any client considering either or both steps. If, however, the client does consider the B Lab imprimatur an essential component of its business strategy, it is worth noting that B Lab does require that B Corps avail themselves of the benefit corporation structure within three years of initial certification if that organizational form choice is an option for the entity in its home state.

Benefit corporation statutes vary significantly in the many ways in which they confront the problem of greenwashing. This chapter focuses on the Pennsylvania statute because it closely follows the model statute written by Philadelphia attorney and benefit corporate form architect, William Clark.

The proponents of another hybrid form, the low-profit limited liability company, have pursued, as yet unsuccessfully, special treatment from the IRS as a safe vehicle for investment from 501(c)(3) private foundations. But those who have advocated for the benefit corporation form have not fought for any special Federal corporate income tax classification, and none appears to be forthcoming as tax-exempt status and nonprofit status seem as strongly linked as ever under Federal tax law.

Federal corporate income tax status is not the only issue on which benefit corporations are still firmly categorized with straightforwardly for-profit entities. The availability of volunteer labor is effectively regulated for all but the smallest of ventures by the U.S. Department of Labor through its administration of the Fair Labor Standards Act. Nonprofit organizations may further their exempt purposes through the use of volunteers as long as they are not displacing employees. The FLSA's imposition of a minimum wage means that for-profit organizations can put volunteers to work only if the placement meets strict training or education requirements. Under the current interpretation of the FLSA, benefit corporations are not treated any differently than other for-profit employers.

DISCUSSION QUESTION 8–A

Now that you have had the chance to familiarize yourself with the characteristics of the nonprofit corporation, the limited liability company, and the benefit corporation, explain which of these options you would present to the team of social entrepreneurs described below. What would you want to know about their goals, their plans for raising capital and their projections as to income and expenses before deciding as to whether the benefit corporation is a viable option for formalizing their new venture?

> Three students on the verge of graduating from a major university have recently returned from a semester in India working on clean water solutions. They have devised a low-cost, high-tech pump that can be accessed using basic cellphone technology. To maximize impact, they are exploring two main options: licensing the idea to a for-profit, nonprofit, or governmental entity with the capital to mass-produce it and distribute the pumps or, in the

alternative, raising the capital needed to manufacture and deploy the pumps themselves.

B. THE BASIC FEATURES OF THE PENNSYLVANIA BENEFIT CORPORATION

Every business that incorporates under the Benefit Corporation statute commits itself to "general public benefit" as defined by the statute. While a benefit corporation is free to pursue one or more specific public benefits listed in the statute, it is the general public benefit requirement together with the mandate to adopt a third-party standard that is the core defining feature of Pennsylvania's approach to setting benefit corporations apart from other for-profit entities. The statute defines "general public benefit" as "[a] material positive impact on society and the environment, taken as a whole and assessed against a third-party standard, from the business and operations of [the] benefit corporation." The definition itself requires an evaluation of the benefit corporation's activities, based upon an independently developed set of criteria, and a conclusion as to whether the social benefits of its activities outweigh their social costs.

The third-party standard has a significantly longer statutory definition, which is reprinted in Article V of the unique-bylaws-provisions form provided at the end of the chapter. By law, the third-party standard must be comprehensive, independently developed, credible, and transparent. To be comprehensive, the standard must evaluate the effect of the corporation's operations on shareholders, workers, customers, any impacted community, the environment, and the corporation itself, including its ability to accomplish general public benefit and any specific public benefits adopted. In order to qualify as independently developed, the standard must be issued by an organization that has no significant overlap in leadership with the benefit corporation and does not receive material financial support from it. For credibility, the development of the standard must involve corporate social responsibility expertise and a public comment period involving multiple stakeholders. Finally, a third-party standard is transparent if and only if certain statutorily specified information about the elements of the standard and the process by which it was created are publicly available.

Note that, even though the criteria by which general public benefit is judged must be independently created, the annual application of those criteria need not be conducted by someone unconnected with the benefit corporation. The statute requires only that an independent benefit director certify compliance with the statute's public benefit requirements including the dissemination of a report articulating how the corporation's activities fared after application of the third-party standard. The requirement that a benefit director be independent disqualifies certain people from holding the position including current or recent employees, family members of current or recent corporate leaders, as well as major stockholders or officers of the corporation or of its affiliates. The statute also specifies requirements for the content and distribution of the annual benefit report. These are also reprinted in Article V of the form at the end of the chapter.

C. CREATING THE ARTICLES

The Pennsylvania statute (as well as the form below) requires only minimal additional information in the articles of incorporation of a benefit corporation. Surprisingly, even if a benefit corporation adopts one or more specified public benefit purposes, these need not be stated in the articles filed with the State. Merely, checking the blank next to "___ Benefit (§ 330)" is all that is needed. That election commits the entity to a general public benefit purpose, which the statute defines as "[a] material positive impact on society and the environment, taken as a whole and assessed against a third-party standard, from the business and operations of a benefit corporation." A benefit corporation wishing to signal a targeted commitment may choose to articulate one or more specific public benefit purposes in addition to its overall commitment by stating in its articles which of the specific public benefits listed in the statute it has selected.

Pennsylvania Articles of Incorporation—For-Profit (Benefit)

PENNSYLVANIA DEPARTMENT OF STATE
BUREAU OF CORPORATIONS AND CHARITABLE ORGANIZATIONS

Articles of Incorporation-For Profit
(15 Pa.C.S.)

___ Business-stock (§ 1306)	___ Management (§ 2703)
___ Business-nonstock (§ 2102)	___ Professional (§ 2903)
___ Business-statutory close (§ 2303)	___ Insurance (§ 3101)
___ Cooperative (§ 7102)	___ Benefit (§ 3303)

Name
Address
City State Zip Code

Document will be returned to the name and address you enter to the left.

Fee: $125

In compliance with the requirements of the applicable provisions (relating to corporations and unincorporated associations), the undersigned, desiring to incorporate a corporation for profit, hereby states that:

1. The name of the corporation *(corporate designator required, i.e., "corporation", "incorporated", "limited" "company" or any abbreviation. "Professional corporation" or "P.C")* :

2. The (a) address of this corporation's current registered office in this Commonwealth *(post office box, alone, is not acceptable)* or (b) name of its commercial registered office provider and the county of venue is:

(a) Number and Street City State Zip County

(b) Name of Commercial Registered Office Provider County

c/o:

3. The corporation is incorporated under the provisions of the Business Corporation Law of 1988.

4. Check and complete one:
___ The corporation is organized on a nonstock basis.
___ The corporation is organized on a stock share basis and the aggregate number of shares authorized is: ________

D. SPECIAL BYLAWS PROVISIONS

The following unique-bylaws provisions form for a Pennsylvania Benefit Corporation closely tracks the statute and goes a long way to articulating how the benefit corporation is structured to balance meaningfully shareholder economic benefit and the benefit corporation's stated general and, if any, specific public benefit purposes. Like the bylaws forms provided in Chapters 3 and 7, benefit corporation bylaws contain many mandatory and discretionary procedure provisions, even if those are not included in the form below, which focuses on provisions unique to benefit corporations. Many such provisions create duties and thus use "shall" in their verb structures. This form also uses tabulation at least as much as any other reprinted in this book.

Unique Provisions for Pennsylvania Benefit Corporation Bylaws

ARTICLE I DEFINITIONS

"General Public Benefit." A material positive impact on society and the environment, taken as a whole and assessed against a third-party standard, from the business and operations of a benefit corporation.

"Independent." When a person has no material relationship with a benefit corporation or any of its subsidiaries, other than the relationship of serving as the benefit director or benefit officer. A material relationship between an individual and a benefit corporation or any of its subsidiaries will be conclusively presumed to exist if:

a. the person is or has been within the last three years an employee of the benefit corporation or any of its subsidiaries, other than as a benefit officer;

b. an immediate family member of the person is or has been within the last three years an executive officer, other than a benefit officer, of the benefit corporation or any of its subsidiaries; or

c. the person, or an association of which the person is a governor or officer or in which the person owns beneficially or of record 5% or more of the outstanding interests, owns beneficially or of record 5% or more of the outstanding shares of the benefit corporation. The percentage of ownership in an association shall be calculated as if all outstanding rights to acquire interests in the association had been exercised.

ARTICLE III DIRECTORS

DISCHARGE OF DUTIES.

Consistent with the corporation's purpose of creating General Public Benefit [and INSERT SPECIFIC PUBLIC BENEFIT PURPOSE(S), IF ANY], in discharging their duties, the directors shall consider the effect of any actions on the following:

a. The ability of the corporation to accomplish its General Public Benefit purpose [and INSERT SPECIFIC PUBLIC BENEFIT PURPOSE(S), IF ANY].

b. The shareholders of the benefit corporation.

c. the employees and work force of the benefit corporation and its subsidiaries and suppliers.

d. The interests of customers as beneficiaries of the General Public Benefit purposes [or INSERT SPECIFIC PUBLIC BENEFIT, IF ANY] of the benefit corporation.

e. Community and societal considerations, including those of any community in which offices or facilities of the benefit corporation or its subsidiaries or suppliers are located.

f. The local and global environment.

g. The short-term and long-term interests of the benefit corporation, including benefits that may accrue to the benefit corporation from its long-term plans and the possibility that these interests may be best served by the continued independence of the benefit corporation.

h. The ability of the benefit corporation to accomplish its General Public Benefit purpose and any specific public benefit purpose.

Directors may also consider the resources, intent, and conduct (past, stated and potential) of any person seeking to acquire control of the corporation, and any other pertinent factors or the interests of any other group that they deem appropriate, consistent with the corporation's purpose to create social benefit.

Directors are not required to give priority to any of the considerations listed above and shall give priority to the interests of any person or group referred to in the immediately preceding paragraph or in paragraphs (a) through (h) over the interests of any other person or group in considering the effect of their actions, as long as such actions are consistent with the benefit corporation's purpose of creating General Public Benefit [and INSERT SPECIFIC PUBLIC BENEFIT PURPOSE, IF ANY].

BENEFIT DIRECTOR

The board of directors shall include a director who:

a. shall be designated as the benefit director; and

b. shall have, in addition to all of the powers, duties, rights and immunities of the other directors of the benefit corporation, the powers, duties, rights and immunities provided in this Article.

The benefit director shall be an individual who is Independent. The benefit director may serve as the benefit officer at the same time as serving as the benefit director.

The benefit director shall prepare, and the benefit corporation shall include in the annual benefit report to shareholders required under section 3331 (relating to annual benefit report), a statement whether, in the opinion of the benefit director, the benefit corporation acted in accordance with its general and any specific public benefit purpose in all material respects during the period covered by the report and whether the directors and officers complied with Pennsylvania Consolidated Statutes sections 3321(a) (relating to standard of conduct for directors) and 3323(a) (relating to standard of conduct for officers), respectively. If, in the opinion of the benefit director, the benefit corporation or its directors or officers failed so to act, then the statement of the benefit director shall include a description of the ways in which the benefit corporation or its directors or officers failed so to act.

ARTICLE IV

BENEFIT OFFICER

The benefit corporation may have an officer designated as the benefit officer who shall have such authority and shall perform such duties in the management of the benefit corporation relating to the purpose of the corporation to create General Public Benefit or specific public benefit9s), if any, as may be provided by or pursuant to these bylaws or, in the absence of controlling provisions in these bylaws, as may be determined by or pursuant to resolutions or orders of the board of directors. If the benefit corporation has a benefit officer, the duties of the benefit officer shall include preparing the benefit report required under Pennsylvania Consolidated Statutes section 3331 (relating to annual benefit report).

ARTICLE V

ANNUAL BENEFIT REPORT

SELECTION OF THIRD-PARTY STANDARD

Each year, the board shall select a third-party standard for use in preparing the annual benefit report. The third-party standard shall be a standard for defining, reporting, and assessing overall corporate social and environmental performance that meets the following criteria:

a. Comprehensive in that it assesses the effect of the business and its operations upon the interests listed in section 3321(a)(1)(ii), (iii), (iv) and (v) (relating to standard of conduct for directors).

b. Developed by an organization that is independent of the benefit corporation and satisfies the following requirements:

i) Not more than one-third of the members of the governing body of the organization are representatives of any of the following:

(A) An association of businesses operating in a specific industry the performance of whose members is measured by the standard.

(B) Businesses from a specific industry or an association of businesses in that industry.

(C) Businesses whose performance is assessed against the standard.

ii) The organization is not materially financed by an association or business described in subparagraph (i).

c. Credible because the standard is developed by a person that both:

i) has access to necessary expertise to assess overall corporate social and environmental performance; and

ii) uses a balanced multi-stakeholder approach, including a public comment period of at least 30 days to develop the standard.

d. Transparent because the following information is publicly available:

i) About the standard:

(A) The criteria considered when measuring the overall social and environmental performance of a business.

(B) The relative weightings, if any, of those criteria.

ii) About the development and revision of the standard:

(A) The identity of the directors, officers, material owners and the governing body of the organization that developed and controls revisions to the standard.

(B) The process by which revisions to the standard and changes to the membership of the governing body are made.

(C) An accounting of the sources of financial support for the organization, with sufficient detail to disclose any relationships that could reasonably be considered to present a potential conflict of interest.

PREPARATION OF ANNUAL BENEFIT REPORT

The Benefit Officer shall prepare, or cause to be prepared, the annual benefit report, which shall:

a. describe the process and rationale for selecting the third-party standard used to prepare the Annual Benefit Report;

b. describe the General Public Benefit and any specific public benefit pursued and created during the year and any circumstances that may have hindered the creation of these benefits;

c. assess the overall social and environmental performance of the benefit corporation against the Third-party standard and state the process and rationale for selecting the third-party standard;

d. give the name and contact information of the Benefit Director and the Benefit Officer, if any;

e. provide the compensation paid to each director;

f. give the name of each person that owns 5% or more of the outstanding shares of the benefit corporation;

g. contain the annual compliance statement of the benefit director described in Pennsylvania Consolidated Statutes section 3322(c); and

h. contain a statement of any connection between the organization that established the third-party standard and the benefit corporation, or their directors, officers or any holder of 5% or more of the governance interests/outstanding shares in either organization, including any financial or governance relationship which might materially affect the credibility of the use of the third-party standard.

DELIVERY AND POSTING OF ANNUAL BENEFIT REPORT

The corporation shall deliver the annual benefit report to each shareholder within one hundred twenty (120) days of the close of the corporation's fiscal year. Additionally, the corporation shall post the most recent annual benefit report to the public portion of its website, if any, except that the compensation paid to directors and any financial or proprietary information included in the benefit report may be omitted from the benefit report as publicly posted.

FILING OF ANNUAL BENEFIT REPORT

Concurrent with the delivery of the annual benefit report to the shareholders no later than one hundred twenty (120) days after the close of the corporation's fiscal year, the corporation shall deliver a copy of the benefit report to the Pennsylvania Department of State for filing, except that the compensation paid to directors and any financial or proprietary information included in the benefit report may be omitted from the benefit report as filed.

APPENDIX

■ ■ ■

REV. MODEL NONPROFIT CORPORATION ACT (1988), CHS. 2–8 (EXCERPT)[1]

CHAPTER 2. ORGANIZATION

Section 2.01. Incorporators.

One or more persons may act as the incorporator or incorporators of a corporation by delivering articles of incorporation to the secretary of state for filing.

Section 2.02. Articles of Incorporation.

(a) The articles of incorporation must set forth:

(1) a corporate name for the corporation that satisfies the requirements of section 4.01;

(2) one of the following statements:

(i) This corporation is a public benefit corporation.

(ii) This corporation is a mutual benefit corporation.

(iii) This corporation is a religious corporation;

(3) the street address of the corporation's initial registered office and the name of its initial registered agent at that office;

(4) the name and address of each incorporator;

(5) whether or not the corporation will have members; and

(6) provisions not inconsistent with law regarding the distribution of assets on dissolution.

(b) The articles of incorporation may set forth:

(1) the purpose or purposes for which the corporation is organized, which may be, either alone or in combination with other purposes, the transaction of any lawful activity;

(2) the names and addresses of the individuals who are to serve as the initial directors;

(3) provisions not inconsistent with law regarding:

(i) managing and regulating the affairs of the corporation;

[1] Reprinted with permission of the American Bar Association.

(ii) defining, limiting, and regulating the powers of the corporation, its board of directors, and members (or any class of members); and

(iii) the characteristics, qualifications, rights, limitations and obligations attaching to each or any class of members.

(4) any provision that under this Act is required or permitted to be set forth in the bylaws.

(c) Each incorporator and director named in the articles must sign the articles.

(d) The articles of incorporation need not set forth any of the corporate powers enumerated in this Act.

Section 2.03. Incorporation.

(a) Unless a delayed effective date is specified, the corporate existence begins when the articles of incorporation are filed.

(b) The secretary of state's filing of the articles of incorporation is conclusive proof that the incorporators satisfied all conditions precedent to incorporation except in a proceeding by the state to cancel or revoke the incorporation or involuntarily dissolve the corporation.

Section 2.04. Liability for Preincorporation Transactions.

All persons purporting to act as or on behalf of a corporation, knowing there was no incorporation under this Act, are jointly and severally liable for all liabilities created while so acting.

Section 2.05. Organization of Corporation.

(a) After incorporation:

(1) if initial directors are named in the articles of incorporation, the initial directors shall hold an organizational meeting, at the call of a majority of the directors, to complete the organization of the corporation by appointing officers, adopting bylaws, and carrying on any other business brought before the meeting;

(2) if initial directors are not named in the articles, the incorporator or incorporators shall hold an organizational meeting at the call of a majority of the incorporators:

(i) to elect directors and complete the organization of the corporation; or

(ii) to elect a board of directors who shall complete the organization of the corporation.

(b) Action required or permitted by this Act to be taken by incorporators at an organizational meeting may be taken without a meeting if the action taken is evidenced by one or more written consents describing the action taken and signed by each incorporator.

(c) An organizational meeting may be held in or out of this state in accordance with section 8.21.

Section 2.06. Bylaws.

(a) The incorporators or board of directors of a corporation shall adopt bylaws for the corporation.

(b) The bylaws may contain any provision for regulating and managing the affairs of the corporation that is not inconsistent with law or the articles of incorporation.

Section 2.07. Emergency Bylaws and Powers.

(a) Unless the articles provide otherwise the directors of a corporation may adopt, amend or repeal bylaws to be effective only in an emergency defined in subsection (d). The emergency bylaws, which are subject to amendment or repeal by the members, may provide special procedures necessary for managing the corporation during the emergency, including:

(1) how to call a meeting of the board;

(2) quorum requirements for the meeting; and

(3) designation of additional or substitute directors.

(b) All provisions of the regular bylaws consistent with the emergency bylaws remain effective during the emergency. The emergency bylaws are not effective after the emergency ends.

(c) Corporate action taken in good faith in accordance with the emergency bylaws:

(1) binds the corporation; and

(2) may not be used to impose liability on a corporate director, officer, employee, or agent.

(d) An emergency exists for purposes of this section if a quorum of the corporation's directors cannot readily be assembled because of some catastrophic event.

CHAPTER 8. DIRECTORS AND OFFICERS

SUBCHAPTER A. BOARD OF DIRECTORS

Section 8.01. Requirement for and Duties of Board.

(a) Each corporation must have a board of directors.

(b) Except as provided in this Act or subsection (c), all corporate powers shall be exercised by or under the authority of, and the affairs of the corporation managed under the direction of, its board.

(c) The articles may authorize a person or persons to exercise some or all of the powers which would otherwise be exercised by a board. To the extent so authorized any such person or persons shall have the duties and responsibilities of the directors, and the directors shall be relieved to that extent from such duties and responsibilities.

Section 8.02. Qualifications of Directors.

All directors must be individuals. The articles or bylaws may prescribe other qualifications for directors.

Section 8.03. Number of Directors.

(a) A board of directors must consist of three or more individuals, with the number specified in or fixed in accordance with the articles or bylaws.

(b) The number of directors may be increased or decreased (but to no fewer than three) from time to time by amendment to or in the manner prescribed in the articles or bylaws.

Section 8.04. Election, Designation and Appointment of Directors.

(a) If the corporation has members, all the directors (except the initial directors) shall be elected at the first annual meeting of members, and at each annual meeting thereafter, unless the articles or bylaws provide some other time or method of election, or provide that some of the directors are appointed by some other person or designated.

(b) If the corporation does not have members, all the directors (except the initial directors) shall be elected, appointed or designated as provided in the articles or bylaws. If no method of designation or appointment is set forth in the articles or bylaws, the directors (other than the initial directors) shall be elected by the board.

Section 8.05. Terms of Directors Generally.

(a) The articles or bylaws must specify the terms of directors. Except for designated or appointed directors, the terms of directors may not exceed five years. In the absence of any term specified in the articles or bylaws, the term of each director shall be one year. Directors may be elected for successive terms.

(b) A decrease in the number of directors or term of office does not shorten an incumbent director's term.

(c) Except as provided in the articles or bylaws:

(1) the term of a director filling a vacancy in the office of a director elected by members expires at the next election of directors by members; and

(2) the term of a director filling any other vacancy expires at the end of the unexpired term that such director is filling.

(d) Despite the expiration of a director's term, the director continues to serve until the director's successor is elected, designated or appointed and qualifies, or until there is a decrease in the number of directors.

Section 8.06. Staggered Terms for Directors.

The articles or bylaws may provide for staggering the terms of directors by dividing the total number of directors into groups. The terms of office of the several groups need not be uniform.

Section 8.07. Resignation of Directors.

(a) A director may resign at any time by delivering written notice to the board of directors, its presiding officer or to the president or secretary.

(b) A resignation is effective when the notice is effective unless the notice specifies a later effective date. If a resignation is made effective at a later date, the board may fill the pending vacancy before the effective date if the board provides that the successor does not take office until the effective date.

Section 8.08. Removal of Directors Elected by Members or Directors.

(a) The members may remove one or more directors elected by them without cause.

(b) If a director is elected by a class, chapter or other organizational unit or by region or other geographic grouping, the director may be removed only by the members of that class, chapter, unit or grouping.

(c) Except as provided in subsection (i), a director may be removed under subsection (a) or (b) only if the number of votes cast to remove the director would be sufficient to elect the director at a meeting to elect directors.

(d) If cumulative voting is authorized, a director may not be removed if the number of votes, or if the director was elected by a class, chapter, unit or grouping of members, the number of votes of that class, chapter, unit or grouping, sufficient to elect the director under cumulative voting is voted against the director's removal.

(e) A director elected by members may be removed by the members only at a meeting called for the purpose of removing the director and the meeting notice must state that the purpose, or one of the purposes, of the meeting is removal of the director.

(f) In computing whether a director is protected from removal under subsections (b)–(d), it should be assumed that the votes against removal are cast in an election for the number of directors of the class to which the director to be removed belonged on the date of that director's election.

(g) An entire board of directors may be removed under subsections (a)–(e).

(h) A director elected by the board may be removed without cause by the vote of two-thirds of the directors then in office or such greater number as is set forth in the articles or bylaws; provided, however, that a director elected by the board to fill the vacancy of a director elected by the members may be removed without cause by the members, but not the board.

(i) If, at the beginning of a director's term on the board, the articles or bylaws provide that the director may be removed for missing a specified number of board meetings, the board may remove the director for failing to attend the specified number of meetings. The director may be removed only if a majority of the directors then in office vote for the removal.

(j) The articles or bylaws of a religious corporation may:

(1) limit the application of this section; and

(2) set forth the vote and procedures by which the board or any person may remove with or without cause a director elected by the members or the board.

Section 8.09. Removal of Designated or Appointed Directors.

(a) A designated director may be removed by an amendment to the articles or bylaws deleting or changing the designation.

(b) Appointed Directors:

(1) Except as otherwise provided in the articles or bylaws, an appointed director may be removed without cause by the person appointing the director;

(2) The person removing the director shall do so by giving written notice of the removal to the director and either the presiding officer of the board or the corporation's president or secretary; and

(3) A removal is effective when the notice is effective unless the notice specifies a future effective date.

Section 8.10. Removal of Directors by Judicial Proceeding.

(a) The [name or describe] court of the county where a corporation's principal office is located may remove any director of the corporation from office in a proceeding commenced either by the corporation, its members holding at least 10 percent of the voting power of any class, or the attorney general in the case of a public benefit corporation, if the court finds that

(1) the director engaged in fraudulent or dishonest conduct, or gross abuse of authority or discretion, with respect to the corporation, [if section 8.13 is adopted, that the provisions of section 8.13 have been violated,] or a final judgment has been entered finding that the director has violated a duty set forth in sections 8.30–8.33, and

(2) removal is in the best interest of the corporation.

(b) The court that removes a director may bar the director from serving on the board for a period prescribed by the court.

(c) If members or the attorney general commence a proceeding under subsection (a), the corporation shall be made a party defendant.

(d) If a public benefit corporation or its members commence a proceeding under subsection (a), they shall give the attorney general written notice of the proceeding.

(e) The articles or bylaws of a religious corporation may limit or prohibit the application of this section.

Section 8.11. Vacancy on Board.

(a) Unless the articles or bylaws provide otherwise, and except as provided in subsections (b) and (c), if a vacancy occurs on a board of directors, including a vacancy resulting from an increase in the number of directors:

(1) the members, if any, may fill the vacancy; if the vacant office was held by a director elected by a class, chapter or other organizational unit or by region or other geographic grouping, only members of the class, chapter, unit or grouping are entitled to vote to fill the vacancy if it is filled by the members;

(2) the board of directors may fill the vacancy; or

(3) if the directors remaining in office constitute fewer than a quorum of the board, they may fill the vacancy by the affirmative vote of a majority of all the directors remaining in office.

(b) Unless the articles or bylaws provide otherwise, if a vacant office was held by an appointed director, only the person who appointed the director may fill the vacancy.

(c) If a vacant office was held by a designated director, the vacancy shall be filled as provided in the articles or bylaws. In the absence of an applicable article or bylaw provision, the vacancy may not be filled by the board.

(d) A vacancy that will occur at a specific later date (by reason of a resignation effective at a later date under section 8.07(b) or otherwise) may be filled before the vacancy occurs but the new director may not take office until the vacancy occurs.

Section 8.12. Compensation of Directors.

Unless the articles or bylaws provide otherwise, a board of directors may fix the compensation of directors.

Section 8.13. Financially Disinterested Majority—Public Benefit Corporations. Optional section.

(a) No more than 49 percent of the individuals serving on the board of any public benefit corporation may be financially interested persons.

(b) For the purposes of this section "financially interested persons" means:

(1) Individuals who have received or are entitled to receive compensation, directly or indirectly, from the corporation for services rendered to it within the previous 12 months, whether as full- or part-time employees, independent contractors, consultants or otherwise, excluding any reasonable payments made to directors for serving as directors; or

(2) Any spouse, brother, sister, parent or child of any such individual.

(c) The failure to comply with the provisions of this section shall not affect the validity or enforceability of any transactions entered into by a corporation.

SUBCHAPTER B. MEETINGS AND ACTION OF THE BOARD

Section 8.20. Regular and Special Meetings.

(a) If the time and place of a directors' meeting is fixed by the bylaws or the board, the meeting is a regular meeting. All other meetings are special meetings.

(b) A board of directors may hold regular or special meetings in or out of this state.

(c) Unless the articles or bylaws provide otherwise, a board may permit any or all directors to participate in a regular or special meeting by, or conduct the meeting through the use of, any means of communication by which all directors participating may simultaneously hear each other during the meeting. A director participating in a meeting by this means is deemed to be present in person at the meeting.

Section 8.21. Action Without Meeting.

(a) Unless the articles or bylaws provide otherwise, action required or permitted by this Act to be taken at a board of directors' meeting may be taken without a meeting if the action is taken by all members of the board. The action must be evidenced by one or more written consents describing the action taken, signed by each director, and included in the minutes filed with the corporate records reflecting the action taken.

(b) Action taken under this section is effective when the last director signs the consent, unless the consent specifies a different effective date.

(c) A consent signed under this section has the effect of a meeting vote and may be described as such in any document.

Section 8.22. Call and Notice of Meetings.

(a) Unless the articles, bylaws or subsection (c) provide otherwise, regular meetings of the board may be held without notice.

(b) Unless the articles, bylaws or subsection (c) provide otherwise, special meetings of the board must be preceded by at least two days' notice to each director of the date, time, and place, but not the purpose, of the meeting.

(c) In corporations without members any board action to remove a director or to approve a matter that would require approval by the members if the corporation had members, shall not be valid unless each director is given at least seven days' written notice that the matter will be voted upon at a directors' meeting or unless notice is waived pursuant to section 8.23.

(d) Unless the articles or bylaws provide otherwise, the presiding officer of the board, the president or twenty percent of the directors then in office may call and give notice of a meeting of the board.

Section 8.23. Waiver of Notice.

(a) A director may at any time waive any notice required by this Act, the articles or bylaws. Except as provided in subsection (b), the waiver must be in writing, signed by the director entitled to the notice, and filed with the minutes or the corporate records.

(b) A director's attendance at or participation in a meeting waives any required notice of the meeting unless the director upon arriving at the meeting or prior to the vote on a matter not noticed in conformity with this Act, the articles or bylaws objects to lack of notice and does not thereafter vote for or assent to the objected to action.

Section 8.24. Quorum and Voting.

(a) Except as otherwise provided in this Act, the articles or bylaws, a quorum of a board of directors consists of a majority of the directors in office immediately before a meeting begins. In no event may the articles or bylaws authorize a quorum of fewer than the greater of one-third of the number of directors in office or two directors.

(b) If a quorum is present when a vote is taken, the affirmative vote of a majority of directors present is the act of the board unless this Act, the articles or bylaws require the vote of a greater number of directors.

Section 8.25. Committees of the Board.

(a) Unless prohibited or limited by the articles or bylaws, a board of directors may create one or more committees of the board and appoint members of the board to serve on them. Each committee shall have two or more directors, who serve at the pleasure of the board.

(b) The creation of a committee and appointment of members to it must be approved by the greater of:

(1) a majority of all the directors in office when the action is taken; or

(2) the number of directors required by the articles or bylaws to take action under section 8.24.

(c) Sections 8.20 through 8.24, which govern meetings, action without meetings, notice and waiver of notice, and quorum and voting requirements of the board, apply to committees of the board and their members as well.

(d) To the extent specified by the board of directors or in the articles or bylaws, each committee of the board may exercise the board's authority under section 8.01.

(e) A committee of the board may not, however:

(1) authorize distributions;

(2) approve or recommend to members dissolution, merger or the sale, pledge or transfer of all or substantially all of the corporation's assets;

(3) elect, appoint or remove directors or fill vacancies on the board or on any of its committees; or

(4) adopt, amend or repeal the articles or bylaws.

(f) The creation of, delegation of authority to, or action by a committee does not alone constitute compliance by a director with the standards of conduct described in section 8.30.

SUBCHAPTER C. STANDARDS OF CONDUCT

Section 8.30. General Standards for Directors.

(a) A director shall discharge his or her duties as a director, including his or her duties as a member of a committee:

(1) in good faith;

(2) with the care an ordinarily prudent person in a like position would exercise under similar circumstances; and

(3) in a manner the director reasonably believes to be in the best interests of the corporation.

(b) In discharging his or her duties, a director is entitled to rely on information, opinions, reports, or statements, including financial statements and other financial data, if prepared or presented by:

(1) one or more officers or employees of the corporation whom the director reasonably believes to be reliable and competent in the matters presented;

(2) legal counsel, public accountants or other persons as to matters the director reasonably believes are within the person's professional or expert competence;

(3) a committee of the board of which the director is not a member, as to matters within its jurisdiction, if the director reasonably believes the committee merits confidence; or

(4) in the case of religious corporations, religious authorities and ministers, priests, rabbis or other persons whose position or duties in the religious organization the director believes justify reliance and confidence and whom the director believes to be reliable and competent in the matters presented.

(c) A director is not acting in good faith if the director has knowledge concerning the matter in question that makes reliance otherwise permitted by subsection (b) unwarranted.

(d) A director is not liable to the corporation, any member, or any other person for any action taken or not taken as a director, if the director acted in compliance with this section.

(e) A director shall not be deemed to be a trustee with respect to the corporation or with respect to any property held or administered by the corporation, including without limit, property that may be subject to restrictions imposed by the donor or transferor of such property.

Section 8.31. Director Conflict of Interest.

(a) A conflict of interest transaction is a transaction with the corporation in which a director of the corporation has a direct or indirect interest. A conflict of interest transaction is not voidable or the basis for imposing liability on the director if the transaction was fair at the time it was entered into or is approved as provided in subsections (b) or (c).

(b) A transaction in which a director of a public benefit or religious corporation has a conflict of interest may be approved:

(1) in advance by the vote of the board of directors or a committee of the board if:

(i) the material facts of the transaction and the director's interest are disclosed or known to the board or committee of the board; and

(ii) the directors approving the transaction in good faith reasonably believe that the transaction is fair to the corporation; or

(2) before or after it is consummated by obtaining approval of the:

(i) attorney general; or

(ii) [describe or name] court in an action in which the attorney general is joined as a party; or

(c) A transaction in which a director of a mutual benefit corporation has a conflict of interest may be approved if;

(1) the material facts of the transaction and the director's interest were disclosed or known to the board of directors or a committee of the board and the board or committee of the board authorized, approved, or ratified the transaction; or

(2) the material facts of the transaction and the director's interest were disclosed or known to the members and they authorized, approved, or ratified the transaction.

(d) For purposes of this section, a director of the corporation has an indirect interest in a transaction if (1) another entity in which the director has a material interest or in which the director is a general partner is a party to the transaction or (2) another entity of which the director is a director, officer, or trustee is a party to the transaction.

(e) For purposes of subsections (b) and (c) a conflict of interest transaction is authorized, approved, or ratified, if it receives the affirmative vote of a majority of the directors on the board or on the committee, who have no direct or indirect interest in the transaction, but a transaction may not be authorized, approved, or ratified under this section by a single director. If a majority of the directors on the board who have no direct or indirect interest in the transaction vote to authorize, approve, or ratify the transaction, a quorum is present for the purpose of taking action under this section. The presence of, or a vote cast by, a director with a direct or indirect interest in the transaction does not affect the validity of any action taken under subsections (b)(1) or (c)(1) if the transaction is otherwise approved as provided in subsection (b) or (c).

(f) For purposes of subsection (c)(2), a conflict of interest transaction is authorized, approved, or ratified by the members if it receives a majority of the votes entitled to be counted under this subsection. Votes cast by or voted under the control of a director who has a direct or indirect interest in the transaction, and votes cast by or voted under the control of an entity described in subsection (d)(1), may not be counted in a vote of members to determine whether to authorize, approve, or ratify a conflict of interest transaction under subsection (c)(2). The vote of these members, however, is counted in determining whether the transaction is approved under other sections of this Act. A majority of the voting power, whether or not present, that are entitled to be counted in a vote on the transaction under this subsection constitutes a quorum for the purpose of taking action under this section.

(g) The articles, bylaws, or a resolution of the board may impose additional requirements on conflict of interest transactions.

Section 8.32. Loans to or Guaranties for Directors and Officers.

(a) A corporation may not lend money to or guaranty the obligation of a director or officer of the corporation.

(b) The fact that a loan or guaranty is made in violation of this section does not affect the borrower's liability on the loan.

Section 8.33. Liability for Unlawful Distributions.

(a) Unless a director complies with the applicable standards of conduct described in section 8.30, a director who votes for or assents to a distribution made in violation of this Act is personally liable to the corporation for the amount of the distribution that exceeds what could have been distributed without violating this Act.

(b) A director held liable for an unlawful distribution under subsection (a) is entitled to contribution:

(1) from every other director who voted for or assented to the distribution without complying with the applicable standards of conduct described in section 8.30; and

(2) from each person who received an unlawful distribution for the amount of the distribution whether or not the person receiving the distribution knew it was made in violation of this Act.

SUBCHAPTER D. OFFICERS

Section 8.40. Required Officers.

(a) Unless otherwise provided in the articles or bylaws, a corporation shall have a president, a secretary, a treasurer and such other officers as are appointed by the board.

(b) The bylaws or the board shall delegate to one of the officers responsibility for preparing minutes of the directors' and members' meetings and for authenticating records of the corporation.

(c) The same individual may simultaneously hold more than one office in a corporation.

Section 8.41. Duties and Authority of Officers.

Each officer has the authority and shall perform the duties set forth in the bylaws or, to the extent consistent with the bylaws, the duties and authority prescribed in a resolution of the board or by direction of an officer authorized by the board to prescribe the duties and authority of other officers.

Section 8.42. Standards of Conduct for Officers.

(a) An officer with discretionary authority shall discharge his or her duties under that authority:

(1) in good faith;

(2) with the care an ordinarily prudent person in a like position would exercise under similar circumstances; and

(3) in a manner the officer reasonably believes to be in the best interests of the corporation and its members, if any.

(b) In discharging his or her duties an officer is entitled to rely on information, opinions, reports, or statements, including financial statements and other financial data, if prepared or presented by:

(1) one or more officers or employees of the corporation who the officer reasonably believes to be reliable and competent in the matters presented;

(2) legal counsel, public accountants or other persons as to matters the officer reasonably believes are within the person's professional or expert competence; or

(3) in the case of religious corporations, religious authorities and ministers, priests, rabbis or other persons whose position or duties in the religious organization the officer believes justify reliance and confidence and who the officer believes to be reliable and competent in the matters presented.

(c) An officer is not acting in good faith if the officer has knowledge concerning the matter in question that makes reliance otherwise permitted by subsection (b) unwarranted.

(d) An officer is not liable to the corporation, any member, or other person for any action taken or not taken as an officer, if the officer acted in compliance with this section.

Section 8.43. Resignation and Removal of Officers.

(a) An officer may resign at any time by delivering notice to the corporation. A resignation is effective when the notice is effective unless the notice specifies a future effective date. If a resignation is made effective at a future date and the corporation accepts the future effective date, its board of directors may fill the pending vacancy before the effective date if the board provides that the successor does not take office until the effective date.

(b) A board may remove any officer at any time with or without cause.

Section 8.44. Contract Rights of Officers.

(a) The appointment of an officer does not itself create contract rights.

(b) An officer's removal does not affect the officer's contract rights, if any, with the corporation. An officer's resignation does not affect the corporation's contract rights, if any, with the officer.

Section 8.45. Officers' Authority To Execute Documents.

Any contract or other instrument in writing executed or entered into between a corporation and any other person is not invalidated as to the corporation by any lack of authority of the signing officers in the absence of actual knowledge on the part of the other person that the signing officers had no authority to execute the contract or other instrument if it is signed by any two officers in Category 1 below or by one officer in Category 1 below and one officer in Category 2 below.

Category 1—The presiding officer of the board and the president.

Category 2—A vice president, the secretary, treasurer and executive director.

SUBCHAPTER E. INDEMNIFICATION

Section 8.50. Subchapter Definitions.

In this subchapter:

(1) "Corporation" includes any domestic or foreign predecessor entity of a corporation in a merger or other transaction in which the predecessor's existence ceased upon consummation of the transaction.

(2) "Director" means an individual who is or was a director of a corporation or an individual who, while a director of a corporation, is or was serving at the corporation's request as a director, officer, partner, trustee, employee, or agent of another foreign or domestic business or nonprofit corporation, partnership, joint venture, trust, employee benefit plan, or other enterprise. A director is considered to be serving an employee benefit plan at the corporation's request if the director's duties to the corporation also impose duties on, or otherwise involve services by, the director to the plan or to participants in or beneficiaries of the plan. "Director" includes, unless the context requires otherwise, the estate or personal representative of a director.

(3) "Expenses" include counsel fees.

(4) "Liability" means the obligation to pay a judgment, settlement, penalty, fine (including an excise tax assessed with respect to an employee benefit plan), or reasonable expenses actually incurred with respect to a proceeding.

(5) "Official capacity" means: (i) when used with respect to a director, the office of director in a corporation; and (ii) when used with respect to an individual other than a director, as contemplated in section 8.56, the office in a corporation held by the officer or the employment or agency relationship undertaken by the employee or agent on behalf of the corporation. "Official capacity" does not include service for any other foreign or domestic business or nonprofit corporation or any partnership, joint venture, trust, employee benefit plan, or other enterprise.

(6) "Party" includes an individual who was, is or is threatened to be made a named defendant or respondent in a proceeding.

(7) "Proceeding" means any threatened, pending, or completed action, suit or proceeding whether civil, criminal, administrative, or investigative and whether formal or informal.

Section 8.51. Authority To Indemnify.

(a) Except as provided in subsection (d), a corporation may indemnify an individual made a party to a proceeding because the individual is or was a director against liability incurred in the proceeding if the individual:

(1) conducted himself or herself in good faith; and

(2) reasonably believed:

(i) in the case of conduct in his or her official capacity with the corporation, that his or her conduct was in its best interests; and

(ii) in all other cases, that his or her conduct was at least not opposed to its best interests; and

(3) in the case of any criminal proceeding, had no reasonable cause to believe his or her conduct was unlawful.

(b) A director's conduct with respect to an employee benefit plan for a purpose the director reasonably believed to be in the interests of the participants in and beneficiaries of the plan is conduct that satisfies the requirements of subsection (a)(2)(ii).

(c) The termination of a proceeding by judgment, order, settlement, conviction, or upon a plea of nolo contendere or its equivalent is not, of itself, determinative that the director did not meet the standard of conduct described in this section.

(d) A corporation may not indemnify a director under this section:

(1) in connection with a proceeding by or in the right of the corporation in which the director was adjudged liable to the corporation; or

(2) in connection with any other proceeding charging improper personal benefit to the director, whether or not involving action in his or her official capacity, in which the director was adjudged liable on the basis that personal benefit was improperly received by the director.

(e) Indemnification permitted under this section in connection with a proceeding by or in the right of the corporation is limited to reasonable expenses incurred in connection with the proceeding.

Section 8.52. Mandatory Indemnification.

Unless limited by its articles of incorporation, a corporation shall indemnify a director who was wholly successful, on the merits or otherwise, in the defense of any proceeding to which the director was a party because he or she is or was a director of the corporation against reasonable expenses actually incurred by the director in connection with the proceeding.

Section 8.53. Advance for Expenses.

(a) A corporation may pay for or reimburse the reasonable expenses incurred by a director who is a party to a proceeding in advance of final disposition of the proceeding if:

(1) the director furnishes the corporation a written affirmation of his or her good faith belief that he or she has met the standard of conduct described in section 8.51;

(2) the director furnishes the corporation a written undertaking, executed personally or on the director's behalf, to repay the advance if it is ultimately determined that the director did not meet the standard of conduct; and

(3) a determination is made that the facts then known to those making the determination would not preclude indemnification under this subchapter.

(b) The undertaking required by subsection (a)(2) must be an unlimited general obligation of the director but need not be secured and may be accepted without reference to financial ability to make repayment.

(c) Determinations and authorizations of payments under this section shall be made in the manner specified in section 8.55.

Section 8.54. Court-Ordered Indemnification.

Unless limited by a corporation's articles of incorporation, a director of the corporation who is a party to a proceeding may apply for indemnification to the court conducting the proceeding or to another court of competent jurisdiction. On receipt of an application, the court after giving any notice the court considers necessary may order indemnification in the amount it considers proper if it determines:

(1) the director is entitled to mandatory indemnification under section 8.52, in which case the court shall also order the corporation to pay the director's reasonable expenses incurred to obtain court-ordered indemnification; or

(2) the director is fairly and reasonably entitled to indemnification in view of all the relevant circumstances, whether or not the director met the standard of conduct set forth in section 8.51(a) or was adjudged liable as described in section 8.51(d), but if the director was adjudged so liable indemnification is limited to reasonable expenses incurred.

Section 8.55. Determination and Authorization of Indemnification.

(a) A corporation may not indemnify a director under section 8.51 unless authorized in the specific case after a determination has been made that indemnification of the director is permissible in the circumstances because the director has met the standard of conduct set forth in section 8.51.

(b) The determination shall be made:

(1) by the board of directors by majority vote of a quorum consisting of directors not at the time parties to the proceeding;

(2) if a quorum cannot be obtained under subdivision (1), by majority vote of a committee duly designated by the board of directors (in which designation directors who are parties may participate), consisting solely of two or more directors not at the time parties to the proceeding;

(3) by special legal counsel:

(i) selected by the board of directors or its committee in the manner prescribed in subdivision (1) or (2); or

(ii) if a quorum of the board cannot be obtained under subdivision (1) and a committee cannot be designated under subdivision (2), selected by majority vote of the full board (in which selection directors who are parties may participate); or

(4) by the members of a mutual benefit corporation, but directors who are at the time parties to the proceeding may not vote on the determination.

(c) Authorization of indemnification and evaluation as to reasonableness of expenses shall be made in the same manner as the determination that indemnification is permissible, except that if the determination is made by special legal counsel, authorization of indemnification and evaluation as to reasonableness of expenses shall be made by those entitled under subsection (b)(3) to select counsel.

(d) A director of a public benefit corporation may not be indemnified until 20 days after the effective date of written notice to the attorney general of the proposed indemnification.

Section 8.56. Indemnification of Officers, Employees and Agents.

Unless limited by a corporation's articles of incorporation:

(1) an officer of the corporation who is not a director is entitled to mandatory indemnification under section 8.52, and is entitled to apply for court-ordered indemnification under section 8.54 in each case, to the same extent as a director;

(2) the corporation may indemnify and advance expenses under this subchapter to an officer, employee, or agent of the corporation who is not a director to the same extent as to a director; and

(3) a corporation may also indemnify and advance expenses to an officer, employee, or agent who is not a director to the extent, consistent with

public policy, that may be provided by its articles of incorporation, bylaws, general or specific action of its board of directors, or contract.

Section 8.57. Insurance.

A corporation may purchase and maintain insurance on behalf of an individual who is or was a director, officer, employee, or agent of the corporation, or who, while a director, officer, employee, or agent of the corporation, is or was serving at the request of the corporation as a director, officer, partner, trustee, employee, or agent of another foreign or domestic business or nonprofit corporation, partnership, joint venture, trust, employee benefit plan, or other enterprise, against liability asserted against or incurred by him or her in that capacity or arising from his or her status as a director, officer, employee, or agent, whether or not the corporation would have power to indemnify the person against the same liability under section 8.51 or 8.52.

Section 8.58. Application of Subchapter.

(a) A provision treating a corporation's indemnification of or advance for expenses to directors that is contained in its articles of incorporation, bylaws, a resolution of its members or board of directors, or in a contract or otherwise, is valid only if and to the extent the provision is consistent with this subchapter. If articles of incorporation limit indemnification or advance for expenses, indemnification and advance for expenses are valid only to the extent consistent with the articles.

(b) This subchapter does not limit a corporation's power to pay or reimburse expenses incurred by a director in connection with appearing as a witness in a proceeding at a time when the director has not been made a named defendant or respondent to the proceeding.

TREASURY REGULATION § 1.501(c)(3)–1 (EXCERPT)

§ 1.501(c)(3)–1 Organizations organized and operated for religious, charitable, scientific, testing for public safety, literary, or educational purposes, or for the prevention of cruelty to children or animals.

(a) Organizational and operational tests. (1) In order to be exempt as an organization described in section 501(c)(3), an organization must be both organized and operated exclusively for one or more of the purposes specified in such section. If an organization fails to meet either the organizational test or the operational test, it is not exempt.

(2) The term exempt purpose or purposes, as used in this section, means any purpose or purposes specified in section 501(c)(3), as defined and elaborated in paragraph (d) of this section.

(b) Organizational test—(1) In general. (i) An organization is organized exclusively for one or more exempt purposes only if its articles of organization (referred to in this section as its articles) as defined in subparagraph (2) of this paragraph:

(a) Limit the purposes of such organization to one or more exempt purposes; and

(b) Do not expressly empower the organization to engage, otherwise than as an insubstantial part of its activities, in activities which in themselves are not in furtherance of one or more exempt purposes.

(ii) In meeting the organizational test, the organization's purposes, as stated in its articles, may be as broad as, or more specific than, the purposes stated in section 501(c)(3). Therefore, an organization which, by the terms of its articles, is formed for literary and scientific purposes within the meaning of section 501(c)(3) of the Code shall, if it otherwise meets the requirements in this paragraph, be considered to have met the organizational test. Similarly, articles stating that the organization is created solely to receive contributions and pay them over to organizations which are described in section 501(c)(3) and exempt from taxation under section 501(a)) are sufficient for purposes of the organizational test. Moreover, it is sufficient if the articles set for the purpose of the organization to be the operation of a school for adult education and describe in detail the manner of the operation of such school. In addition, if the articles state that the organization is formed for charitable purposes, such articles ordinarily shall be sufficient for purposes of the organizational test (see subparagraph (5) of this paragraph for rules relating to construction of terms).

(iii) An organization is not organized exclusively for one or more exempt purposes if its articles expressly empower it to carry on, otherwise than as an insubstantial part of its activities, activities which are not in furtherance of one or more exempt purposes, even though such organization is, by the terms of such articles, created for a purpose that is no broader than the purposes specified in section 501(c)(3). Thus, an organization that is empowered by its articles to engage in a manufacturing business, or to engage in the operation of a social club does not meet the organizational test regardless of the fact that its articles may state that such organization is created for charitable purposes within the meaning of section 501(c)(3) of the Code.

(iv) In no case shall an organization be considered to be organized exclusively for one or more exempt purposes, if, by the terms of its articles, the purposes for which such organization is created are broader than the purposes specified in section 501(c)(3). The fact that the actual operations of such an organization have been exclusively in furtherance of one or more exempt purposes shall not be sufficient to permit the organization to meet the organizational test. Similarly, such an organization will not meet the organizational test as a result of statements or other evidence that the members thereof intend to operate only in furtherance of one or more exempt purposes.

(v) Unless otherwise prescribed by applicable regulations or other guidance published in the Internal Revenue Bulletin, an organization must, in order to establish its exemption, submit a detailed statement of its proposed activities with and as a part of its application for exemption (see § 1.501(a)–1(b)).

(2) Articles of organization. For purposes of this section, the term articles of organization or articles includes the trust instrument, the corporate charter, the articles of association, or any other written instrument by which an organization is created.

(3) Authorization of legislative or political activities. An organization is not organized exclusively for one or more exempt purposes if its articles expressly empower it:

(i) To devote more than an insubstantial part of its activities to attempting to influence legislation by propaganda or otherwise; or

(ii) Directly or indirectly to participate in, or intervene in (including the publishing or distributing of statements), any political campaign on behalf of or in opposition to any candidate for public office; or

(iii) To have objectives and to engage in activities which characterize it as an action organization as defined in paragraph (c)(3) of this section.

The terms used in subdivisions (i), (ii), and (iii) of this subparagraph shall have the meanings provided in paragraph (c)(3) of this section. An organization's articles will not violate the provisions of paragraph (b)(3)(i) of this section even though the organization's articles expressly empower it to make the election provided for in section 501(h) with respect to influencing legislation and, only if it so elects, to make lobbying or grass roots expenditures that do not normally exceed the ceiling amounts prescribed by section 501(h)(2)(B) and (D).

(4) Distribution of assets on dissolution. An organization is not organized exclusively for one or more exempt purposes unless its assets are dedicated to an exempt purpose. An organization's assets will be considered dedicated to an exempt purpose, for example, if, upon dissolution, such assets would, by reason of a provision in the organization's articles or by operation of law, be distributed for one or more exempt purposes, or to the Federal Government, or to a State or local government, for a public purpose, or would be distributed by a court to another organization to be used in such manner as in the judgment of the court will best accomplish the general purposes for which the dissolved organization was organized. However, an organization does not meet the organizational test if its articles or the law

of the State in which it was created provide that its assets would, upon dissolution, be distributed to its members or shareholders.

(5) Construction of terms. The law of the State in which an organization is created shall be controlling in construing the terms of its articles. However, any organization which contends that such terms have under State law a different meaning from their generally accepted meaning must establish such special meaning by clear and convincing reference to relevant court decisions, opinions of the State attorney-general, or other evidence of applicable State law.

(6) Applicability of the organizational test. A determination by the Commissioner that an organization is described in section 501(c)(3) and exempt under section 501(a) will not be granted after July 26, 1959, regardless of when the application is filed, unless such organization meets the organizational test prescribed by this paragraph (b). If, before July 27, 1959, an organization has been determined by the Commissioner or district director to be exempt as an organization described in section 501(c)(3) or in a corresponding provision of prior law and such determination has not been revoked before such date, the fact that such organization does not meet the organizational test prescribed by this paragraph (b) shall not be a basis for revoking such determination. Accordingly, an organization that has been determined to be exempt before July 27, 1959, and which does not seek a new determination of exemption is not required to amend its articles of organization to conform to the rules of this paragraph (b), but any organization that seeks a determination of exemption after July 26, 1959, must have articles of organization that meet the rules of this paragraph (b). For the rules relating to whether an organization determined to be exempt before July 27, 1959, is organized exclusively for one or more exempt purposes, see 26 CFR (1939) 39.101(6)–1 (Regulations 118) as made applicable to the Code by Treasury Decision 6091, approved August 16, 1954 (19 FR 5167; 1954–2 CB 47).

. . .

(d) Exempt purposes—(1) In general. (i) An organization may be exempt as an organization described in section 501(c)(3) if it is organized and operated exclusively for one or more of the following purposes:

(a) Religious,

(b) Charitable,

(c) Scientific,

(d) Testing for public safety,

(e) Literary,

(f) Educational, or

(g) Prevention of cruelty to children or animals.

(ii) An organization is not organized or operated exclusively for one or more of the purposes specified in subdivision (i) of this subparagraph unless it serves a public rather than a private interest. Thus, to meet the requirement of this subdivision, it is necessary for an organization to establish that it is not organized or operated for the benefit of private interests such as designated individuals, the creator or his family, shareholders of the organization, or persons controlled, directly or indirectly, by such private interests.

. . .

(2) Charitable defined. The term charitable is used in section 501(c)(3) in its generally accepted legal sense and is, therefore, not to be construed as limited by the separate enumeration in section 501(c)(3) of other tax-exempt purposes which may fall within the broad outlines of charity as developed by judicial decisions. Such term includes: Relief of the poor and distressed or of the underprivileged; advancement of religion; advancement of education or science; erection or maintenance of public buildings, monuments, or works; lessening of the burdens of Government; and promotion of social welfare by organizations designed to accomplish any of the above purposes, or (i) to lessen neighborhood tensions; (ii) to eliminate prejudice and discrimination; (iii) to defend human and civil rights secured by law; or (iv) to combat community deterioration and juvenile delinquency. The fact that an organization which is organized and operated for the relief of indigent persons may receive voluntary contributions from the persons intended to be relieved will not necessarily prevent such organization from being exempt as an organization organized and operated exclusively for charitable purposes. The fact that an organization, in carrying out its primary purpose, advocates social or civic changes or presents opinion on controversial issues with the intention of molding public opinion or creating public sentiment to an acceptance of its views does not preclude such organization from qualifying under section 501(c)(3) so long as it is not an action organization of any one of the types described in paragraph (c)(3) of this section.

(3) Educational defined—(i) In general. The term educational, as used in section 501(c)(3), relates to:

(a) The instruction or training of the individual for the purpose of improving or developing his capabilities; or

(b) The instruction of the public on subjects useful to the individual and beneficial to the community.

An organization may be educational even though it advocates a particular position or viewpoint so long as it presents a sufficiently full and fair exposition of the pertinent facts as to permit an individual or the public to form an independent opinion or conclusion. On the other hand, an organization is not educational if its principal function is the mere presentation of unsupported opinion.

(ii) Examples of educational organizations. The following are examples of organizations which, if they otherwise meet the requirements of this section, are educational:

Example 1. An organization, such as a primary or secondary school, a college, or a professional or trade school, which has a regularly scheduled curriculum, a regular faculty, and a regularly enrolled body of students in attendance at a place where the educational activities are regularly carried on.

Example 2. An organization whose activities consist of presenting public discussion groups, forums, panels, lectures, or other similar programs. Such programs may be on radio or television.

Example 3. An organization which presents a course of instruction by means of correspondence or through the utilization of television or radio.

Example 4. Museums, zoos, planetariums, symphony orchestras, and other similar organizations.

INDIANA CODE TITLE 23, ART. 18, CHS. 2, 4–6 (EXCERPT)

IC 23–18–2 Chapter 2. Organization and Powers

IC 23–18–2–1 Organization; purpose; regulation

Sec. 1.(a) A limited liability company may:

(1) be organized under this article for any business, personal, or nonprofit purpose; and

(2) conduct business in any state for any lawful purpose;

unless a more limited purpose is set forth in its articles of organization.

(b) A limited liability company must comply with any statute that regulates the limited liability company's business.

As added by P.L. 8–1993, SEC. 301. Amended by P.L. 40–2013, SEC. 6.

IC 23–18–2–2 Powers

Sec. 2. Unless the limited liability company's articles of organization provide otherwise, every limited liability company has the same powers as an individual to do all things necessary or convenient to carry out its business and affairs, including the following:

(1) Sue, be sued, complain, and defend in its name.

(2) Make and amend operating agreements, not inconsistent with its articles of organization or with the laws of this state, for managing the business and regulating the affairs of the limited liability company.

(3) Purchase, receive, lease, or otherwise acquire and own, hold, improve, use, and otherwise deal with real or personal property, or any legal or equitable interest in property, wherever located.

(4) Sell, convey, mortgage, pledge, lease, exchange, and otherwise dispose of all or any part of its property.

(5) Except as otherwise prohibited by this article:

(A) purchase, receive, subscribe for, or otherwise acquire;

(B) own, hold, vote, use, sell, mortgage, lend, pledge, or otherwise dispose of; and

(C) deal in and with shares, interests, obligations, or other securities of;

any corporation, partnership, association, limited liability company, foreign limited liability company, or business trust.

(6) Make contracts and guarantees, incur liabilities, borrow money, and issue notes, bonds, and other obligations, and secure any of its obligations by mortgage or pledge of any of its property, franchises, or income.

(7) Lend money, invest and reinvest its funds, and receive and hold real and personal property as security for repayment.

(8) Be a promoter, a stockholder, a partner, a member, a manager, an associate, or an agent of any corporation, partnership, limited liability company, foreign limited liability company, joint venture, trust, or other enterprise.

(9) Conduct its business, locate offices, and exercise the powers granted by this article within or outside Indiana.

(10) Elect or appoint managers, agents, and employees, define their duties, fix their compensation, and lend them money and credit.

(11) Pay pensions and establish and administer pension plans, pension trusts, profit-sharing plans, welfare plans, qualified and nonqualified retirement plans, and benefit or incentive plans for any or all of its current or former managers, employees, and agents.

(12) Make donations for public welfare, charitable, scientific, or educational purposes.

(13) Transact any lawful business that will aid governmental policy.

(14) Indemnify and hold harmless any member, manager, agent, or employee from and against any and all claims and demands, except in the case of action or failure to act by the member, agent, or employee which constitutes willful misconduct or recklessness and subject to any standards and restrictions set forth in a written operating agreement.

(15) To the extent authorized by the licensing authority (as defined in IC 23–1.5–1–9) provide professional services (as defined in IC 23–1.5–1–11).

(16) Make payments or donations or do any other act that furthers the business and affairs of the limited liability company.

(17) Adopt, either in the limited liability company's articles of organization or written operating agreement, a provision establishing exclusive jurisdiction in the circuit or superior courts of any county in Indiana or in the United States district courts of Indiana, for:

(A) any action asserting a claim for breach of a fiduciary duty owed by any director, officer, employee, or agent of the limited liability company to the limited liability company;

(B) any action asserting a claim arising under:

(i) any provision of this article; or

(ii) the limited liability company's articles of organization or operating agreement; or

(C) any actions otherwise relating to the internal affairs of the limited liability company.

As added by P.L. 8–1993, SEC. 301. Amended by P.L. 63–2014, SEC. 28.

IC 23–18–2–3 Professional licensing or regulatory authorities; powers

Sec. 3. Except for the prohibitions in this article concerning the personal liability of members, managers, employees, and agents of a limited liability company organized under this article, nothing in this article is intended to restrict or limit in any manner the authority and duty of any licensing authority (as defined in IC 23–1.5–1–9) or to regulate the provision of professional services (as defined in IC 23–1.5–1–11) within Indiana, notwithstanding that the member, manager, or employee of a limited liability company is providing professional services or engaging in the practice of a profession through the limited liability company.

As added by P.L. 8–1993, SEC. 301.

IC 23–18–2–4 Formation; articles of organization; contents

Sec. 4.(a) At least one (1) person may form a limited liability company by causing articles of organization to be executed and filed for record with the office of the secretary of state. A person does not need to be a member of the limited liability company at the time of formation or after formation has occurred.

(b) Articles of organization shall contain the following:

(1) The name of the limited liability company.

(2) The street address of the limited liability company's registered office in Indiana and the name of the limited liability company's registered agent at that office.

(3) The latest date upon which the limited liability company is to dissolve, or a statement that the duration of the limited liability company is perpetual until dissolution in accordance with this article.

(4) If the articles of organization provide for a manager or managers, a statement to that effect.

(5) Any other matters not inconsistent with this article that the members agree to include, including any matters that are required to be or may be included in an operating agreement under this article.

As added by P.L. 8–1993, SEC. 301.

IC 23–18–2–5 Amendment of articles of organization

Sec. 5.(a) Articles of organization of a limited liability company may be amended by filing articles of amendment of the articles of organization in the office of the secretary of state. The articles of amendment must contain the following:

(1) The name of the limited liability company.

(2) The date the articles of organization were filed.

(3) The amendment to the articles of organization.

(b) Articles of organization of a limited liability company may be amended at any time that the members determine provided that the articles of organization as amended contain only provisions that may be lawfully contained in articles of organization at the time the amendment is made.

As added by P.L. 8–1993, SEC. 301.

IC 23–18–2–6 Restated articles of organization

Sec. 6.(a) Articles of organization may be restated at any time. Restated articles of organization must:

(1) be filed with the secretary of state;

(2) be specifically designated as "restated articles of organization"; and

(3) state in the heading or in a separate paragraph the limited liability company's present name, and if the name has been changed, all of its former names and the date of filing of its original articles of organization.

(b) A restated articles of organization may include one (1) or more amendments to the articles of organization. If the restated articles of organization include an amendment, the amendment must be adopted as provided in section 5 of this chapter.

As added by P.L. 8–1993, SEC. 301. Amended by P.L. 121–1994, SEC. 2.

IC 23–18–2–7 Filing articles with secretary of state; notice

Sec. 7. The fact that articles of organization of a limited liability company are on file in the office of the secretary of state is notice that the limited liability company has been organized and is notice of all other facts that are required to be set forth in the articles of organization under section 4 of this chapter and that are set forth in the articles of organization.

As added by P.L. 8–1993, SEC. 301.

IC 23–18–2–8 Name

Note: This version of section effective until 1-1-2018. See also following repeal of this section, effective 1-1-2018.

Sec. 8.(a) The name of each limited liability company as set forth in its articles of organization:

(1) must contain the words "limited liability company" or either of the following abbreviations:

(A) "L.L.C."; or

(B) "LLC";

(2) may contain the name of a member or manager; and

(3) except as provided in subsection (b), must be such as to distinguish the name upon the records of the office of the secretary of state from the name of any limited liability company or other business entity reserved or organized under the laws of Indiana or authorized to transact business in Indiana.

(b) A limited liability company may apply to the secretary of state to use a name that is not distinguishable upon the secretary of state's records from one (1) or more of the names described in subsection (a). The secretary of state shall authorize the use of the name applied for if:

(1) the other domestic or foreign limited liability company or other business entity files its written consent to the use of its name; or

(2) the applicant delivers to the secretary of state a certified copy of a final court judgment from a circuit or superior court in the state of Indiana establishing the applicant's right to use the name applied for in Indiana.

As added by P.L. 8–1993, SEC. 301. Amended by P.L. 178–2002, SEC. 105; P.L. 119–2015, SEC. 70; P.L. 170–2016, SEC. 15.

IC 23–18–2–9 Reserve exclusive use of name; transfer

Note: This version of section effective until 1-1-2018. See also following repeal of this section, effective 1-1-2018.

Sec. 9.(a) A person may reserve the exclusive right to the use of a name by delivering an electronic application to the secretary of state. The application must set forth the name and address of the applicant and the name to be reserved. If the secretary of state finds that the name is available, the secretary of state shall reserve the name for the exclusive use of the applicant for renewable one hundred twenty (120) day periods.

(b) The owner of a reserved name may transfer the reservation to another person by delivering to the office of the secretary of state, electronically, a signed notice of the transfer that states the name and address of the transferee.

As added by P.L. 8–1993, SEC. 301. Amended by P.L. 277–2001, SEC. 22; P.L. 119–2015, SEC. 71; P.L. 170–2016, SEC. 16.

IC 23–18–2–10 Maintenance of registered office and registered agent; agent's consent; communications contact information; resignation

Note: This version of section effective until 1-1-2018. See also following repeal of this section, effective 1-1-2018.

Sec. 10.(a) A limited liability company must continuously maintain in Indiana the following:

(1) A registered office.

(2) A registered agent, who must be one (1) of the following:

(A) An individual who resides in Indiana and whose business office is identical with the registered office.

(B) A domestic limited liability company, domestic corporation, or nonprofit domestic corporation whose business office is identical with the registered office.

(C) A foreign limited liability company, foreign corporation, or nonprofit foreign corporation authorized to transact business in Indiana whose business office is identical with the registered office.

(b) Each limited liability company organized after June 30, 2014, under the laws of Indiana shall file with the secretary of state:

(1) the registered agent's written consent; or

(2) a representation that the registered agent has consented.

(c) Each limited liability company formed under the laws of Indiana shall provide to the limited liability company's registered agent, and update from time to time as necessary, the name, business address, and business telephone number of a natural person who is:

(1) an officer, a director, an employee, or a designated agent of the limited liability company; and

(2) authorized to receive communications from the registered agent.

The natural person is considered to be the communications contact for the limited liability company.

(d) A registered agent shall retain, in paper or electronic form, the information provided by a limited liability company under subsection (c).

(e) If a limited liability company fails to provide the registered agent with the information required under subsection (c), the registered agent may resign, as provided in section 12 of this chapter, as the registered agent for the limited liability company.

As added by P.L. 8–1993, SEC. 301. Amended by P.L. 63–2014, SEC. 29.

IC 23–18–2–11 Change of registered office or agent

Note: This version of section effective until 1-1-2018. See also following repeal of this section, effective 1-1-2018.

Sec. 11.(a) A limited liability company may change its registered office or registered agent by delivering to the secretary of state for filing a statement of change that sets forth the following:

(1) The name of the limited liability company.

(2) The street address of its current registered office.

(3) If the current registered office is to be changed, the street address of the new registered office.

(4) The name of its current registered agent.

(5) If the current registered agent is to be changed, the name of the new registered agent and the new registered agent's written consent or a representation that the new registered agent has consented either on the statement or attached to the statement to the appointment.

(6) That after the change or changes are made, the street addresses of its registered office and the business office of its registered agent will be identical.

(b) If a registered agent changes the street address of the registered agent's business office, the registered agent may change the street address of the registered office of any limited liability company that the registered agent serves by notifying the limited liability company in writing of the change and signing either manually or in facsimile and delivering to the secretary of state for filing a statement that complies with the requirements of subsection (a) and states that the limited liability company has been notified of the change.

As added by P.L. 8–1993, SEC. 301.

IC 23–18–2–12 Resignation of agency; discontinuance of office

Note: This version of section effective until 1-1-2018. See also following repeal of this section, effective 1-1-2018.

Sec. 12.(a) A registered agent may resign the agency appointment by signing and delivering to the secretary of state for filing as described in IC 23–18–12 a statement of resignation. The statement may include a statement that the registered office is also discontinued.

(b) After filing the statement, the secretary of state shall mail one (1) copy to the limited liability company at the limited liability company's principal office and one (1) copy to the registered office, if not discontinued.

(c) The agency appointment is terminated and the registered office discontinued, if discontinued under the statement, thirty-one (31) days after the statement was filed.

As added by P.L. 8–1993, SEC. 301. Amended by P.L. 228–1995, SEC. 26.

IC 23–18–2–13 Service of process; perfection; nonexclusive means

Note: This version of section effective until 1-1-2018. See also following repeal of this section, effective 1-1-2018.

Sec. 13.(a) A limited liability company's registered agent is the limited liability company's agent for service of process, notice, or demand required or permitted by law to be served on the limited liability company.

(b) If a limited liability company does not have a registered agent or the agent cannot with reasonable diligence be served, the limited liability company may be served by registered or certified mail, return receipt requested, addressed to the limited liability company at the limited liability company's principal office. Service is perfected under this subsection at the earliest of the following:

(1) The date the limited liability company receives the mail.

(2) The date shown on the return receipt, if signed on behalf of the limited liability company.

(3) Five (5) days after the deposit of the service in the United States mail, if mailed postpaid and correctly addressed.

(c) This section does not prescribe the only means, or necessarily the required means, of serving a limited liability company.

As added by P.L. 8–1993, SEC. 301.

. . .

IC 23–18–4 Chapter 4. Rights and Duties of Members and Managers

IC 23–18–4–1 Authority of members or managers

Sec. 1.(a) Unless the articles of organization provide for a manager or managers, management of the business or affairs of the limited liability company is vested in the members. Subject to any provisions in the operating agreement or this article restricting or enlarging the management rights and duties of any person or group or class of persons, the members have the right and authority to manage the affairs and make all decisions of the limited liability company.

(b) If the articles of organization provide for a manager or managers, except to the extent that the operating agreement reserves the authority to any members or class or group of members, the manager or managers have the authority to manage the business or affairs of the limited liability company. Unless otherwise provided in a written operating agreement, a manager or managers:

(1) must be designated, appointed, elected, removed, or replaced by a vote, approval, or consent of a majority in interest of the members;

(2) do not need to be members of the limited liability company or natural persons; and

(3) unless they have been earlier removed or have earlier resigned, shall act as managers until their successors have been elected and qualified.

As added by P.L. 8–1993, SEC. 301.

IC 23–18–4 Chapter 4. Rights and Duties of Members and Managers

IC 23–18–4–2 Acts and omissions liability; trustee for personal benefits derived through company; duties of member in company providing for manager

Sec. 2.(a) Unless otherwise provided in a written operating agreement, a member or manager is not liable for damages to the limited liability company or to the members of the limited liability company for any action taken or failure to act on behalf of the limited liability company, unless the act or omission constitutes willful misconduct or recklessness.

(b) Unless otherwise provided in a written operating agreement, each member and manager must account to the limited liability company and hold as trustee for it any profit or benefit derived by the manager or member without the consent of a majority of the disinterested managers or members or other persons participating in the management of the business or affairs of the limited liability company from:

(1) a transaction connected with the conduct or winding up of the limited liability company; or

(2) any use by the manager or member of the limited liability company's property, including confidential or proprietary information of the limited liability company or other matters entrusted to the manager or member because of the manager's or member's status as manager or member.

(c) Unless otherwise provided in a written operating agreement, a member of a limited liability company in which the articles of organization provide for a manager or managers and who is not a manager has no duties to the limited liability company or to the other members solely by reason of acting in the capacity as a member.

As added by P.L. 8–1993, SEC. 301.

IC 23–18–4–3 Affirmative vote, approval, or consent; requirements

Sec. 3.(a) Unless the articles of organization provide for a manager or managers, and except as otherwise provided in a written operating agreement or this article and subject to subsection (c), the affirmative vote, approval, or consent of a majority in interest of the members is required to decide a matter connected with the business or affairs of the limited liability company.

(b) If the articles of organization provide for more than one (1) manager and except as provided otherwise in a written operating agreement or this article, the affirmative vote, approval, or consent of a majority of the managers shall be required to decide any matter that requires the approval of the managers.

(c) Except as provided otherwise in a written operating agreement, the affirmative vote, approval, or consent of all members is required to do the following:

(1) Amend the operating agreement.

(2) Authorize a manager, a member, or another person to do an act on behalf of the limited liability company that contravenes the operating agreement, including a written provision of the operating agreement that expressly limits the purpose, business, affairs, or conduct of the limited liability company.

As added by P.L. 8–1993, SEC. 301.

IC 23–18–4–4 Written operating agreement

Sec. 4.(a) A written operating agreement may do one (1) or more of the following:

(1) Modify, increase, decrease, limit, or eliminate the duties (including fiduciary duties) or the liability of a member or manager for breach of the duties set forth in section 2(a) of this chapter.

(2) Provide for indemnification of a member or manager for judgments, settlements, penalties, fines, or expenses incurred in a proceeding to which a person is a party because the person is or was a member or manager.

(3) Provide for officers of a limited liability company that is:

(A) managed by a manager or managers; or

(B) managed by a member or members;

by specifying the title, powers, duties, and term of office (either perpetual or for a specific term) for each officer and the means by which each officer is to be appointed, elected, or reelected, or by authorizing in the written operating agreement the authority of the manager or managers of a manager-managed limited liability company or the member or members of a member-managed limited liability company to otherwise establish officers and the titles, powers, duties, and terms of office of the officers.

(4) Provide that one (1) or more persons who are not members or managers have the right to approve or disapprove any of one (1) or more specified actions with respect to the limited liability company, including:

(A) voluntary dissolution;

(B) merger; or

(C) amending the written operating agreement.

(b) If a person who is not a member or manager is given the right to approve or disapprove specified actions as permitted by subsection (a)(4), the person does not have the general right to vote with the members or managers regarding any matters unless specifically provided otherwise in the written operating agreement.

As added by P.L. 8–1993, SEC. 301. Amended by P.L. 40–2013, SEC. 8; P.L. 63–2014, SEC. 32.

IC 23–18–4–5 Operating agreements; objectives

Sec. 5. Members may enter into an operating agreement to regulate or establish any aspect of the affairs of the limited liability company or the relations of the members and managers, if any, including provisions establishing the following:

(1) The manner in which the business and affairs of the limited liability company shall be managed, controlled, and operated, which may include the granting of exclusive authority to manage, control, and operate the limited liability company to managers who are not members.

(2) The manner in which the members will share in distributions of the assets and the profits or losses of the limited liability company.

(3) The rights of members to assign all or a portion of their interests in the limited liability company.

(4) Classes or groups of at least one (1) member having certain relative rights, powers, and duties, including voting rights, and may provide for the future creation, in the manner provided in the operating agreement, of additional classes or groups of members

having certain relative rights, powers, or duties, including voting rights, expressed either in the operating agreement or at the time the classes or groups are created, including rights, powers, or duties senior to those of at least one (1) existing class or group of members.

(5) Classes or groups of at least one (1) manager having certain relative rights, powers, and duties, including voting rights, and may provide for the future creation, in the manner provided in the operating agreement, of additional classes or groups of managers having certain relative rights, powers, or duties, including voting rights, expressed either in the operating agreement or at the time the classes or groups are created, including rights, powers, or duties senior to those of at least one (1) existing class or group of managers.

(6) The circumstances in which an assignee of a member's interest may be admitted as a member of the limited liability company.

(7) The procedure for the following:

(A) The right to have a member's interest in the limited liability company evidenced by a certificate issued by the limited liability company.

(B) Assignment, pledge, or transfer of an interest represented by the certificate.

(C) Any other provisions dealing with the certificate.

(8) The method by which the operating agreement may be amended.

As added by P.L. 8–1993, SEC. 301.

IC 23–18–4–6 Initial operating agreement; amendments; power of attorney

Sec. 6.(a) The initial operating agreement must be agreed to by all persons who are members at the time the initial agreement is accepted.

(b) An amendment to an oral operating agreement must be approved by the unanimous consent of all members.

(c) An amendment to a written operating agreement must be in writing and must, unless otherwise provided in the operating agreement before the amendment, be approved by the unanimous consent of all members.

(d) A copy of any written amendment to an operating agreement must be delivered to each member who did not consent to the amendment and to each assignee who has not been admitted as a member.

(e) A person may sign articles of organization, an operating agreement, or an amendment to articles of organization or an operating agreement as an attorney in fact. A power of attorney relating to the signing of a document under this subsection by an attorney in fact may but is not required to be:

(1) sworn to, verified, or acknowledged;

(2) signed in the presence of a notary public;

(3) filed with the secretary of state; or

(4) included in another written agreement.

However, the power of attorney must be retained in the records of the limited liability company.

As added by P.L. 8–1993, SEC. 301. Amended by P.L. 130–2006, SEC. 27.

IC 23–18–4–7 Enforcement of operating agreement; injunctive or other relief

Sec. 7.(a) A court may enforce an operating agreement by injunction or by granting other relief that the court in its discretion determines to be fair and appropriate in the circumstances.

(b) As an alternative to injunctive or other equitable relief, when the provisions under IC 23–18–9–2 are applicable, the court may order dissolution of the limited liability company.

As added by P.L. 8–1993, SEC. 301.

IC 23–18–4–8 Records; inspection; full disclosure; omissions

Sec. 8.(a) A limited liability company must keep at its principal office the following records and information:

(1) A list with the full name and last known mailing address of each member and manager, if any, of the limited liability company from the date of organization.

(2) A copy of the articles of organization and all amendments.

(3) Copies of the limited liability company's federal, state, and local income tax returns and financial statements, if any, for the three (3) most recent years, or if the returns and statements were not prepared, copies of the information and statements provided to or that should have been provided to the members to enable them to prepare their federal, state, and local tax returns for the same period.

(4) Copies of any written operating agreements and all amendments and copies of any written operating agreements no longer in effect.

(5) Unless otherwise set forth in a written operating agreement, a writing setting out the following:

(A) The amount of cash, if any, and a statement of the agreed value of other property or services contributed by each member and the times at which or events upon the happening of which any additional contributions agreed to be made by each member are to be made.

(B) The events, if any, upon the happening of which the limited liability company is to be dissolved and its affairs wound up.

(C) Other writings, if any, required by the operating agreement.

(b) A member may, at the member's own expense, inspect and copy the limited liability company records described in subsection (a) where the records are located during ordinary business hours if the member gives the limited liability company written notice of the member's request at least five (5) business days before the date on which the member wishes to inspect and copy the records.

(c) Unless greater rights of access to records or other information are provided in a written operating agreement, members or managers, if any, shall give to the extent the circumstances allow just, reasonable, true, and full information of all things affecting the members to any member or to the legal representative of any deceased member or of any member under legal disability upon reasonable demand for any purpose reasonably related to a member's interest as a member of the limited liability company.

(d) If a limited liability company is managed by one (1) or more managers, a member or the legal representative of a deceased member or a member under a legal disability may obtain information under subsection (c) only if:

(1) the member makes the request at least five (5) business days before the date on which the member wishes to obtain the information;

(2) the member makes the request in good faith and for a proper purpose;

(3) the member describes with reasonable particularity the member's purpose and the information that the member wishes to obtain; and

(4) the information is directly connected to the member's purpose.

(e) Failure of the limited liability company to keep or maintain the records or information required by this section is not grounds for imposing liability on any member for the debts and obligations of the limited liability company.

As added by P.L. 8–1993, SEC. 301. Amended by P.L. 130–2006, SEC. 28; P.L. 1–2007, SEC. 163.

IC 23–18–4–9 Managerial omissions; penalties or consequences

Sec. 9. If set forth in writing, an operating agreement may provide that:

(1) a manager who fails to perform and comply with the terms and conditions of the operating agreement is subject to penalties or consequences specified in the operating agreement; and

(2) at the time or upon the happening of events specified in the operating agreement, a manager is subject to penalties or consequences specified in the operating agreement.

As added by P.L. 8–1993, SEC. 301.

IC 23–18–4–10 Good faith reliance on records by members or managers; liability

Sec. 10. A member or manager of a limited liability company is not liable when relying in good faith upon the records of the limited liability company and on the information, opinions, reports, or statements presented to the limited liability company by its other managers, members, agents, or employees, or by any other person, concerning matters the member or manager reasonably believes are within the other person's professional or expert competence and who has been selected with reasonable care by or on behalf of the limited liability company, including information, opinions, reports, or statements concerning the value and amount of the assets, liabilities, profits, or losses of the limited liability company or other facts pertinent to the existence and amount of assets from which distributions to members might properly be paid.

As added by P.L. 8–1993, SEC. 301.

IC 23–18–4–11 Resignation of manager

Sec. 11.(a) A manager may resign as a manager of a limited liability company at the time or upon the happening of events specified in an operating agreement and in accordance with the operating agreement.

(b) A written operating agreement may provide that a manager does not have the right to resign as a manager of a limited liability company. Notwithstanding any provision in an operating agreement to the contrary, a manager may resign as a manager of a limited liability company at any time by giving written notice to the members and other managers. If the resignation of a manager violates the operating agreement, in addition to any remedies otherwise available under applicable law, a limited liability company may recover from the resigning manager damages for breach of the operating agreement and offset the damages against the amount payable to the resigning manager.

As added by P.L. 8–1993, SEC. 301.

IC 23–18–4–12 Business between company and member or manager

Sec. 12. Except when prohibited in a written operating agreement, a member or manager may lend money to and transact other business with the limited liability company and, subject to other applicable law, has the same rights and obligations with respect to the transaction as a person who is not a member or manager.

As added by P.L. 8–1993, SEC. 301.

IC 23–18–4–13 Policy

Sec. 13. The policy of this article is to give the maximum effect to the principle of freedom of contract and to the enforceability of operating agreements of limited liability companies.

As added by P.L. 40–2013, SEC. 9.

IC 23–18–5 Chapter 5. Finance

IC 23–18–5–1 Promises to contribute property or services; enforceability

Sec. 1.(a) A promise by a member to make a contribution to the limited liability company is not enforceable unless the promise is written and signed by the member.

(b) Except as otherwise provided in a written operating agreement, a member is obligated to the limited liability company to perform any enforceable promise to contribute cash or property or to perform services, even if the member is unable to perform for any reason, including death and disability.

(c) If a member does not make the required contribution of property or services, the member is obligated, at the option of the limited liability company, to contribute cash equal to the value of that portion of the contribution that has not been made. This option is in addition to and not in lieu of any other rights, including the right to specific performance, that the limited liability company may have against the member under the operating agreement or applicable law.

As added by P.L. 8–1993, SEC. 301.

IC 23–18–5–2 Obligation to make capital contribution or other payment; compromise; effect; remedies or consequences of nonpayment

Sec. 2.(a) The obligation of a member to make a capital contribution or return money or other property paid or distributed in violation of this article may be compromised only:

(1) in compliance with a written operating agreement; or

(2) if a written operating agreement does not so provide, with the unanimous consent of the members.

(b) Any compromise does not affect the rights, if any, of any creditor of a limited liability company who, before the compromise, extends credit or acts in reliance on the obligation after the member signs a writing that reflects the obligation.

(c) An operating agreement may provide that a member who fails to make a capital contribution or other payment that the member is required to make is subject to specified remedies for or specified consequences of the failure. The remedy or consequence may include the following form:

(1) Reducing the defaulting member's interest in the limited liability company.

(2) Subordinating the defaulting member's interest in the limited liability company to that of nondefaulting members.

(3) A forced sale of the defaulting member's interest in the limited liability company.

(4) Forfeiture of the defaulting member's interest in the limited liability company.

(5) A loan by the nondefaulting members of the amount necessary to meet the commitment.

(6) A determination of the value of the member's interest in the limited liability company by appraisal or by formula and redemption and sale of the defaulting member's interest in the limited liability company at that value.

As added by P.L. 8–1993, SEC. 301.

IC 23–18–5–3 Allocation of profits and losses

Sec. 3. Unless otherwise provided in the operating agreement, profits and losses must be allocated on the basis of the agreed value, as stated in the records of the limited liability company, of the contributions made by each member to the extent the contributions have been received by the limited liability company and not previously returned.

As added by P.L. 8–1993, SEC. 301.

IC 23–18–5–4 Shared distributions of cash or other assets

Sec. 4. Except as provided in section 5 or 5.1 of this chapter and IC 23–18–9–6, distributions of cash or other assets of a limited liability company must be shared among the members and among classes of members in the manner provided in the operating agreement. If the operating agreement does not provide otherwise, distributions must be allocated on the basis of the agreed value, as stated in the records of the limited liability company, of the contributions made by each member to the extent the contributions have been received by the limited liability company and not previously returned. A member is entitled to receive distributions described in this section from a limited liability company to the extent and at the times or upon the happening of the events specified in the operating agreement or at the times determined by the members or managers, if any, voting under IC 23–18–4–3.

As added by P.L. 8–1993, SEC. 301. Amended by P.L. 269–1999, SEC. 3.

IC 23–18–5–5 Dissociation; companies existing on or before June 30, 1999

Sec. 5.(a) Unless otherwise provided in a written operating agreement, a limited liability company existing under this article on or before June 30, 1999, is governed by this section.

(b) Upon the occurrence of an event of dissociation under IC 23–18–6–5 that does not cause dissolution, a dissociating member is entitled to receive:

(1) any distribution that the member is entitled to under this article or the operating agreement; and

(2) unless otherwise provided in the operating agreement, within a reasonable time after dissociation, the fair value of the member's interest in the limited liability company as of the date of dissociation based on the member's right to share in distributions from the limited liability company, less a distribution received under subdivision (1).

As added by P.L. 8–1993, SEC. 301. Amended by P.L. 269–1999, SEC. 4; P.L. 130–2006, SEC. 29.

IC 23–18–5–5.1 Dissociation; companies formed after June 30, 1999

Sec. 5.1.(a) A limited liability company formed under this article after June 30, 1999, is governed by this section.

(b) Upon the occurrence of an event of dissociation under IC 23–18–6–5, a dissociating member is entitled to receive:

(1) any distribution that the member is entitled to under this article or the operating agreement; and

(2) unless otherwise provided in the operating agreement, within a reasonable time after dissociation, the fair value of the member's interest in the limited liability company as of the date of dissociation based on the member's right to share in distributions from the limited liability company, less a distribution received under subdivision (1).

As added by P.L. 269–1999, SEC. 5. Amended by P.L. 130–2006, SEC. 30.

IC 23–18–5–6 Distributions

Sec. 6.(a) A distribution may not be made if after giving effect to the distribution:

(1) the limited liability company would not be able to pay its debts as the debts become due in the usual course of business; or

(2) the limited liability company's total assets would be less than the sum of its total liabilities plus, unless the operating agreement permits otherwise, the amount that would be needed if the affairs of the limited liability company were to be wound up at the time of the distribution to satisfy any preferential rights that are superior to the rights of members receiving the distribution.

(b) The limited liability company may base a determination that a distribution is not prohibited under subsection (a) upon one (1) of the following:

(1) Financial statements prepared on the basis of accounting practices and principles that are reasonable under the circumstances.

(2) A fair valuation of assets and liabilities or other reasonable method approved by the members or managers, if any.

(c) Except as provided in subsection (e), the effect of a distribution under subsection (a) is measured as of:

(1) the date the distribution is authorized if the payment occurs not more than one hundred twenty (120) days after the date of authorization; or

(2) the date the payment is made if it occurs more than one hundred twenty (120) days after the date of authorization.

(d) A limited liability company's indebtedness to a member incurred by reason of an obligation to make a distribution in accordance with this section is at parity with the limited liability company's indebtedness to its general unsecured creditors, except to the extent subordinated by agreement.

(e) If terms of the indebtedness provide that payment of principal and interest is to be made only if and to the extent that payment of a distribution to members could then be made under this section, indebtedness of a limited liability company, including indebtedness issued as a distribution, is not a liability for purposes of determinations made under subsection (b).

(f) If the indebtedness is issued as a distribution, each payment of principal or interest on the indebtedness is treated as a distribution, the effect of which is measured on the date the payment is actually made.

As added by P.L. 8–1993, SEC. 301.

IC 23–18–5–7 Unlawful distributions; liability

Sec. 7.(a) A member or manager who votes for or assents to a distribution in violation of the operating agreement or section 6 of this chapter is personally liable to the limited liability company for the amount of the distribution that exceeds the amount that could have been distributed without violating the operating agreement or section 6 of this chapter or if it is established that the member or manager did not act in compliance with section 6 of this chapter.

(b) Each member or manager held liable under subsection (a) for an unlawful distribution is entitled to contribution from the following:

(1) Each other member or manager who could be held liable under subsection (a) for the unlawful distribution.

(2) Each member for the amount the member received knowing that the distribution was made in violation of the operating agreement or section 6 of this chapter.

(c) A proceeding under this section is barred unless it is commenced not more than two (2) years after the date on which the effect of the distribution is measured under section 6 of this chapter.

As added by P.L. 8–1993, SEC. 301.

IC 23–18–5–8 Distributions in kind

Sec. 8.(a) Except as provided in the operating agreement, a member, regardless of the nature of the member's contribution, does not have a right to demand and receive a distribution from a limited liability company in a form other than cash.

(b) Except as provided in the operating agreement, a member may not be compelled to accept a distribution in kind from a limited liability company to the extent that the member's percentage interest in the assets being distributed in kind exceeds the percentage of distributions that the member is entitled to receive under section 4 of this chapter.

As added by P.L. 8–1993, SEC. 301.

IC 23–18–5–9 Status of member entitled to receive distribution

Sec. 9. At the time a member becomes entitled to receive a distribution, the member has the status of and is entitled to all remedies available to a creditor of the limited liability company with respect to the distribution.

As added by P.L. 8–1993, SEC. 301.

IC 23-18-6 Chapter 6. Membership

IC 23–18–6–0.5 Minimum membership

Note: This version of section effective until 1-1-2018. See also following version of this section, effective 1-1-2018.

Sec. 0.5. A limited liability company formed under this article or a foreign limited liability company admitted to transact business in Indiana under IC 23–18–11 may have at least one (1) member.

As added by P.L. 34–1997, SEC. 16.

IC 23–18–6–0.5 Minimum membership

Note: This version of section effective 1-1-2018. See also preceding version of this section, effective until 1-1-2018.

Sec. 0.5. A limited liability company formed under this article or a foreign limited liability company admitted to transact business in Indiana under IC 23–0.5–5 may have at least one (1) member.

As added by P.L. 34–1997, SEC. 16. Amended by P.L. 118–2017, SEC. 104.

IC 23–18–6–1 Acquisition of membership

Sec. 1.(a) Subject to subsection (b), a person may become a member in a limited liability company:

(1) in the case of a person acquiring an interest directly from the limited liability company, upon compliance with the operating agreement or if the operating agreement does not provide in writing, upon the written consent of all members; and

(2) in the case of an assignee of an interest, as provided in section 4 or 4.1 of this chapter.

(b) The effective time of admission of a member to a limited liability company is the later of the following:

(1) The date the limited liability company is organized.

(2) The time provided in the operating agreement, or if no time is provided, when the person's admission is reflected in the records of the limited liability company.

As added by P.L. 8–1993, SEC. 301. Amended by P.L. 269–1999, SEC. 6.

IC 23–18–6–2 Interest of member; nature

Sec. 2. The interest of a member in a limited liability company is personal property.

As added by P.L. 8–1993, SEC. 301.

IC 23–18–6–2.5 Member interest designated as transfer on death property or held in joint tenancy

Sec. 2.5.(a) Unless otherwise limited or prohibited in a written operating agreement, any member interest in a limited liability company:

(1) may be designated as a transfer on death property under IC 32–17–14, with:

(A) the member as the owner of the interest; and

(B) one (1) or more transfer on death beneficiaries designated; or

(2) may be titled and held in joint tenancy with right of survivorship between two (2) or more individuals.

(b) The following apply upon the death of a person who is the owner of a member interest designated as a transfer on death property:

(1) Each surviving transfer on death beneficiary has the status of an assignee of all or a fractional or percentage portion of the entire member interest owned by the deceased owner, depending on the number of surviving transfer on death beneficiaries, consistent with the transfer on death beneficiary designation, until that transfer on death beneficiary is admitted as a member of the limited liability company.

(2) The rights and obligations of each surviving transfer on death beneficiary with respect to the member interest are subject to all:

(A) transfer restrictions;

(B) redemption options; or

(C) other provisions;

that apply to the member's interest or member interests generally under a written operating agreement.

(c) The following apply upon the death of a person who is the owner of a member interest held in joint tenancy:

(1) Each surviving joint tenant has the status of an assignee of all or a fractional or percentage portion of the entire member interest, depending on the number of surviving joint tenants, until the surviving joint tenant is admitted as a member of the limited liability company unless the surviving joint tenant was already a member under subsection (d) before the death of each other joint tenant.

(2) The rights and obligations of each surviving joint tenant with respect to the member interest are subject to all:

(A) transfer restrictions;

(B) redemption options; or

(C) other provisions;

that apply to the member interest generally under a written operating agreement.

(d) If a member interest in a limited liability company is originally and initially issued in joint tenancy form to two (2) or more individuals, each joint tenant has the voting rights of a member unless otherwise provided in the written operating agreement. If an individual member:

(1) receives and holds a member interest as the sole owner; and

(2) at a later date, makes a lawful transfer of the member interest to be held in joint tenancy between the member and one (1) or more other persons;

then, unless otherwise provided in a written operating agreement, each other person, while all joint tenants are alive, has the status of an assignee of a fractional part of the member interest until the other person is admitted as a member of the limited liability company.

As added by P.L. 40–2013, SEC. 10. Amended by P.L. 63–2014, SEC. 33.

IC 23–18–6–3 Assignment of interest; companies existing on or before June 30, 1999

Sec. 3.(a) Unless otherwise provided in a written operating agreement, a limited liability company existing under this article on or before June 30, 1999, is governed by this section.

(b) Except as provided in a written operating agreement:

(1) an interest is assignable in whole or in part;

(2) an assignment entitles the assignee to receive, to the extent assigned, only the distributions to which the assignor would be entitled;

(3) an assignment of an interest does not of itself dissolve the limited liability company or entitle the assignee to participate in the management and affairs of the limited liability company or to become or exercise any rights of a member;

(4) until the assignee of an interest becomes a member, the assignor continues to be a member and to have the power to exercise any rights of a member, subject to the other members' right to remove the assignor under section 5(a)(3)(B) of this chapter;

(5) until an assignee of an interest becomes a member, the assignee has no liability as a member solely as a result of the assignment; and

(6) the assignor of an interest is not released from liability as a member solely as a result of the assignment.

(c) Unless otherwise provided in an operating agreement, the pledge of or granting of a security interest, lien, or other encumbrance in or against any or all of the interest of a member is not an assignment and does not cause the member to cease to be a member or to cease to have the power to exercise any rights or powers of a member.

As added by P.L. 8–1993, SEC. 301. Amended by P.L. 269–1999, SEC. 7.

IC 23–18–6–3.1 Assignment of interest; companies formed after June 30, 1999

Sec. 3.1.(a) A limited liability company formed under this article after June 30, 1999, is governed by this section.

(b) Except as provided in a written operating agreement:

(1) an interest is assignable in whole or in part;

(2) an assignment entitles the assignee to receive, to the extent assigned, only the distributions to which the assignor would be entitled;

(3) an assignment of an interest does not of itself dissolve the limited liability company or entitle the assignee to participate in the management and affairs of the limited liability company or to become or exercise any rights of a member;

(4) until an assignee of an interest becomes a member, the assignee has no liability as a member solely as a result of the assignment; and

(5) the assignor of an interest is not released from liability as a member solely as a result of the assignment.

(c) Unless otherwise provided in an operating agreement, the pledge of or granting of a security interest, lien, or other encumbrance in or against any or all of the interest of a member is not an assignment and does not cause the member to cease to be a member or to cease to have the power to exercise any rights or powers of a member.

As added by P.L. 269–1999, SEC. 8. Amended by P.L. 14–2000, SEC. 54.

IC 23–18–6–4 Assignee membership; companies existing on or before June 30, 1999

Sec. 4.(a) Unless otherwise provided in a written operating agreement, a limited liability company existing under this article on or before June 30, 1999, is governed by this section.

(b) Except as otherwise provided in a written operating agreement, an assignee of an interest may become a member only if the other members unanimously consent. The consent of a member may be evidenced in any manner specified in writing in an operating agreement, but in the absence of a specification, consent must be evidenced by a written instrument, dated and signed by the member.

(c) An assignee who becomes a member:

(1) has, to the extent assigned, the rights and powers and is subject to the restrictions and liabilities of a member under the articles of organization, any operating agreement, and this article; and

(2) is liable for any obligations of the member's assignor for unpaid contributions under IC 23–18–5–1 or for any wrongful distributions under IC 23–18–5–7.

However, the assignee is not obligated for liabilities of which the assignee had no knowledge at the time the assignee became a member and that could not be ascertained from a written operating agreement.

(d) Whether or not an assignee of an interest becomes a member, the assignor is not released from the assignor's liability to the limited liability company for unpaid contributions under IC 23–18–5–1 or for any wrongful distributions under IC 23–18–5–7 that are solely a result of the assignment.

(e) Unless otherwise provided in a written operating agreement, a member who assigns the member's entire interest in the limited liability company ceases to be a member or to have the power to exercise any rights of a member when an assignee of the member's interest becomes a member with respect to the assigned interest.

As added by P.L. 8–1993, SEC. 301. Amended by P.L. 269–1999, SEC. 9.

IC 23–18–6–4.1 Assignee membership; companies formed after June 30, 1999

Sec. 4.1.(a) A limited liability company formed under this article after June 30, 1999, is governed by this section.

(b) Except as otherwise provided in a written operating agreement, if a limited liability company has at least two (2) members, an assignee of an interest may become a member only if the other members unanimously consent. The consent of a member may be evidenced in any manner specified in writing in an operating agreement, but in the absence of a specification, consent must be evidenced by a written instrument, dated and signed by the member. If a limited liability company has one (1) member, an assignee of an interest may become a member in accordance with the terms of an agreement between the assignor and the assignee.

(c) An assignee who becomes a member:

(1) has, to the extent assigned, the rights and powers and is subject to the restrictions and liabilities of a member under the articles of organization, any operating agreement, and this article; and

(2) is liable for any obligations of the member's assignor for unpaid contributions under IC 23–18–5–1 or for any wrongful distributions under IC 23–18–5–7.

However, the assignee is not obligated for liabilities of which the assignee had no knowledge at the time the assignee became a member and that could not be ascertained from a written operating agreement.

(d) Whether or not an assignee of an interest becomes a member, the assignor is not released from the assignor's liability to the limited liability company for unpaid contributions under IC 23–18–5–1 or for any wrongful distributions under IC 23–18–5–7 that are solely a result of the assignment.

(e) Unless otherwise provided in a written operating agreement, a member who assigns the member's entire interest in the limited liability company ceases to be a member or to have the power to exercise any rights of a member.

As added by P.L. 269–1999, SEC. 10.

IC 23–18–6–5 Cessation of membership

Sec. 5.(a) A person ceases to be a member of a limited liability company upon the occurrence of any of the following events:

(1) The person withdraws from the limited liability company as provided in section 6 of this chapter.

(2) The person ceases to be a member as provided in section 4(e) or 4.1(e) of this chapter.

(3) The person is removed as a member:

(A) in accordance with the operating agreement; or

(B) unless otherwise provided in a written operating agreement, by the affirmative vote, approval, or consent of a majority in interest of the members after the member has assigned the member's entire interest in the limited liability company.

(4) Unless otherwise provided in a written operating agreement or with the written consent of all other members, in the case of a member who is an individual, the individual's death.

(5) Unless otherwise provided in a written operating agreement or with the written consent of all other members, in the case of a member who is acting as a member by virtue of being a trustee of a trust, the termination of the trust, but not merely the substitution of a new trustee.

(6) Unless otherwise provided in a written operating agreement or with the written consent of all other members, in the case of a member that is a partnership, limited partnership, or another limited liability company, the dissolution and commencement of winding up of the partnership, limited partnership, or limited liability company.

(7) Unless otherwise provided in a written operating agreement or with the written consent of all other members, in the case of a member that is a corporation, the dissolution of the corporation.

(8) Unless otherwise provided in a written operating agreement or with the written consent of all other members, in the case of a member that is an estate, the distribution by the fiduciary of the estate's entire interest in the limited liability company.

(b) A written operating agreement may provide for other events that result in a person ceasing to be a member of the limited liability company, including insolvency, bankruptcy, and adjudicated incompetency.

As added by P.L. 8–1993, SEC. 301. Amended by P.L. 269–1999, SEC. 11.

IC 23–18–6–6 Withdrawal of member; companies existing on or before June 30, 1999

Sec. 6.(a) Unless otherwise provided in a written operating agreement, a limited liability company existing under this article on or before June 30, 1999, is governed by this section.

(b) Unless a written operating agreement provides that a member does not have the power to withdraw by voluntary act from a limited liability company, the member may do so at any time by giving thirty (30) days written notice to the other members or other notice required under the operating agreement. If the member has the power to withdraw but the withdrawal is a breach of the operating agreement, or the withdrawal occurs as a result of otherwise wrongful conduct of the member, the limited liability company may recover from the withdrawing member damages for breach of the operating agreement, including the reasonable cost of obtaining the replacement of services that the withdrawn member was obligated to perform. The limited liability company may offset the damages against amounts otherwise distributable to the withdrawn member, in addition to pursuing any remedies provided for in the operating agreement or available under applicable law.

(c) Unless otherwise provided in a written operating agreement, in the case of a limited liability company for a definite term or particular undertaking, a withdrawal by a member before the expiration of the term is a breach of the operating agreement.

As added by P.L. 8–1993, SEC. 301. Amended by P.L. 269–1999, SEC. 12.

IC 23–18–6–6.1 Withdrawal of member; companies formed after June 30, 1999

Sec. 6.1.(a) A limited liability company formed under this article after June 30, 1999, is governed by this section.

(b) Unless otherwise provided in a written operating agreement, a member may not withdraw from a limited liability company before the dissolution and winding up of the limited liability company. A member may withdraw from a limited liability company only at the time or upon the occurrence of events specified in the operating agreement and in accordance with the operating agreement.

As added by P.L. 269–1999, SEC. 13.

IC 23–18–6–7 Judgment creditors of members; rights

Sec. 7.(a) On application to a court with jurisdiction by a judgment creditor of a member, the court may charge the interest of the member in the limited liability company with the payment of the unsatisfied amount of the judgment with interest.

(b) To the extent the court charges under subsection (a), the judgment creditor has only the rights of an assignee of the member's interest in the limited liability company.

(c) This article does not deprive a member of the benefit of any exemption laws applicable to the member's interest in the limited liability company.

As added by P.L. 8–1993, SEC. 301.

DELAWARE GEN. CORPORATION LAW CHAPTERS 1–2 (EXCERPT)

D. CHAPTER 1. GENERAL CORPORATION LAW

4. Subchapter I. Formation

§ 101 Incorporators; how corporation formed; purposes.

(a) Any person, partnership, association or corporation, singly or jointly with others, and without regard to such person's or entity's residence, domicile or state of incorporation, may incorporate or organize a corporation under this chapter by filing with the Division of Corporations in the Department of State a certificate of incorporation which shall be executed, acknowledged and filed in accordance with § 103 of this title.

(b) A corporation may be incorporated or organized under this chapter to conduct or promote any lawful business or purposes, except as may otherwise be provided by the Constitution or other law of this State.

(c) Corporations for constructing, maintaining and operating public utilities, whether in or outside of this State, may be organized under this chapter, but corporations for constructing, maintaining and operating public utilities within this State shall be subject to, in addition to this chapter, the special provisions and requirements of Title 26 applicable to such corporations.

8 Del. C. 1953, § 101; 56 Del. Laws, c. 50; 70 Del. Laws, c. 186, § 1; 70 Del. Laws, c. 587, § 1; 71 Del. Laws, c. 339, § 1.;

§ 102 Contents of certificate of incorporation.

(a) The certificate of incorporation shall set forth:

(1) The name of the corporation, which (i) shall contain 1 of the words "association," "company," "corporation," "club," "foundation," "fund," "incorporated," "institute," "society," "union," "syndicate," or "limited," (or abbreviations thereof, with or without punctuation), or words (or abbreviations thereof, with or without punctuation) of like import of foreign countries or jurisdictions (provided they are written in roman characters or letters); provided, however, that the Division of Corporations in the Department of State may waive such requirement (unless it determines that such name is, or might otherwise appear to be, that of a natural person) if such corporation executes, acknowledges and files with the Secretary of State in accordance with § 103 of this title a certificate stating that its total assets, as defined in § 503(i) of this title, are not less than $10,000,000, or, in the sole discretion of the Division of Corporations in the Department of State, if the corporation is both a nonprofit nonstock corporation and an association of professionals, (ii) shall be such as to distinguish it upon the records in the office of the Division of Corporations in the Department of State from the names that are reserved on such records and from the names on such records of each other corporation, partnership, limited partnership, limited liability company or statutory trust organized or registered as a domestic or foreign corporation, partnership, limited partnership, limited liability company or statutory trust under the laws of this State, except with the written consent of the person who has reserved such name or such other foreign corporation or domestic or foreign partnership, limited partnership, limited liability company or statutory trust, executed, acknowledged and filed with the Secretary of State in accordance with § 103 of this title, or except that, without prejudicing any rights of the person who has reserved such name or such other foreign corporation or domestic or foreign partnership, limited partnership, limited liability company or statutory trust, the Division of Corporations in the Department of State may waive such requirement if the corporation demonstrates to the satisfaction of the Secretary of State that the corporation or a predecessor entity previously has made substantial use of such name or a substantially similar name, that the corporation has made reasonable efforts to secure such written consent, and that such waiver is in the interest of the State, (iii) except as permitted by § 395 of this title, shall not contain the word "trust," and (iv) shall not contain the word "bank," or any variation thereof, except for the name of a bank reporting to and under the supervision of the State Bank Commissioner of this State or a subsidiary of a bank or savings association (as those terms are defined in the Federal Deposit Insurance Act, as

amended, at 12 U.S.C. § 1813), or a corporation regulated under the Bank Holding Company Act of 1956, as amended, 12 U.S.C. § 1841 et seq., or the Home Owners' Loan Act, as amended, 12 U.S.C. § 1461 et seq.; provided, however, that this section shall not be construed to prevent the use of the word "bank," or any variation thereof, in a context clearly not purporting to refer to a banking business or otherwise likely to mislead the public about the nature of the business of the corporation or to lead to a pattern and practice of abuse that might cause harm to the interests of the public or the State as determined by the Division of Corporations in the Department of State;

(2) The address (which shall be stated in accordance with § 131(c) of this title) of the corporation's registered office in this State, and the name of its registered agent at such address;

(3) The nature of the business or purposes to be conducted or promoted. It shall be sufficient to state, either alone or with other businesses or purposes, that the purpose of the corporation is to engage in any lawful act or activity for which corporations may be organized under the General Corporation Law of Delaware, and by such statement all lawful acts and activities shall be within the purposes of the corporation, except for express limitations, if any;

(4) If the corporation is to be authorized to issue only 1 class of stock, the total number of shares of stock which the corporation shall have authority to issue and the par value of each of such shares, or a statement that all such shares are to be without par value. If the corporation is to be authorized to issue more than 1 class of stock, the certificate of incorporation shall set forth the total number of shares of all classes of stock which the corporation shall have authority to issue and the number of shares of each class and shall specify each class the shares of which are to be without par value and each class the shares of which are to have par value and the par value of the shares of each such class. The certificate of incorporation shall also set forth a statement of the designations and the powers, preferences and rights, and the qualifications, limitations or restrictions thereof, which are permitted by § 151 of this title in respect of any class or classes of stock or any series of any class of stock of the corporation and the fixing of which by the certificate of incorporation is desired, and an express grant of such authority as it may then be desired to grant to the board of directors to fix by resolution or resolutions any thereof that may be desired but which shall not be fixed by the certificate of incorporation. The foregoing provisions of this paragraph shall not apply to nonstock corporations. In the case of nonstock corporations, the fact that they are not authorized to issue capital stock shall be stated in the certificate of incorporation. The conditions of membership, or other criteria for identifying members, of nonstock corporations shall likewise be stated in the certificate of incorporation or the bylaws. Nonstock corporations

shall have members, but failure to have members shall not affect otherwise valid corporate acts or work a forfeiture or dissolution of the corporation. Nonstock corporations may provide for classes or groups of members having relative rights, powers and duties, and may make provision for the future creation of additional classes or groups of members having such relative rights, powers and duties as may from time to time be established, including rights, powers and duties senior to existing classes and groups of members. Except as otherwise provided in this chapter, nonstock corporations may also provide that any member or class or group of members shall have full, limited, or no voting rights or powers, including that any member or class or group of members shall have the right to vote on a specified transaction even if that member or class or group of members does not have the right to vote for the election of the members of the governing body of the corporation. Voting by members of a nonstock corporation may be on a per capita, number, financial interest, class, group, or any other basis set forth. The provisions referred to in the 3 preceding sentences may be set forth in the certificate of incorporation or the bylaws. If neither the certificate of incorporation nor the bylaws of a nonstock corporation state the conditions of membership, or other criteria for identifying members, the members of the corporation shall be deemed to be those entitled to vote for the election of the members of the governing body pursuant to the certificate of incorporation or bylaws of such corporation or otherwise until thereafter otherwise provided by the certificate of incorporation or the bylaws;

(5) The name and mailing address of the incorporator or incorporators;

(6) If the powers of the incorporator or incorporators are to terminate upon the filing of the certificate of incorporation, the names and mailing addresses of the persons who are to serve as directors until the first annual meeting of stockholders or until their successors are elected and qualify.

(b) In addition to the matters required to be set forth in the certificate of incorporation by subsection (a) of this section, the certificate of incorporation may also contain any or all of the following matters:

(1) Any provision for the management of the business and for the conduct of the affairs of the corporation, and any provision creating, defining, limiting and regulating the powers of the corporation, the directors, and the stockholders, or any class of the stockholders, or the governing body, members, or any class or group of members of a nonstock corporation; if such provisions are not contrary to the laws of this State. Any provision which is required or permitted by any section of this chapter to be stated in the bylaws may instead be stated in the certificate of incorporation;

(2) The following provisions, in haec verba, (i), for a corporation other than a nonstock corporation, viz:

"Whenever a compromise or arrangement is proposed between this corporation and its creditors or any class of them and/or between this corporation and its stockholders or any class of them, any court of equitable jurisdiction within the State of Delaware may, on the application in a summary way of this corporation or of any creditor or stockholder thereof or on the application of any receiver or receivers appointed for this corporation under § 291 of Title 8 of the Delaware Code or on the application of trustees in dissolution or of any receiver or receivers appointed for this corporation under § 279 of Title 8 of the Delaware Code order a meeting of the creditors or class of creditors, and/or of the stockholders or class of stockholders of this corporation, as the case may be, to be summoned in such manner as the said court directs. If a majority in number representing three fourths in value of the creditors or class of creditors, and/or of the stockholders or class of stockholders of this corporation, as the case may be, agree to any compromise or arrangement and to any reorganization of this corporation as consequence of such compromise or arrangement, the said compromise or arrangement and the said reorganization shall, if sanctioned by the court to which the said application has been made, be binding on all the creditors or class of creditors, and/or on all the stockholders or class of stockholders, of this corporation, as the case may be, and also on this corporation"; or

(ii), for a nonstock corporation, viz:

"Whenever a compromise or arrangement is proposed between this corporation and its creditors or any class of them and/or between this corporation and its members or any class of them, any court of equitable jurisdiction within the State of Delaware may, on the application in a summary way of this corporation or of any creditor or member thereof or on the application of any receiver or receivers appointed for this corporation under § 291 of Title 8 of the Delaware Code or on the application of trustees in dissolution or of any receiver or receivers appointed for this corporation under § 279 of Title 8 of the Delaware Code order a meeting of the creditors or class of creditors, and/or of the members or class of members of this corporation, as the case may be, to be summoned in such manner as the said court directs. If a majority in number representing three fourths in value of the creditors or class of creditors, and/or of the members or class of members of this corporation, as the case may be, agree to any compromise or arrangement and to any reorganization of this corporation as consequence of such compromise or arrangement, the said compromise or arrangement and the said reorganization shall, if sanctioned by the court to which the said application has been made, be binding on all the creditors or class of creditors, and/or on all the members or class of members, of this corporation, as the case may be, and also on this corporation";

(3) Such provisions as may be desired granting to the holders of the stock of the corporation, or the holders of any class or series of a class thereof, the preemptive right to subscribe to any or all additional issues of stock of the corporation of any or all classes or series thereof, or to any securities of the corporation convertible into such stock. No stockholder shall have any preemptive right to subscribe to an additional issue of stock or to any security convertible into such stock unless, and except to the extent that, such right is expressly granted to such stockholder in the certificate of incorporation. All such rights in existence on July 3, 1967, shall remain in existence unaffected by this paragraph unless and until changed or terminated by appropriate action which expressly provides for the change or termination;

(4) Provisions requiring for any corporate action, the vote of a larger portion of the stock or of any class or series thereof, or of any other securities having voting power, or a larger number of the directors, than is required by this chapter;

(5) A provision limiting the duration of the corporation's existence to a specified date; otherwise, the corporation shall have perpetual existence;

(6) A provision imposing personal liability for the debts of the corporation on its stockholders to a specified extent and upon specified conditions; otherwise, the stockholders of a corporation shall not be personally liable for the payment of the corporation's debts except as they may be liable by reason of their own conduct or acts;

(7) A provision eliminating or limiting the personal liability of a director to the corporation or its stockholders for monetary damages for breach of fiduciary duty as a director, provided that such provision shall not eliminate or limit the liability of a director: (i) For any breach of the director's duty of loyalty to the corporation or its stockholders; (ii) for acts or omissions not in good faith or which involve intentional misconduct or a knowing violation of law; (iii) under § 174 of this title; or (iv) for any transaction from which the director derived an improper personal benefit. No such provision shall eliminate or limit the liability of a director for any act or omission occurring prior to the date when such provision becomes effective. All references in this paragraph to a director shall also be deemed to refer to such other person or persons, if any, who, pursuant to a provision of the certificate of incorporation in accordance with § 141(a) of this title, exercise or perform any of the powers or duties otherwise conferred or imposed upon the board of directors by this title.

(c) It shall not be necessary to set forth in the certificate of incorporation any of the powers conferred on corporations by this chapter.

(d) Except for provisions included pursuant to paragraphs (a)(1), (a)(2), (a)(5), (a)(6), (b)(2), (b)(5), (b)(7) of this section, and provisions included pursuant to paragraph (a)(4) of this section specifying the classes, number of shares, and par value of shares a corporation other than a nonstock corporation is authorized to issue, any provision of the certificate of incorporation may be made dependent upon facts ascertainable outside such instrument, provided that the manner in which such facts shall operate upon the provision is clearly and explicitly set forth therein. The term "facts," as used in this subsection, includes, but is not limited to, the occurrence of any event, including a determination or action by any person or body, including the corporation.

(e) The exclusive right to the use of a name that is available for use by a domestic or foreign corporation may be reserved by or on behalf of:

(1) Any person intending to incorporate or organize a corporation with that name under this chapter or contemplating such incorporation or organization;

(2) Any domestic corporation or any foreign corporation qualified to do business in the State of Delaware, in either case, intending to change its name or contemplating such a change;

(3) Any foreign corporation intending to qualify to do business in the State of Delaware and adopt that name or contemplating such qualification and adoption; and

(4) Any person intending to organize a foreign corporation and have it qualify to do business in the State of Delaware and adopt that name or contemplating such organization, qualification and adoption.

The reservation of a specified name may be made by filing with the Secretary of State an application, executed by the applicant, certifying that the reservation is made by or on behalf of a domestic corporation, foreign corporation or other person described in paragraphs (e)(1)–(4) of this section above, and specifying the name to be reserved and the name and address of the applicant. If the Secretary of State finds that the name is available for use by a domestic or foreign corporation, the Secretary shall reserve the name for the use of the applicant for a period of 120 days. The same applicant may renew for successive 120-day periods a reservation of a specified name by filing with the Secretary of State, prior to the expiration of such reservation (or renewal thereof), an application for renewal of such reservation, executed by the applicant, certifying that the reservation is renewed by or on behalf of a domestic corporation, foreign corporation or other person described in paragraphs (e)(1)–(4) of this section above and specifying the name reservation to be renewed and the name and address of the applicant. The right to the exclusive use of a reserved name may be transferred to any other person by filing in the office of the Secretary of State a notice of the transfer, executed by the applicant for whom the name was reserved, specifying the name reservation to be transferred and the name and address of the transferee. The reservation of a specified name may be cancelled by filing with the Secretary of State a notice of cancellation, executed by the applicant or transferee, specifying the name reservation to be cancelled and the name and address of the applicant or transferee. Unless the Secretary of State finds that any application, application for renewal, notice of transfer, or notice of cancellation filed with the Secretary of State as required by this subsection does not conform to law, upon receipt of all filing fees required by law the Secretary of State shall prepare and return to the person who filed such instrument a copy of the filed instrument with a notation thereon of the action taken by the Secretary of State. A fee as set forth in § 391 of this title shall be paid at the time of the reservation of any name, at the time of the renewal of any such reservation and at the time of the filing of a notice of the transfer or cancellation of any such reservation.

(f) The certificate of incorporation may not contain any provision that would impose liability on a stockholder for the attorneys' fees or expenses of the corporation or any other party in connection with an internal corporate claim, as defined in § 115 of this title.

8 Del. C. 1953, § 102; 56 Del. Laws, c. 50; 57 Del. Laws, c. 148, § 1; 65 Del. Laws, c. 127, § 1; 65 Del. Laws, c. 289, §§ 1, 2; 66 Del. Laws, c. 136, § 1; 66 Del. Laws, c. 352, § 1; 67 Del. Laws, c. 376, § 1; 69 Del. Laws, c. 61, § 1; 70 Del. Laws, c. 79, §§ 1–3; 71 Del. Laws, c. 120, § 1; 71 Del. Laws, c. 339, § 2; 72 Del. Laws, c. 123, § 1; 72 Del. Laws, c. 343, § 1; 73 Del. Laws, c. 82, § 1; 73 Del. Laws, c. 329, § 43; 74 Del. Laws, c. 326, § 1; 75 Del. Laws, c. 306, §§ 1, 2; 77 Del. Laws, c. 253, §§ 1–7; 78 Del. Laws, c. 96, §§ 1–3; 80 Del. Laws, c. 40, §§ 1, 2.;

§ 103 Execution, acknowledgment, filing, recording and effective date of original certificate of incorporation and other instruments; exceptions.

(a) Whenever any instrument is to be filed with the Secretary of State or in accordance with this section or chapter, such instrument shall be executed as follows:

(1) The certificate of incorporation, and any other instrument to be filed before the election of the initial board of directors if the initial directors were not named in the certificate of incorporation, shall be signed by the incorporator or incorporators (or, in the case of any such other instrument, such incorporator's or incorporators' successors and assigns). If any incorporator is not available then any such other instrument may be signed, with the same effect as if such incorporator had signed it, by any person for whom or on whose behalf such incorporator, in executing the certificate of incorporation, was acting directly or indirectly as employee or agent, provided that such other instrument shall state that such incorporator is not available and the reason therefor, that such incorporator in executing the certificate of incorporation was acting directly or indirectly as employee or agent for or on behalf of such person,

and that such person's signature on such instrument is otherwise authorized and not wrongful.

(2) All other instruments shall be signed:

a. By any authorized officer of the corporation; or

b. If it shall appear from the instrument that there are no such officers, then by a majority of the directors or by such directors as may be designated by the board; or

c. If it shall appear from the instrument that there are no such officers or directors, then by the holders of record, or such of them as may be designated by the holders of record, of a majority of all outstanding shares of stock; or

d. By the holders of record of all outstanding shares of stock.

(b) Whenever this chapter requires any instrument to be acknowledged, such requirement is satisfied by either:

(1) The formal acknowledgment by the person or 1 of the persons signing the instrument that it is such person's act and deed or the act and deed of the corporation, and that the facts stated therein are true. Such acknowledgment shall be made before a person who is authorized by the law of the place of execution to take acknowledgments of deeds. If such person has a seal of office such person shall affix it to the instrument.

(2) The signature, without more, of the person or persons signing the instrument, in which case such signature or signatures shall constitute the affirmation or acknowledgment of the signatory, under penalties of perjury, that the instrument is such person's act and deed or the act and deed of the corporation, and that the facts stated therein are true.

(c) Whenever any instrument is to be filed with the Secretary of State or in accordance with this section or chapter, such requirement means that:

(1) The signed instrument shall be delivered to the office of the Secretary of State;

(2) All taxes and fees authorized by law to be collected by the Secretary of State in connection with the filing of the instrument shall be tendered to the Secretary of State; and

(3) Upon delivery of the instrument, the Secretary of State shall record the date and time of its delivery. Upon such delivery and tender of the required taxes and fees, the Secretary of State shall certify that the instrument has been filed in the Secretary of State's office by endorsing upon the signed instrument the word "Filed", and the date and time of its filing. This endorsement is the "filing date" of the instrument, and is conclusive of the date and time of its filing in the absence of actual fraud. The Secretary of State shall file and index the endorsed instrument. Except

as provided in paragraph (c)(4) of this section and in subsection (i) of this section, such filing date of an instrument shall be the date and time of delivery of the instrument.

(4) Upon request made upon or prior to delivery, the Secretary of State may, to the extent deemed practicable, establish as the filing date of an instrument a date and time after its delivery. If the Secretary of State refuses to file any instrument due to an error, omission or other imperfection, the Secretary of State may hold such instrument in suspension, and in such event, upon delivery of a replacement instrument in proper form for filing and tender of the required taxes and fees within 5 business days after notice of such suspension is given to the filer, the Secretary of State shall establish as the filing date of such instrument the date and time that would have been the filing date of the rejected instrument had it been accepted for filing. The Secretary of State shall not issue a certificate of good standing with respect to any corporation with an instrument held in suspension pursuant to this subsection. The Secretary of State may establish as the filing date of an instrument the date and time at which information from such instrument is entered pursuant to paragraph (c)(8) of this section if such instrument is delivered on the same date and within 4 hours after such information is entered.

(5) The Secretary of State, acting as agent for the recorders of each of the counties, shall collect and deposit in a separate account established exclusively for that purpose a county assessment fee with respect to each filed instrument and shall thereafter weekly remit from such account to the recorder of each of the said counties the amount or amounts of such fees as provided for in paragraph (c)(6) of this section or as elsewhere provided by law. Said fees shall be for the purposes of defraying certain costs incurred by the counties in merging the information and images of such filed documents with the document information systems of each of the recorder's offices in the counties and in retrieving, maintaining and displaying such information and images in the offices of the recorders and at remote locations in each of such counties. In consideration for its acting as the agent for the recorders with respect to the collection and payment of the county assessment fees, the Secretary of State shall retain and pay over to the General Fund of the State an administrative charge of 1 percent of the total fees collected.

(6) The assessment fee to the counties shall be $24 for each 1-page instrument filed with the Secretary of State in accordance with this section and $9.00 for each additional page for instruments with more than 1 page. The recorder's office to receive the assessment fee shall be the recorder's office in the county in which the corporation's registered office in this State is, or is to be, located, except that an assessment fee shall not be charged for either a certificate of dissolution qualifying for treatment under

§ 391(a)(5)b. of this title or a document filed in accordance with subchapter XVI of this chapter.

(7) The Secretary of State, acting as agent, shall collect and deposit in a separate account established exclusively for that purpose a courthouse municipality fee with respect to each filed instrument and shall thereafter monthly remit funds from such account to the treasuries of the municipalities designated in § 301 of Title 10. Said fees shall be for the purposes of defraying certain costs incurred by such municipalities in hosting the primary locations for the Delaware courts. The fee to such municipalities shall be $20 for each instrument filed with the Secretary of State in accordance with this section. The municipality to receive the fee shall be the municipality designated in § 301 of Title 10 in the county in which the corporation's registered office in this State is, or is to be, located, except that a fee shall not be charged for a certificate of dissolution qualifying for treatment under § 391(a)(5)b. of this title, a resignation of agent without appointment of a successor under § 136 of this title, or a document filed in accordance with subchapter XVI of this chapter.

(8) The Secretary of State shall cause to be entered such information from each instrument as the Secretary of State deems appropriate into the Delaware Corporation Information System or any system which is a successor thereto in the office of the Secretary of State, and such information and a copy of each such instrument shall be permanently maintained as a public record on a suitable medium. The Secretary of State is authorized to grant direct access to such system to registered agents subject to the execution of an operating agreement between the Secretary of State and such registered agent. Any registered agent granted such access shall demonstrate the existence of policies to ensure that information entered into the system accurately reflects the content of instruments in the possession of the registered agent at the time of entry.

(d) Any instrument filed in accordance with subsection (c) of this section shall be effective upon its filing date. Any instrument may provide that it is not to become effective until a specified time subsequent to the time it is filed, but such time shall not be later than a time on the ninetieth day after the date of its filing. If any instrument filed in accordance with subsection (c) of this section provides for a future effective date or time and if the transaction is terminated or its terms are amended to change the future effective date or time prior to the future effective date or time, the instrument shall be terminated or amended by the filing, prior to the future effective date or time set forth in such instrument, of a certificate of termination or amendment of the original instrument, executed in accordance with subsection (a) of this section, which shall identify the instrument which has been terminated or amended and shall state that the instrument has been terminated or the manner in which it has been amended.

(e) If another section of this chapter specifically prescribes a manner of executing, acknowledging or filing a specified instrument or a time when such instrument shall become effective which differs from the corresponding provisions of this section, then such other section shall govern.

(f) Whenever any instrument authorized to be filed with the Secretary of State under any provision of this title, has been so filed and is an inaccurate record of the corporate action therein referred to, or was defectively or erroneously executed, sealed or acknowledged, the instrument may be corrected by filing with the Secretary of State a certificate of correction of the instrument which shall be executed, acknowledged and filed in accordance with this section. The certificate of correction shall specify the inaccuracy or defect to be corrected and shall set forth the portion of the instrument in corrected form. In lieu of filing a certificate of correction the instrument may be corrected by filing with the Secretary of State a corrected instrument which shall be executed, acknowledged and filed in accordance with this section. The corrected instrument shall be specifically designated as such in its heading, shall specify the inaccuracy or defect to be corrected, and shall set forth the entire instrument in corrected form. An instrument corrected in accordance with this section shall be effective as of the date the original instrument was filed, except as to those persons who are substantially and adversely affected by the correction and as to those persons the instrument as corrected shall be effective from the filing date.

(g) Notwithstanding that any instrument authorized to be filed with the Secretary of State under this title is when filed inaccurately, defectively or erroneously executed, sealed or acknowledged, or otherwise defective in any respect, the Secretary of State shall have no liability to any person for the preclearance for filing, the acceptance for filing or the filing and indexing of such instrument by the Secretary of State.

(h) Any signature on any instrument authorized to be filed with the Secretary of State under this title may be a facsimile, a conformed signature or an electronically transmitted signature.

(i)(1) If:

a. Together with the actual delivery of an instrument and tender of the required taxes and fees, there is delivered to the Secretary of State a separate affidavit (which in its heading shall be designated as an "affidavit of extraordinary condition") attesting, on the basis of personal knowledge of the affiant or a reliable source of knowledge identified in the affidavit, that an earlier effort to deliver such instrument and tender such taxes and fees was made in good faith, specifying the nature, date and time of such good faith effort and requesting that the Secretary of State establish such date and time as the filing date of such instrument; or

b. Upon the actual delivery of an instrument and tender of the required taxes and fees, the Secretary of State in the Secretary's discretion provides a written waiver of the requirement for such an affidavit stating that it appears to the Secretary of State that an earlier effort to deliver such instrument and tender such taxes and fees was made in good faith and specifying the date and time of such effort; and

c. The Secretary of State determines that an extraordinary condition existed at such date and time, that such earlier effort was unsuccessful as a result of the existence of such extraordinary condition, and that such actual delivery and tender were made within a reasonable period (not to exceed 2 business days) after the cessation of such extraordinary condition,

then the Secretary of State may establish such date and time as the filing date of such instrument. No fee shall be paid to the Secretary of State for receiving an affidavit of extraordinary condition.

(2) For purposes of this subsection, an "extraordinary condition" means: any emergency resulting from an attack on, invasion or occupation by foreign military forces of, or disaster, catastrophe, war or other armed conflict, revolution or insurrection, or rioting or civil commotion in, the United States or a locality in which the Secretary of State conducts its business or in which the good faith effort to deliver the instrument and tender the required taxes and fees is made, or the immediate threat of any of the foregoing; or any malfunction or outage of the electrical or telephone service to the Secretary of State's office, or weather or other condition in or about a locality in which the Secretary of State conducts its business, as a result of which the Secretary of State's office is not open for the purpose of the filing of instruments under this chapter or such filing cannot be effected without extraordinary effort. The Secretary of State may require such proof as it deems necessary to make the determination required under paragraph (i)(1)c. of this section, and any such determination shall be conclusive in the absence of actual fraud.

(3) If the Secretary of State establishes the filing date of an instrument pursuant to this subsection, the date and time of delivery of the affidavit of extraordinary condition or the date and time of the Secretary of State's written waiver of such affidavit shall be endorsed on such affidavit or waiver and such affidavit or waiver, so endorsed, shall be attached to the filed instrument to which it relates. Such filed instrument shall be effective as of the date and time established as the filing date by the Secretary of State pursuant to this subsection, except as to those persons who are substantially and adversely affected by such establishment and, as to those persons, the instrument shall be effective from the date and time endorsed on the affidavit of extraordinary condition or written waiver attached thereto.

(j) Notwithstanding any other provision of this chapter, it shall not be necessary for any corporation to amend its certificate of incorporation, or any other document, that has been filed prior to August 1, 2011, to comply with § 131(c) of this title, provided that any certificate or other document filed under this chapter on or after August 1, 2011, and changing the address of a registered office shall comply with § 131(c) of this title.

8 Del. C. 1953, § 103; 56 Del. Laws, c. 50; 56 Del. Laws, c. 186, § 1; 57 Del. Laws, c. 148, § 2; 58 Del. Laws, c. 235, § 1; 64 Del. Laws, c. 112, § 2; 66 Del. Laws, c. 352, §§ 1, 2; 67 Del. Laws, c. 190, §§ 1–3; 68 Del. Laws, c. 211, §§ 1–4; 69 Del. Laws, c. 221, § 1; 69 Del. Laws, c. 235, §§ 1–3; 70 Del. Laws, c. 79, § 4; 70 Del. Laws, c. 186, § 1; 70 Del. Laws, c. 349, § 1; 70 Del. Laws, c. 587, §§ 2–6; 71 Del. Laws, c. 339, §§ 3–5; 72 Del. Laws, c. 343, § 2; 73 Del. Laws, c. 298, § 1; 74 Del. Laws, c. 9, §§ 1–7; 74 Del. Laws, c. 118, § 1; 78 Del. Laws, c. 96, § 4; 79 Del. Laws, c. 122, §§ 1, 2; 79 Del. Laws, c. 327, § 1.;

§ 104 Certificate of incorporation; definition.

The term "certificate of incorporation," as used in this chapter, unless the context requires otherwise, includes not only the original certificate of incorporation filed to create a corporation but also all other certificates, agreements of merger or consolidation, plans of reorganization, or other instruments, howsoever designated, which are filed pursuant to § 102, §§ 133–136, § 151, §§ 241–243, § 245, §§ 251–258, §§ 263–264, § 267, § 303, §§ 311–313, or any other section of this title, and which have the effect of amending or supplementing in some respect a corporation's certificate of incorporation.

8 Del. C. 1953, § 104; 56 Del. Laws, c. 50; 67 Del. Laws, c. 376, § 2; 69 Del. Laws, c. 61, § 2; 77 Del. Laws, c. 290, § 1; 80 Del. Laws, c. 265, § 1.;

§ 105 Certificate of incorporation and other certificates; evidence.

A copy of a certificate of incorporation, or a restated certificate of incorporation, or of any other certificate which has been filed in the office of the Secretary of State as required by any provision of this title shall, when duly certified by the Secretary of State, be received in all courts, public offices and official bodies as prima facie evidence of:

(1) Due execution, acknowledgment and filing of the instrument;

(2) Observance and performance of all acts and conditions necessary to have been observed and performed precedent to the instrument becoming effective; and

(3) Any other facts required or permitted by law to be stated in the instrument.

8 Del. C. 1953, § 105; 56 Del. Laws, c. 50; 70 Del. Laws, c. 587, § 7.;

§ 106 Commencement of corporate existence.

Upon the filing with the Secretary of State of the certificate of incorporation, executed and acknowledged in accordance with § 103 of this title, the incorporator or incorporators who signed the certificate, and such incorporator's or incorporators' successors and assigns, shall, from the date of such filing, be and constitute a body corporate, by the name set forth in the certificate, subject to § 103(d) of this title and subject to dissolution or other termination of its existence as provided in this chapter.

8 Del. C. 1953, § 106; 56 Del. Laws, c. 50; 71 Del. Laws, c. 339, § 6.;

§ 107 Powers of incorporators.

If the persons who are to serve as directors until the first annual meeting of stockholders have not been named in the certificate of incorporation, the incorporator or incorporators, until the directors are elected, shall manage the affairs of the corporation and may do whatever is necessary and proper to perfect the organization of the corporation, including the adoption of the original bylaws of the corporation and the election of directors.

8 Del. C. 1953, § 107; 56 Del. Laws, c. 50.;

§ 108 Organization meeting of incorporators or directors named in certificate of incorporation.

(a) After the filing of the certificate of incorporation an organization meeting of the incorporator or incorporators, or of the board of directors if the initial directors were named in the certificate of incorporation, shall be held, either within or without this State, at the call of a majority of the incorporators or directors, as the case may be, for the purposes of adopting bylaws, electing directors (if the meeting is of the incorporators) to serve or hold office until the first annual meeting of stockholders or until their successors are elected and qualify, electing officers if the meeting is of the directors, doing any other or further acts to perfect the organization of the corporation, and transacting such other business as may come before the meeting.

(b) The persons calling the meeting shall give to each other incorporator or director, as the case may be, at least 2 days' written notice thereof by any usual means of communication, which notice shall state the time, place and purposes of the meeting as fixed by the persons calling it. Notice of the meeting need not be given to anyone who attends the meeting or who signs a waiver of notice either before or after the meeting.

(c) Any action permitted to be taken at the organization meeting of the incorporators or directors, as the case may be, may be taken without a meeting if each incorporator or director, where there is more than 1, or the sole incorporator or director where there is only 1, signs an instrument which states the action so taken.

(d) If any incorporator is not available to act, then any person for whom or on whose behalf the incorporator was acting directly or indirectly as employee or agent, may take any action that such incorporator would have been authorized to take under this section or § 107 of this title; provided that any instrument signed by such other person, or any record of the proceedings of a meeting in which such person participated, shall state that such incorporator is not available and the reason therefor, that such incorporator was acting directly or indirectly as employee or agent for or on behalf of such person, and that such person's signature on such instrument or participation in such meeting is otherwise authorized and not wrongful.

8 Del. C. 1953, § 108; 56 Del. Laws, c. 50; 79 Del. Laws, c. 327, § 2.;

§ 109 Bylaws.

(a) The original or other bylaws of a corporation may be adopted, amended or repealed by the incorporators, by the initial directors of a corporation other than a nonstock corporation or initial members of the governing body of a nonstock corporation if they were named in the certificate of incorporation, or, before a corporation other than a nonstock corporation has received any payment for any of its stock, by its board of directors. After a corporation other than a nonstock corporation has received any payment for any of its stock, the power to adopt, amend or repeal bylaws shall be in the stockholders entitled to vote. In the case of a nonstock corporation, the power to adopt, amend or repeal bylaws shall be in its members entitled to vote. Notwithstanding the foregoing, any corporation may, in its certificate of incorporation, confer the power to adopt, amend or repeal bylaws upon the directors or, in the case of a nonstock corporation, upon its governing body. The fact that such power has been so conferred upon the directors or governing body, as the case may be, shall not divest the stockholders or members of the power, nor limit their power to adopt, amend or repeal bylaws.

(b) The bylaws may contain any provision, not inconsistent with law or with the certificate of incorporation, relating to the business of the corporation, the conduct of its affairs, and its rights or powers or the rights or powers of its stockholders, directors, officers or employees. The bylaws may not contain any provision that would impose liability on a stockholder for the attorneys' fees or expenses of the corporation or any other party in connection with an internal corporate claim, as defined in § 115 of this title.

8 Del. C. 1953, § 109; 56 Del. Laws, c. 50; 59 Del. Laws, c. 437, § 1; 77 Del. Laws, c. 253, § 8; 80 Del. Laws, c. 40, § 3.;

§ 110 Emergency bylaws and other powers in emergency.

(a) The board of directors of any corporation may adopt emergency bylaws, subject to repeal or change by action of the stockholders, which shall notwithstanding any different provision elsewhere in this chapter or in Chapters 3 [repealed] and 5 [repealed] of Title 26, or in Chapter 7 of Title 5, or in the certificate of incorporation or bylaws, be operative during any emergency resulting from an attack on the United States or on a locality in which the corporation conducts its business or customarily holds meetings of its board of directors or its stockholders, or during any nuclear or atomic disaster, or during the existence of any catastrophe, or other similar emergency condition, as a result of which a quorum of the board of directors or a standing committee thereof cannot readily be convened for action. The emergency bylaws may make any provision that may be practical and necessary for the circumstances of the emergency, including provisions that:

(1) A meeting of the board of directors or a committee thereof may be called by any officer or director in such manner and under such conditions as shall be prescribed in the emergency bylaws;

(2) The director or directors in attendance at the meeting, or any greater number fixed by the emergency bylaws, shall constitute a quorum; and

(3) The officers or other persons designated on a list approved by the board of directors before the emergency, all in such order of priority and subject to such conditions and for such period of time (not longer than reasonably necessary after the termination of the emergency) as may be provided in the emergency bylaws or in the resolution approving the list, shall, to the extent required to provide a quorum at any meeting of the board of directors, be deemed directors for such meeting.

(b) The board of directors, either before or during any such emergency, may provide, and from time to time modify, lines of succession in the event that during such emergency any or all officers or agents of the corporation shall for any reason be rendered incapable of discharging their duties.

(c) The board of directors, either before or during any such emergency, may, effective in the emergency, change the head office or designate several alternative head offices or regional offices, or authorize the officers so to do.

(d) No officer, director or employee acting in accordance with any emergency bylaws shall be liable except for wilful misconduct.

(e) To the extent not inconsistent with any emergency bylaws so adopted, the bylaws of the corporation shall remain in effect during any emergency and upon its termination the emergency bylaws shall cease to be operative.

(f) Unless otherwise provided in emergency bylaws, notice of any meeting of the board of directors during such an emergency may be given only to such of the directors as it may be feasible to reach at the time and by such means as may be feasible at the time, including publication or radio.

(g) To the extent required to constitute a quorum at any meeting of the board of directors during such an emergency, the officers of the corporation who are present shall, unless otherwise provided in emergency bylaws, be deemed, in order of rank and within the same rank in order of seniority, directors for such meeting.

(h) Nothing contained in this section shall be deemed exclusive of any other provisions for emergency powers consistent with other sections of this title which have been or may be adopted by corporations created under this chapter.

8 Del. C. 1953, § 110; 56 Del. Laws, c. 50.;

. . .

§ 115 Forum selection provisions.

The certificate of incorporation or the bylaws may require, consistent with applicable jurisdictional requirements, that any or all internal corporate claims shall be brought solely and exclusively in any or all of the courts in this State, and no provision of the certificate of incorporation or the bylaws may prohibit bringing such claims in the courts of this State. "Internal corporate claims" means claims, including claims in the right of the corporation, (i) that are based upon a violation of a duty by a current or former director or officer or stockholder in such capacity, or (ii) as to which this title confers jurisdiction upon the Court of Chancery.

80 Del. Laws, c. 40, § 5.;

. . .

5. Subchapter IV. Directors and Officers

§ 141 Board of directors; powers; number, qualifications, terms and quorum; committees; classes of directors; nonstock corporations; reliance upon books; action without meeting; removal.

(a) The business and affairs of every corporation organized under this chapter shall be managed by or under the direction of a board of directors, except as may be otherwise provided in this chapter or in its certificate of incorporation. If any such provision is made in the certificate of incorporation, the powers and duties conferred or imposed upon the board of directors by this chapter shall be exercised or performed to such extent and by such person or persons as shall be provided in the certificate of incorporation.

(b) The board of directors of a corporation shall consist of 1 or more members, each of whom shall be a natural person. The number of directors shall be fixed by, or in the manner provided in, the bylaws, unless the certificate of incorporation fixes the number of directors, in which case a change in the number of directors shall be made only by amendment of the certificate. Directors need not be stockholders unless so required by the certificate of incorporation or the bylaws. The certificate of incorporation or bylaws may prescribe other qualifications for directors. Each director shall hold office until such director's successor is elected and qualified or until such director's earlier resignation or removal. Any director may resign at any time upon notice given in writing or by electronic transmission to the corporation. A resignation is effective when the resignation is delivered unless the resignation specifies a later effective date or an effective date determined upon the happening of an event or events. A resignation which is conditioned upon the director failing to receive a specified vote for reelection as a director may provide that it is irrevocable. A majority of the total number of directors shall constitute a quorum for the transaction of business unless the certificate of incorporation or the bylaws require a greater number. Unless the certificate of incorporation provides otherwise, the bylaws may provide that a number less than a majority shall constitute a quorum which in no case shall be less than 1/3 of the total number of directors. The vote of the majority of the directors present at a meeting at which a quorum is present shall be the act of the board of directors unless the certificate of incorporation or the bylaws shall require a vote of a greater number.

(c)(1) All corporations incorporated prior to July 1, 1996, shall be governed by this paragraph (c)(1) of this section, provided that any such corporation may by a resolution adopted by a majority of the whole board elect to be governed by paragraph (c)(2) of this section, in which case this paragraph (c)(1) of this section shall not apply to such corporation. All corporations incorporated on or after July 1, 1996, shall be governed by paragraph (c)(2) of this section. The board of directors may, by resolution passed by a majority of the whole board, designate 1 or more committees, each committee to consist of 1 or more of the directors of the corporation. The board may designate 1 or more directors as alternate members of any committee, who may replace any absent or disqualified member at any meeting of the committee. The bylaws may provide that in the absence or disqualification of a member of a committee, the member or members present at any meeting and not disqualified from voting, whether or not the member or members present constitute a quorum, may unanimously appoint another member of the board of directors to act at the meeting in the place of any such absent or disqualified member. Any such committee, to the extent provided in the resolution of the board of directors, or in the bylaws of the corporation, shall have and may exercise all the powers and authority of the board of directors in the management of the business and affairs of the corporation, and may authorize the seal of the corporation to be affixed to all papers which may require it; but no such committee shall have the power or authority in reference to amending the certificate of incorporation (except that a committee may, to the extent authorized in the resolution or resolutions providing for the issuance of shares of stock adopted by the board of directors as provided in § 151(a) of this title, fix the designations and any of the preferences or rights of such shares relating to dividends, redemption, dissolution, any distribution of assets of the corporation or the conversion into, or the exchange of such shares for, shares of any other class or classes or any other series of the same or any other class or classes of stock of the corporation or fix the number of shares of any series of stock or authorize the increase or decrease of the shares of any series), adopting an agreement of merger or consolidation under § 251, § 252, § 254, § 255, § 256, § 257, § 258, § 263 or § 264 of this title, recommending to the stockholders the sale, lease or exchange of all or substantially all of the corporation's property and assets, recommending to the stockholders a dissolution of the corporation or a revocation of a dissolution, or amending the bylaws of the corporation; and, unless the resolution, bylaws or certificate of incorporation expressly so provides, no such committee shall have the power or authority to declare a dividend, to authorize the issuance of stock or to adopt a certificate of ownership and merger pursuant to § 253 of this title.

(2) The board of directors may designate 1 or more committees, each committee to consist of 1 or more of the directors of the corporation. The board may designate 1 or more directors as alternate members of any committee, who may replace any absent or disqualified member at any meeting of the committee. The bylaws may provide that in the absence or disqualification of a member of a committee, the member or members present at any meeting and not disqualified from voting, whether or not such member or members constitute a quorum, may unanimously appoint another member of the board of directors to act at the meeting in the place of any such absent or disqualified member. Any such committee, to the extent provided in the resolution of the board of directors, or in the bylaws of the corporation, shall have and may exercise all the powers and authority of the board of directors in the management of the business and affairs of the corporation, and may authorize the seal of the corporation to be affixed to all papers which may require it; but no such committee shall have the power or authority in reference to the following matter: (i) approving or adopting, or recommending to the stockholders, any action or matter (other than the election or removal of directors) expressly required by this chapter to be submitted to stockholders for approval or (ii) adopting, amending or repealing any bylaw of the corporation.

(3) Unless otherwise provided in the certificate of incorporation, the bylaws or the resolution of the board of directors designating the committee, a committee may create 1 or more subcommittees, each subcommittee to consist of 1 or more members of the committee, and delegate to a subcommittee any or all of the powers and authority of the committee. Except for references to committees and members of

committees in subsection (c) of this section, every reference in this chapter to a committee of the board of directors or a member of a committee shall be deemed to include a reference to a subcommittee or member of a subcommittee.

(4) A majority of the directors then serving on a committee of the board of directors or on a subcommittee of a committee shall constitute a quorum for the transaction of business by the committee or subcommittee, unless the certificate of incorporation, the bylaws, a resolution of the board of directors or a resolution of a committee that created the subcommittee requires a greater or lesser number, provided that in no case shall a quorum be less than 1/3 of the directors then serving on the committee or subcommittee. The vote of the majority of the members of a committee or subcommittee present at a meeting at which a quorum is present shall be the act of the committee or subcommittee, unless the certificate of incorporation, the bylaws, a resolution of the board of directors or a resolution of a committee that created the subcommittee requires a greater number.

(d) The directors of any corporation organized under this chapter may, by the certificate of incorporation or by an initial bylaw, or by a bylaw adopted by a vote of the stockholders, be divided into 1, 2 or 3 classes; the term of office of those of the first class to expire at the first annual meeting held after such classification becomes effective; of the second class 1 year thereafter; of the third class 2 years thereafter; and at each annual election held after such classification becomes effective, directors shall be chosen for a full term, as the case may be, to succeed those whose terms expire. The certificate of incorporation or bylaw provision dividing the directors into classes may authorize the board of directors to assign members of the board already in office to such classes at the time such classification becomes effective. The certificate of incorporation may confer upon holders of any class or series of stock the right to elect 1 or more directors who shall serve for such term, and have such voting powers as shall be stated in the certificate of incorporation. The terms of office and voting powers of the directors elected separately by the holders of any class or series of stock may be greater than or less than those of any other director or class of directors. In addition, the certificate of incorporation may confer upon 1 or more directors, whether or not elected separately by the holders of any class or series of stock, voting powers greater than or less than those of other directors. Any such provision conferring greater or lesser voting power shall apply to voting in any committee, unless otherwise provided in the certificate of incorporation or bylaws. If the certificate of incorporation provides that 1 or more directors shall have more or less than 1 vote per director on any matter, every reference in this chapter to a majority or other proportion of the directors shall refer to a majority or other proportion of the votes of the directors.

(e) A member of the board of directors, or a member of any committee designated by the board of directors, shall, in the performance of such member's duties, be fully protected in relying in good faith upon the records of the corporation and upon such information, opinions, reports or statements presented to the corporation by any of the corporation's officers or employees, or committees of the board of directors, or by any other person as to matters the member reasonably believes are within such other person's professional or expert competence and who has been selected with reasonable care by or on behalf of the corporation.

(f) Unless otherwise restricted by the certificate of incorporation or bylaws, any action required or permitted to be taken at any meeting of the board of directors or of any committee thereof may be taken without a meeting if all members of the board or committee, as the case may be, consent thereto in writing, or by electronic transmission and the writing or writings or electronic transmission or transmissions are filed with the minutes of proceedings of the board, or committee. Such filing shall be in paper form if the minutes are maintained in paper form and shall be in electronic form if the minutes are maintained in electronic form. Any person (whether or not then a director) may provide, whether through instruction to an agent or otherwise, that a consent to action will be effective at a future time (including a time determined upon the happening of an event), no later than 60 days after such instruction is given or such provision is made and such consent shall be deemed to have been given for purposes of this subsection at such effective time so long as such person is then a director and did not revoke the consent prior to such time. Any such consent shall be revocable prior to its becoming effective.

(g) Unless otherwise restricted by the certificate of incorporation or bylaws, the board of directors of any corporation organized under this chapter may hold its meetings, and have an office or offices, outside of this State.

(h) Unless otherwise restricted by the certificate of incorporation or bylaws, the board of directors shall have the authority to fix the compensation of directors.

(i) Unless otherwise restricted by the certificate of incorporation or bylaws, members of the board of directors of any corporation, or any committee designated by the board, may participate in a meeting of such board, or committee by means of conference telephone or other communications equipment by means of which all persons participating in the meeting can hear each other, and participation in a meeting pursuant to this subsection shall constitute presence in person at the meeting.

(j) The certificate of incorporation of any nonstock corporation may provide that less than 1/3 of the members of the governing body may constitute a quorum thereof and may otherwise provide that the business and affairs of the corporation shall be managed in a manner different from that provided in this section. Except as may be otherwise provided by the certificate of incorporation, this section shall apply to such a corporation, and when so applied, all references to the board of directors, to members thereof, and to stockholders shall be deemed to refer to the governing body of the corporation, the members thereof and the members of the corporation, respectively; and all references to stock, capital stock, or shares thereof shall be deemed to refer to memberships of a nonprofit nonstock corporation and to membership interests of any other nonstock corporation.

(k) Any director or the entire board of directors may be removed, with or without cause, by the holders of a majority of the shares then entitled to vote at an election of directors, except as follows:

(1) Unless the certificate of incorporation otherwise provides, in the case of a corporation whose board is classified as provided in subsection (d) of this section, stockholders may effect such removal only for cause; or

(2) In the case of a corporation having cumulative voting, if less than the entire board is to be removed, no director may be removed without cause if the votes cast against such director's removal would be sufficient to elect such director if then cumulatively voted at an election of the entire board of directors, or, if there be classes of directors, at an election of the class of directors of which such director is a part.

Whenever the holders of any class or series are entitled to elect 1 or more directors by the certificate of incorporation, this subsection shall apply, in respect to the removal without cause of a director or directors so elected, to the vote of the holders of the outstanding shares of that class or series and not to the vote of the outstanding shares as a whole.

8 Del. C. 1953, § 141; 56 Del. Laws, c. 50; 56 Del. Laws, c. 186, § 3; 57 Del. Laws, c. 148, §§ 5, 6; 57 Del. Laws, c. 421, § 1; 59 Del. Laws, c. 437, §§ 2–5; 64 Del. Laws, c. 112, § 6; 65 Del. Laws, c. 127, § 3; 66 Del. Laws, c. 136, §§ 2, 3; 70 Del. Laws, c. 79, § 7; 70 Del. Laws, c. 186, § 1; 70 Del. Laws, c. 349, § 2; 71 Del. Laws, c. 339, §§ 11–13; 72 Del. Laws, c. 343, §§ 4–6; 73 Del. Laws, c. 298, § 2; 74 Del. Laws, c. 84, § 2; 74 Del. Laws, c. 326, § 2; 75 Del. Laws, c. 30, § 1; 75 Del. Laws, c. 306, §§ 3, 4; 76 Del. Laws, c. 145, § 1; 77 Del. Laws, c. 253, §§ 10–12; 79 Del. Laws, c. 327, § 3; 80 Del. Laws, c. 265, §§ 3–5.;

§ 142 Officers; titles, duties, selection, term; failure to elect; vacancies.

(a) Every corporation organized under this chapter shall have such officers with such titles and duties as shall be stated in the bylaws or in a resolution of the board of directors which is not inconsistent with the bylaws and as may be necessary to enable it to sign instruments and stock certificates which comply with §§ 103(a)(2) and 158 of this title. One of the officers shall have the duty to record the proceedings of the meetings of the stockholders and directors in a book to be kept for that purpose. Any number of offices may be held by the same person unless the certificate of incorporation or bylaws otherwise provide.

(b) Officers shall be chosen in such manner and shall hold their offices for such terms as are prescribed by the bylaws or determined by the board of directors or other governing body. Each officer shall hold office until such officer's successor is elected and qualified or until such officer's earlier resignation or removal. Any officer may resign at any time upon written notice to the corporation.

(c) The corporation may secure the fidelity of any or all of its officers or agents by bond or otherwise.

(d) A failure to elect officers shall not dissolve or otherwise affect the corporation.

(e) Any vacancy occurring in any office of the corporation by death, resignation, removal or otherwise, shall be filled as the bylaws provide. In the absence of such provision, the vacancy shall be filled by the board of directors or other governing body.

8 Del. C. 1953, § 142; 56 Del. Laws, c. 50; 56 Del. Laws, c. 186, § 4; 57 Del. Laws, c. 649, § 2; 59 Del. Laws, c. 437, § 6; 71 Del. Laws, c. 339, § 14.;

§ 143 Loans to employees and officers; guaranty of obligations of employees and officers.

Any corporation may lend money to, or guarantee any obligation of, or otherwise assist any officer or other employee of the corporation or of its subsidiary, including any officer or employee who is a director of the corporation or its subsidiary, whenever, in the judgment of the directors, such loan, guaranty or assistance may reasonably be expected to benefit the corporation. The loan, guaranty or other assistance may be with or without interest, and may be unsecured, or secured in such manner as the board of directors shall approve, including, without limitation, a pledge of shares of stock of the corporation. Nothing in this section contained shall be deemed to deny, limit or restrict the powers of guaranty or warranty of any corporation at common law or under any statute.

8 Del. C. 1953, § 143; 56 Del. Laws, c. 50.;

§ 144 Interested directors; quorum.

(a) No contract or transaction between a corporation and 1 or more of its directors or officers, or between a corporation and any other corporation, partnership, association, or other organization in which 1 or more of its directors or officers, are directors or officers, or have a financial interest, shall be void or voidable solely for this reason, or solely because the director or officer is present at or participates in the meeting of the board or committee which authorizes the contract or transaction, or solely because any such director's or officer's votes are counted for such purpose, if:

(1) The material facts as to the director's or officer's relationship or interest and as to the contract or transaction are disclosed or are known to the board of directors or the committee, and the board or committee in good faith authorizes the contract or transaction by the affirmative votes of a majority of the disinterested directors, even though the disinterested directors be less than a quorum; or

(2) The material facts as to the director's or officer's relationship or interest and as to the contract or transaction are disclosed or are known to the stockholders entitled to vote thereon, and the contract or transaction is specifically approved in good faith by vote of the stockholders; or

(3) The contract or transaction is fair as to the corporation as of the time it is authorized, approved or ratified, by the board of directors, a committee or the stockholders.

(b) Common or interested directors may be counted in determining the presence of a quorum at a meeting of the board of directors or of a committee which authorizes the contract or transaction.

8 Del. C. 1953, § 144; 56 Del. Laws, c. 50; 56 Del. Laws, c. 186, § 5; 57 Del. Laws, c. 148, § 7; 71 Del. Laws, c. 339, §§ 15–17; 77 Del. Laws, c. 253, §§ 13, 14.;

§ 145 Indemnification of officers, directors, employees and agents; insurance.

(a) A corporation shall have power to indemnify any person who was or is a party or is threatened to be made a party to any threatened, pending or completed action, suit or proceeding, whether civil, criminal, administrative or investigative (other than an action by or in the right of the corporation) by reason of the fact that the person is or was a director, officer, employee or agent of the corporation, or is or was serving at the request of the corporation as a director, officer, employee or agent of another corporation, partnership, joint venture, trust or other enterprise, against expenses (including attorneys' fees), judgments, fines and amounts paid in settlement actually and reasonably incurred by the person in connection with such action, suit or proceeding if the person acted in good faith and in a manner the person reasonably believed to be in or not opposed to the best interests of the corporation, and, with respect to any criminal action or proceeding, had no reasonable cause to believe the person's conduct was unlawful. The termination of any action, suit or proceeding by judgment, order, settlement, conviction, or upon a plea of nolo contendere or its equivalent, shall not, of itself, create a presumption that the person did not act in good faith and in a manner which the person reasonably believed to be in or not opposed to the best interests of the corporation, and, with respect to any criminal action or proceeding, had reasonable cause to believe that the person's conduct was unlawful.

(b) A corporation shall have power to indemnify any person who was or is a party or is threatened to be made a party to any threatened, pending or completed action or suit by or in the right of the corporation to procure a judgment in its favor by reason of the fact that the person is or was a director, officer, employee or agent of the corporation, or is or was serving at the request of the corporation as a director, officer, employee or agent of another corporation, partnership, joint venture, trust or other enterprise against expenses (including attorneys' fees) actually and reasonably incurred by the person in connection with the defense or settlement of such action or suit if the person acted in good faith and in a manner the person reasonably believed to be in or not opposed to the best interests of the corporation and except that no indemnification shall be made in respect of any claim, issue or matter as to which such person shall have been adjudged to be liable to the corporation unless and only to the extent that the Court of Chancery or the court in which such action or suit was brought shall determine upon application that, despite the adjudication of liability but in view of all the circumstances of the case, such person is fairly and reasonably entitled to indemnity for such expenses which the Court of Chancery or such other court shall deem proper.

(c) To the extent that a present or former director or officer of a corporation has been successful on the merits or otherwise in defense of any action, suit or proceeding referred to in subsections (a) and (b) of this section, or in defense of any claim, issue or matter therein, such person shall be indemnified against expenses (including attorneys' fees) actually and reasonably incurred by such person in connection therewith.

(d) Any indemnification under subsections (a) and (b) of this section (unless ordered by a court) shall be made by the corporation only as authorized in the specific case upon a determination that indemnification of the present or former director, officer, employee or agent is proper in the circumstances because the person has met the applicable standard of conduct set forth in subsections (a) and (b) of this section. Such determination shall be made, with respect to a person who is a director or officer of the corporation at the time of such determination:

(1) By a majority vote of the directors who are not parties to such action, suit or proceeding, even though less than a quorum; or

(2) By a committee of such directors designated by majority vote of such directors, even though less than a quorum; or

(3) If there are no such directors, or if such directors so direct, by independent legal counsel in a written opinion; or

(4) By the stockholders.

(e) Expenses (including attorneys' fees) incurred by an officer or director of the corporation in defending any civil, criminal, administrative or investigative action, suit or proceeding may be paid by the corporation in advance of the final disposition of such action, suit or proceeding upon receipt of an undertaking by or on behalf of such director or officer to repay such amount if it shall ultimately be determined that such person is not entitled to be indemnified by the corporation as authorized in this section. Such expenses (including attorneys' fees) incurred by former directors and officers or other employees and agents of the corporation or by persons serving at the request of the corporation as directors, officers, employees or agents of another corporation, partnership, joint venture, trust or other enterprise may be so paid upon such terms and conditions, if any, as the corporation deems appropriate.

(f) The indemnification and advancement of expenses provided by, or granted pursuant to, the other subsections of this section shall not be deemed exclusive of any other rights to which those seeking indemnification or advancement of expenses may be entitled under any bylaw, agreement, vote of stockholders or disinterested directors or otherwise, both as to action in such person's official capacity and as to action in another capacity while holding such office. A right to indemnification or to advancement of expenses arising under a provision of the certificate of incorporation or a bylaw shall not be eliminated or impaired by an amendment to the certificate of incorporation or the bylaws after the occurrence of the act or omission that is the subject of the civil, criminal, administrative or investigative action, suit or proceeding for which indemnification or advancement of expenses is sought, unless the provision in effect at the time of such act or omission explicitly authorizes such elimination or impairment after such action or omission has occurred.

(g) A corporation shall have power to purchase and maintain insurance on behalf of any person who is or was a director, officer, employee or agent of the corporation, or is or was serving at the request of the corporation as a director, officer, employee or agent of another corporation, partnership, joint venture, trust or other enterprise against any liability asserted against such person and incurred by such person in any such capacity, or arising out of such person's status as such, whether or not the corporation would have the power to indemnify such person against such liability under this section.

(h) For purposes of this section, references to "the corporation" shall include, in addition to the resulting corporation, any constituent corporation (including any constituent of a constituent) absorbed in a consolidation or merger which, if its separate existence had continued, would have had power and authority to indemnify its directors, officers, and employees or agents, so that any person who is or was a director, officer, employee or agent of such constituent corporation, or is or was serving at the request of such constituent corporation as a director, officer, employee or agent of another corporation, partnership, joint venture, trust or other enterprise, shall stand in the same position under this section with respect to the resulting or surviving corporation as such person would have with respect to such constituent corporation if its separate existence had continued.

(i) For purposes of this section, references to "other enterprises" shall include employee benefit plans; references to "fines" shall include any excise taxes assessed on a person with respect to any employee benefit plan; and references to "serving at the request of the corporation" shall include any service as a director, officer, employee or agent of the corporation which imposes duties on, or involves services by, such director, officer, employee or agent with respect to an employee benefit plan, its participants or beneficiaries; and a person who acted in good faith and in a manner such person reasonably believed to be in the interest of the participants and beneficiaries of an employee benefit plan shall be deemed to have acted in a manner "not opposed to the best interests of the corporation" as referred to in this section.

(j) The indemnification and advancement of expenses provided by, or granted pursuant to, this section shall, unless otherwise provided when authorized or ratified, continue as to a person who has ceased to be a director, officer, employee or agent and shall inure to the benefit of the heirs, executors and administrators of such a person.

(k) The Court of Chancery is hereby vested with exclusive jurisdiction to hear and determine all actions for advancement of expenses or indemnification brought under this section or under any bylaw, agreement, vote of stockholders or disinterested directors, or otherwise. The Court of Chancery may summarily determine a corporation's obligation to advance expenses (including attorneys' fees).

8 Del. C. 1953, § 145; 56 Del. Laws, c. 50; 56 Del. Laws, c. 186, § 6; 57 Del. Laws, c. 421, § 2; 59 Del. Laws, c. 437, § 7; 63 Del. Laws, c. 25, § 1; 64 Del. Laws, c. 112, § 7; 65 Del. Laws, c. 289, §§ 3–6; 67 Del. Laws, c. 376, § 3; 69 Del. Laws, c. 261, §§ 1, 2; 70 Del. Laws, c. 186, § 1; 71 Del. Laws, c. 120, §§ 3–11; 77 Del. Laws, c. 14, § 3; 77 Del. Laws, c. 290, §§ 5, 6; 78 Del. Laws, c. 96, § 6.;

§ 146 Submission of matters for stockholder vote.

A corporation may agree to submit a matter to a vote of its stockholders whether or not the board of directors determines at any time subsequent to approving such matter that such matter is no longer advisable and recommends that the stockholders reject or vote against the matter.

74 Del. Laws, c. 84, § 3.;

. . .

6. Subchapter VII. Meetings, Elections, Voting and Notice

§ 211 Meetings of stockholders.

(a)(1) Meetings of stockholders may be held at such place, either within or without this State as may be designated by or in the manner provided in the certificate of incorporation or bylaws, or if not so designated, as determined by the board of directors. If, pursuant to this paragraph or the certificate of incorporation or the bylaws of the corporation, the board of directors is authorized to determine the place of a meeting of stockholders, the board of directors may, in its sole discretion, determine that the meeting shall not be held at any place, but may instead be held solely by means of remote communication as authorized by paragraph (a)(2) of this section.

(2) If authorized by the board of directors in its sole discretion, and subject to such guidelines and procedures as the board of directors may adopt, stockholders and proxyholders not physically present at a meeting of stockholders may, by means of remote communication:

a. Participate in a meeting of stockholders; and

b. Be deemed present in person and vote at a meeting of stockholders, whether such meeting is to be held at a designated place or solely by means of remote communication, provided that (i) the corporation shall implement reasonable measures to verify that each person deemed present and permitted to vote at the meeting by means of remote communication is a stockholder or proxyholder, (ii) the corporation shall implement reasonable measures to provide such stockholders and proxyholders a reasonable opportunity to participate in the meeting and to vote on matters submitted to the stockholders, including an opportunity to read or hear the proceedings of the meeting substantially concurrently with such proceedings, and (iii) if any stockholder or proxyholder votes or takes other action at the meeting by means of remote communication, a record of such vote or other action shall be maintained by the corporation.

(b) Unless directors are elected by written consent in lieu of an annual meeting as permitted by this subsection, an annual meeting of stockholders shall be held for the election of directors on a date and at a time designated by or in the manner provided in the bylaws. Stockholders may, unless the certificate of incorporation otherwise provides, act by written consent to elect directors; provided, however, that, if such consent is less than unanimous, such action by written consent may be in lieu of holding an annual meeting only if all of the directorships to which directors could be elected at an annual meeting held at the effective time of such action are vacant and are filled by such action. Any other proper business may be transacted at the annual meeting.

(c) A failure to hold the annual meeting at the designated time or to elect a sufficient number of directors to conduct the business of the corporation shall not affect otherwise valid corporate acts or work a forfeiture or dissolution of the corporation except as may be otherwise specifically provided in this chapter. If the annual meeting for election of directors is not held on the date designated therefor or action by written consent to elect directors in lieu of an annual meeting has not been taken, the directors shall cause the meeting to be held as soon as is convenient. If there be a failure to hold the annual meeting or to take action by written consent to elect directors in lieu of an annual meeting for a period of 30 days after the date designated for the annual meeting, or if no date has been designated, for a period of 13 months after the latest to occur of the organization of the corporation, its last annual meeting or the last action by written consent to elect directors in lieu of an annual meeting, the Court of Chancery may summarily order a meeting to be held upon the application of any stockholder or director. The shares of stock represented at such meeting, either in person or by proxy, and entitled to vote thereat, shall constitute a quorum for the purpose of such meeting, notwithstanding any provision of the certificate of incorporation or bylaws to the contrary. The Court of Chancery may issue such orders as may be appropriate, including, without limitation, orders designating the time and place of such meeting, the record date or dates for determination of stockholders entitled to notice of the meeting and to vote thereat, and the form of notice of such meeting.

(d) Special meetings of the stockholders may be called by the board of directors or by such person or persons as may be authorized by the certificate of incorporation or by the bylaws.

(e) All elections of directors shall be by written ballot unless otherwise provided in the certificate of incorporation; if authorized by the board of directors, such requirement of a written ballot shall be satisfied by a ballot submitted by electronic transmission, provided that any such electronic transmission must either set forth or be submitted with information from which it can be determined that the electronic transmission was authorized by the stockholder or proxy holder.

8 Del. C. 1953, § 211; 56 Del. Laws, c. 50; 56 Del. Laws, c. 186, § 12; 63 Del. Laws, c. 25, § 4; 71 Del. Laws, c. 120, §§ 12, 13; 72 Del. Laws, c. 343, §§ 7, 8; 77 Del. Laws, c. 14, § 4.;

§ 212 Voting rights of stockholders; proxies; limitations.

(a) Unless otherwise provided in the certificate of incorporation and subject to § 213 of this title, each stockholder shall be entitled to 1 vote for each share of capital stock held by such stockholder. If the certificate of incorporation provides for more or less than 1 vote for any share, on any matter, every reference in this chapter to a majority or other proportion of stock, voting stock or shares shall refer to such majority or other proportion of the votes of such stock, voting stock or shares.

(b) Each stockholder entitled to vote at a meeting of stockholders or to express consent or dissent to corporate action in writing without a meeting may authorize another person or persons to act for such stockholder by proxy, but no such proxy shall be voted or acted upon after 3 years from its date, unless the proxy provides for a longer period.

(c) Without limiting the manner in which a stockholder may authorize another person or persons to act for such stockholder as proxy pursuant to subsection (b) of this section, the following shall constitute a valid means by which a stockholder may grant such authority:

(1) A stockholder may execute a writing authorizing another person or persons to act for such stockholder as proxy. Execution may be accomplished by the stockholder or such stockholder's authorized officer, director, employee or agent signing such writing or causing such person's signature to be affixed to such writing by any reasonable means including, but not limited to, by facsimile signature.

(2) A stockholder may authorize another person or persons to act for such stockholder as proxy by transmitting or authorizing the transmission of a telegram, cablegram, or other means of electronic transmission to the person who will be the holder of the proxy or to a proxy solicitation firm, proxy support service organization or like agent duly authorized by the person who will be the holder of the proxy to receive such transmission, provided that any such telegram, cablegram or other means of electronic transmission must either set forth or be submitted with information from which it can be determined that the telegram, cablegram or other electronic transmission was authorized by the stockholder. If it is determined that such telegrams, cablegrams or other electronic transmissions are valid, the inspectors or, if there are no inspectors, such other persons making that determination shall specify the information upon which they relied.

(d) Any copy, facsimile telecommunication or other reliable reproduction of the writing or transmission created pursuant to subsection (c) of this section may be substituted or used in lieu of the original writing or transmission for any and all purposes for which the original writing or transmission could be used, provided that such copy, facsimile telecommunication or other reproduction shall be a complete reproduction of the entire original writing or transmission.

(e) A duly executed proxy shall be irrevocable if it states that it is irrevocable and if, and only as long as, it is coupled with an interest sufficient in law to support an irrevocable power. A proxy may be made irrevocable regardless of whether the interest with which it is coupled is an interest in the stock itself or an interest in the corporation generally.

8 Del. C. 1953, § 212; 56 Del. Laws, c. 50; 57 Del. Laws, c. 148, § 12; 67 Del. Laws, c. 376, § 6; 71 Del. Laws, c. 339, §§ 28–31; 73 Del. Laws, c. 298, § 7.;

§ 213 Fixing date for determination of stockholders of record.

(a) In order that the corporation may determine the stockholders entitled to notice of any meeting of stockholders or any adjournment thereof, the board of directors may fix a record date, which record date shall not precede the date upon which the resolution fixing the record date is adopted by the board of directors, and which record date shall not be more than 60 nor less than 10 days before the date of such meeting. If the board of directors so fixes a date, such date shall also be the record date for determining the stockholders entitled to vote at such meeting unless the board of directors determines, at the time it fixes such record date, that a later date on or before the date of the meeting shall be the date for making such determination. If no record date is fixed by the board of directors, the record date for determining stockholders entitled to notice of and to vote at a meeting of stockholders shall be at the close of business on the day next preceding the day on which notice is given, or, if notice is waived, at the close of business on the day next preceding the day on which the meeting is held. A determination of stockholders of record entitled to notice of or to vote at a meeting of stockholders shall apply to any adjournment of the meeting; provided, however, that the board of directors may fix a new record date for determination of stockholders entitled to vote at the adjourned meeting, and in such case shall also fix as the record date for stockholders entitled to notice of such adjourned meeting the same or an earlier date as that fixed for determination of stockholders entitled to vote in accordance with the foregoing provisions of this subsection (a) at the adjourned meeting.

(b) In order that the corporation may determine the stockholders entitled to consent to corporate action in writing without a meeting, the board of directors may fix a record date, which record date shall not precede the date upon which the resolution fixing the record date is adopted by the board of directors, and which date shall not be more than 10 days after the date upon which the resolution fixing the record date is adopted by the board of directors. If no record date has been fixed by the board of directors, the record date for determining stockholders entitled to consent to corporate action in writing without a meeting, when no prior action by the board of directors is required by this chapter, shall be the first date on which a signed written consent setting forth the action taken or proposed to be taken is delivered to the corporation by delivery to its registered office in this State, its principal place of business or an officer or agent of the corporation having custody of the book in which proceedings of meetings of stockholders are recorded. Delivery made to a corporation's registered office shall be by hand or by certified or registered mail, return receipt requested. If no record date has been fixed by the board of directors and prior action by the board of directors is required by this chapter, the record date for determining stockholders entitled to consent to corporate action in writing without a meeting shall be at the close of business on the day on which the board of directors adopts the resolution taking such prior action.

(c) In order that the corporation may determine the stockholders entitled to receive payment of any dividend or other distribution or allotment of any rights or the stockholders entitled to exercise any rights in respect of any change, conversion or exchange of stock, or for the purpose of any other lawful action, the board of directors may fix a record date, which record date shall not precede the date upon which the resolution fixing the record date is adopted, and which record date shall be not more than 60 days prior to such action. If no record date is fixed, the record date for determining stockholders for any such purpose shall be at the close of business on the day on which the board of directors adopts the resolution relating thereto.

8 Del. C. 1953, § 213; 56 Del. Laws, c. 50; 57 Del. Laws, c. 148, § 13; 66 Del. Laws, c. 136, §§ 7–9; 77 Del. Laws, c. 14, § 5.;

§ 214 Cumulative voting.

The certificate of incorporation of any corporation may provide that at all elections of directors of the corporation, or at elections held under specified circumstances, each holder of stock or of any class or classes or of a series or series thereof shall be entitled to as many votes as shall equal the number of votes which (except for such provision as to cumulative voting) such holder would be entitled to cast for the election of directors with respect to such holder's shares of stock multiplied by the number of directors to be elected by such holder, and that such holder may cast all of such votes for a single director or may distribute them among the number to be voted for, or for any 2 or more of them as such holder may see fit.

8 Del. C. 1953, § 214; 56 Del. Laws, c. 50; 57 Del. Laws, c. 148, § 37; 57 Del. Laws, c. 421, § 5; 71 Del. Laws, c. 339, § 32.;

§ 215 Voting rights of members of nonstock corporations; quorum; proxies.

(a) Sections 211 through 214 and 216 of this title shall not apply to nonstock corporations, except that § 211(a) and (d) of this title and § 212(c), (d), and (e) of this title shall apply to such corporations, and, when so applied, all references therein to stockholders and to the board of directors shall be deemed to refer to the members and the governing body of a nonstock corporation, respectively; and all references to stock, capital stock, or shares thereof shall be deemed to refer to memberships of a nonprofit nonstock corporation and to membership interests of any other nonstock corporation.

(b) Unless otherwise provided in the certificate of incorporation or the bylaws of a nonstock corporation, and subject to subsection (f) of this section, each member shall be entitled at every meeting of members to 1 vote on each matter submitted to a vote of members. A member may exercise such voting rights in person or by proxy, but no proxy shall be voted on after 3 years from its date, unless the proxy provides for a longer period.

(c) Unless otherwise provided in this chapter, the certificate of incorporation or bylaws of a nonstock corporation may specify the number of members having voting power who shall be present or represented by proxy at any meeting in order to constitute a quorum for, and the votes that shall be necessary for, the transaction of any business. In the absence of such specification in the certificate of incorporation or bylaws of a nonstock corporation:

(1) One-third of the members of such corporation shall constitute a quorum at a meeting of such members;

(2) In all matters other than the election of the governing body of such corporation, the affirmative vote of a majority of such members present in person or represented by proxy at the meeting and entitled to vote on the subject matter shall be the act of the members, unless the vote of a greater number is required by this chapter;

(3) Members of the governing body shall be elected by a plurality of the votes of the members of the corporation present in person or represented by proxy at the meeting and entitled to vote thereon; and

(4) Where a separate vote by a class or group or classes or groups is required, a majority of the members of such class or group or classes or groups, present in person or represented by proxy, shall constitute a quorum entitled to take action with respect to that vote on that matter and, in all matters other than the election of members of the governing body, the affirmative vote of the majority of the members of such class or group or classes or groups present in person or represented by proxy at the meeting shall be the act of such class or group or classes or groups.

(d) If the election of the governing body of any nonstock corporation shall not be held on the day designated by the bylaws, the governing body shall cause the election to be held as soon thereafter as convenient. The failure to hold such an election at the designated time shall not work any forfeiture or dissolution of the corporation, but the Court of Chancery may summarily order such an election to be held upon the application of any member of the corporation. At any election pursuant to such order the persons entitled to vote in such election who shall be present at such meeting, either in person or by proxy, shall constitute a quorum for such meeting, notwithstanding any provision of the certificate of incorporation or the bylaws of the corporation to the contrary.

(e) If authorized by the governing body, any requirement of a written ballot shall be satisfied by a ballot submitted by electronic transmission, provided that any such electronic transmission must either set forth or be submitted with information from which it can be determined that the electronic transmission was authorized by the member or proxy holder.

(f) Except as otherwise provided in the certificate of incorporation, in the bylaws, or by resolution of the governing body, the record date for any meeting or corporate action shall be deemed to be the date of such meeting or corporate action; provided, however, that no record date may precede any action by the governing body fixing such record date.

8 Del. C. 1953, § 215; 56 Del. Laws, c. 50; 63 Del. Laws, c. 25, §§ 5, 6; 71 Del. Laws, c. 339, § 33; 73 Del. Laws, c. 82, §§ 8, 9; 77 Del. Laws, c. 253, § 19.;

§ 216 Quorum and required vote for stock corporations.

Subject to this chapter in respect of the vote that shall be required for a specified action, the certificate of incorporation or bylaws of any corporation authorized to issue stock may specify the number of shares and/or the amount of other securities having voting power the holders of which shall be present or represented by proxy at any meeting in order to constitute a quorum for, and the votes that shall be necessary for, the transaction of any business, but in no event shall a quorum consist of less than 1/3 of the shares entitled to vote at the meeting, except that, where a separate vote by a class or series or classes or series is required, a quorum shall consist of no less than 1/3 of the shares of such class or series or classes or series. In the absence of such specification in the certificate of incorporation or bylaws of the corporation:

(1) A majority of the shares entitled to vote, present in person or represented by proxy, shall constitute a quorum at a meeting of stockholders;

(2) In all matters other than the election of directors, the affirmative vote of the majority of shares present in person or represented by proxy at the meeting and entitled to vote on the subject matter shall be the act of the stockholders;

(3) Directors shall be elected by a plurality of the votes of the shares present in person or represented by proxy at the meeting and entitled to vote on the election of directors; and

(4) Where a separate vote by a class or series or classes or series is required, a majority of the outstanding shares of such class or series or classes or series, present in person or represented by proxy, shall constitute a quorum entitled to take action with respect to that vote on that matter and, in all matters other than the election of directors, the affirmative vote of the majority of shares of such class or series or classes or series present in person or represented by proxy at the meeting shall be the act of such class or series or classes or series.

A bylaw amendment adopted by stockholders which specifies the votes that shall be necessary for the election of directors shall not be further amended or repealed by the board of directors.

8 Del. C. 1953, § 216; 56 Del. Laws, c. 50; 63 Del. Laws, c. 25, § 7; 64 Del. Laws, c. 112, § 21; 66 Del. Laws, c. 136, §§ 10, 11; 71 Del. Laws, c. 339, §§ 34, 35; 75 Del. Laws, c. 306, § 5; 76 Del. Laws, c. 145, § 3.;

§ 217 Voting rights of fiduciaries, pledgors and joint owners of stock.

(a) Persons holding stock in a fiduciary capacity shall be entitled to vote the shares so held. Persons whose stock is pledged shall be entitled to vote, unless in the transfer by the pledgor on the books of the corporation such person has expressly empowered the pledgee to vote thereon, in which case only the pledgee, or such pledgee's proxy, may represent such stock and vote thereon.

(b) If shares or other securities having voting power stand of record in the names of 2 or more persons, whether fiduciaries, members of a partnership, joint tenants, tenants in common, tenants by the entirety or otherwise, or if 2 or more persons have the same fiduciary relationship respecting the same shares, unless the secretary of the corporation is given written notice to the contrary and is furnished with a copy of the instrument or order appointing them or creating the relationship wherein it is so provided, their acts with respect to voting shall have the following effect:

(1) If only 1 votes, such person's act binds all;

(2) If more than 1 vote, the act of the majority so voting binds all;

(3) If more than 1 vote, but the vote is evenly split on any particular matter, each faction may vote the securities in question proportionally, or any person voting the shares, or a beneficiary, if any, may apply to the Court of Chancery or such other court as may have jurisdiction to appoint an additional person to act with the persons so voting the shares, which shall then be voted as determined by a majority of such

persons and the person appointed by the Court. If the instrument so filed shows that any such tenancy is held in unequal interests, a majority or even split for the purpose of this subsection shall be a majority or even split in interest.

8 Del. C. 1953, § 217; 56 Del. Laws, c. 50; 71 Del. Laws, c. 339, §§ 36, 37.;

§ 218 Voting trusts and other voting agreements.

(a) One stockholder or 2 or more stockholders may by agreement in writing deposit capital stock of an original issue with or transfer capital stock to any person or persons, or entity or entities authorized to act as trustee, for the purpose of vesting in such person or persons, entity or entities, who may be designated voting trustee, or voting trustees, the right to vote thereon for any period of time determined by such agreement, upon the terms and conditions stated in such agreement. The agreement may contain any other lawful provisions not inconsistent with such purpose. After delivery of a copy of the agreement to the registered office of the corporation in this State or the principal place of business of the corporation, which copy shall be open to the inspection of any stockholder of the corporation or any beneficiary of the trust under the agreement daily during business hours, certificates of stock or uncertificated stock shall be issued to the voting trustee or trustees to represent any stock of an original issue so deposited with such voting trustee or trustees, and any certificates of stock or uncertificated stock so transferred to the voting trustee or trustees shall be surrendered and cancelled and new certificates or uncertificated stock shall be issued therefore to the voting trustee or trustees. In the certificate so issued, if any, it shall be stated that it is issued pursuant to such agreement, and that fact shall also be stated in the stock ledger of the corporation. The voting trustee or trustees may vote the stock so issued or transferred during the period specified in the agreement. Stock standing in the name of the voting trustee or trustees may be voted either in person or by proxy, and in voting the stock, the voting trustee or trustees shall incur no responsibility as stockholder, trustee or otherwise, except for their own individual malfeasance. In any case where 2 or more persons or entities are designated as voting trustees, and the right and method of voting any stock standing in their names at any meeting of the corporation are not fixed by the agreement appointing the trustees, the right to vote the stock and the manner of voting it at the meeting shall be determined by a majority of the trustees, or if they be equally divided as to the right and manner of voting the stock in any particular case, the vote of the stock in such case shall be divided equally among the trustees.

(b) Any amendment to a voting trust agreement shall be made by a written agreement, a copy of which shall be delivered to the registered office of the corporation in this State or principal place of business of the corporation.

(c) An agreement between 2 or more stockholders, if in writing and signed by the parties thereto, may provide that in exercising any voting rights, the shares held by them shall be voted as provided by the agreement, or as the parties may agree, or as determined in accordance with a procedure agreed upon by them.

(d) This section shall not be deemed to invalidate any voting or other agreement among stockholders or any irrevocable proxy which is not otherwise illegal.

8 Del. C. 1953, § 218; 56 Del. Laws, c. 50; 56 Del. Laws, c. 186, § 13; 57 Del. Laws, c. 148, § 14; 63 Del. Laws, c. 25, § 8; 64 Del. Laws, c. 112, § 22; 69 Del. Laws, c. 263, §§ 1–6; 70 Del. Laws, c. 186, § 1; 71 Del. Laws, c. 339, § 38; 73 Del. Laws, c. 82, § 10; 79 Del. Laws, c. 327, § 4.;

§ 219 List of stockholders entitled to vote; penalty for refusal to produce; stock ledger.

(a) The corporation shall prepare, at least 10 days before every meeting of stockholders, a complete list of the stockholders entitled to vote at the meeting; provided, however, if the record date for determining the stockholders entitled to vote is less than 10 days before the meeting date, the list shall reflect the stockholders entitled to vote as of the tenth day before the meeting date, arranged in alphabetical order, and showing the address of each stockholder and the number of shares registered in the name of each stockholder. Nothing contained in this section shall require the corporation to include electronic mail addresses or other electronic contact information on such list. Such list shall be open to the examination of any stockholder for any purpose germane to the meeting for a period of at least 10 days prior to the meeting: (i) on a reasonably accessible electronic network, provided that the information required to gain access to such list is provided with the notice of the meeting, or (ii) during ordinary business hours, at the principal place of business of the corporation. In the event that the corporation determines to make the list available on an electronic network, the corporation may take reasonable steps to ensure that such information is available only to stockholders of the corporation. If the meeting is to be held at a place, then a list of stockholders entitled to vote at the meeting shall be produced and kept at the time and place of the meeting during the whole time thereof and may be examined by any stockholder who is present. If the meeting is to be held solely by means of remote communication, then such list shall also be open to the examination of any stockholder during the whole time of the meeting on a reasonably accessible electronic network, and the information required to access such list shall be provided with the notice of the meeting.

(b) If the corporation, or an officer or agent thereof, refuses to permit examination of the list by a stockholder, such stockholder may apply to the Court of Chancery for an order to compel the corporation to permit such examination. The burden of proof shall be on the corporation to establish that the examination such stockholder seeks is for a purpose not germane to the meeting. The Court may summarily order the corporation to permit examination of the list upon such conditions as the Court may deem appropriate, and may make such additional orders as may be appropriate, including, without limitation, postponing the meeting or voiding the results of the meeting.

(c) For purposes of this chapter, "stock ledger" means 1 or more records administered by or on behalf of the corporation in which the names of all of the corporation's stockholders of record, the address and number of shares registered in the name of each such stockholder, and all issuances and transfers of stock of the corporation are recorded in accordance with § 224 of this title. The stock ledger shall be the only evidence as to who are the stockholders entitled by this section to examine the list required by this section or to vote in person or by proxy at any meeting of stockholders.

8 Del. C. 1953, § 219; 56 Del. Laws, c. 50; 72 Del. Laws, c. 343, §§ 9, 10; 74 Del. Laws, c. 84, § 4; 76 Del. Laws, c. 252, §§ 1, 2; 77 Del. Laws, c. 14, § 6; 81 Del. Laws, c. 86, §§ 5, 6.;

§ 220 Inspection of books and records.

(a) As used in this section:

(1) "Stockholder" means a holder of record of stock in a stock corporation, or a person who is the beneficial owner of shares of such stock held either in a voting trust or by a nominee on behalf of such person.

(2) "Subsidiary" means any entity directly or indirectly owned, in whole or in part, by the corporation of which the stockholder is a stockholder and over the affairs of which the corporation directly or indirectly exercises control, and includes, without limitation, corporations, partnerships, limited partnerships, limited liability partnerships, limited liability companies, statutory trusts and/or joint ventures.

(3) "Under oath" includes statements the declarant affirms to be true under penalty of perjury under the laws of the United States or any state.

(b) Any stockholder, in person or by attorney or other agent, shall, upon written demand under oath stating the purpose thereof, have the right during the usual hours for business to inspect for any proper purpose, and to make copies and extracts from:

(1) The corporation's stock ledger, a list of its stockholders, and its other books and records; and

(2) A subsidiary's books and records, to the extent that:

a. The corporation has actual possession and control of such records of such subsidiary; or

b. The corporation could obtain such records through the exercise of control over such subsidiary, provided that as of the date of the making of the demand:

1. The stockholder inspection of such books and records of the subsidiary would not constitute a breach of an agreement between the corporation or the subsidiary and a person or persons not affiliated with the corporation; and

2. The subsidiary would not have the right under the law applicable to it to deny the corporation access to such books and records upon demand by the corporation.

In every instance where the stockholder is other than a record holder of stock in a stock corporation, or a member of a nonstock corporation, the demand under oath shall state the person's status as a stockholder, be accompanied by documentary evidence of beneficial ownership of the stock, and state that such documentary evidence is a true and correct copy of what it purports to be. A proper purpose shall mean a purpose reasonably related to such person's interest as a stockholder. In every instance where an attorney or other agent shall be the person who seeks the right to inspection, the demand under oath shall be accompanied by a power of attorney or such other writing which authorizes the attorney or other agent to so act on behalf of the stockholder. The demand under oath shall be directed to the corporation at its registered office in this State or at its principal place of business.

(c) If the corporation, or an officer or agent thereof, refuses to permit an inspection sought by a stockholder or attorney or other agent acting for the stockholder pursuant to subsection (b) of this section or does not reply to the demand within 5 business days after the demand has been made, the stockholder may apply to the Court of Chancery for an order to compel such inspection. The Court of Chancery is hereby vested with exclusive jurisdiction to determine whether or not the person seeking inspection is entitled to the inspection sought. The Court may summarily order the corporation to permit the stockholder to inspect the corporation's stock ledger, an existing list of stockholders, and its other books and records, and to make copies or extracts therefrom; or the Court may order the corporation to furnish to the stockholder a list of its stockholders as of a specific date on condition that the stockholder first pay to the corporation the reasonable cost of obtaining and furnishing such list and on such other conditions as the Court deems appropriate. Where the stockholder seeks to inspect the corporation's books and records, other than its stock ledger or list of stockholders, such stockholder shall first establish that:

(1) Such stockholder is a stockholder;

(2) Such stockholder has complied with this section respecting the form and manner of making demand for inspection of such documents; and

(3) The inspection such stockholder seeks is for a proper purpose.

Where the stockholder seeks to inspect the corporation's stock ledger or list of stockholders and establishes that such stockholder is a stockholder and has complied with this section respecting the form and manner of making demand for inspection of such documents, the burden of proof shall be upon the corporation to establish that the inspection such stockholder seeks is for an improper purpose. The Court may, in its discretion, prescribe any limitations or conditions with reference to the inspection, or award such other or further relief as the Court may deem just and proper. The Court may order books, documents and records, pertinent extracts therefrom, or duly authenticated copies thereof, to be brought within this State and kept in this State upon such terms and conditions as the order may prescribe.

(d) Any director shall have the right to examine the corporation's stock ledger, a list of its stockholders and its other books and records for a purpose reasonably related to the director's position as a director. The Court of Chancery is hereby vested with the exclusive jurisdiction to determine whether a director is entitled to the inspection sought. The Court may summarily order the corporation to permit the director to inspect any and all books and records, the stock ledger and the list of stockholders and to make copies or extracts therefrom. The burden of proof shall be upon the corporation to establish that the inspection such director seeks is for an improper purpose. The Court may, in its discretion, prescribe any limitations or conditions with reference to the inspection, or award such other and further relief as the Court may deem just and proper.

8 Del. C. 1953, § 220; 56 Del. Laws, c. 50; 63 Del. Laws, c. 25, § 9; 70 Del. Laws, c. 79, §§ 11, 12; 70 Del. Laws, c. 186, § 1; 71 Del. Laws, c. 339, § 39; 74 Del. Laws, c. 84, §§ 5–8; 77 Del. Laws, c. 253, §§ 20–23.;

§ 221 Voting, inspection and other rights of bondholders and debenture holders.

Every corporation may in its certificate of incorporation confer upon the holders of any bonds, debentures or other obligations issued or to be issued by the corporation the power to vote in respect to the corporate affairs and management of the corporation to the extent and in the manner provided in the certificate of incorporation and may confer upon such holders of bonds, debentures or other obligations the same right of inspection of its books, accounts and other records, and also any other rights, which the stockholders of the corporation have or may have by reason of this chapter or of its certificate of incorporation. If the certificate of incorporation so provides, such holders of bonds, debentures or other obligations shall be deemed to be stockholders, and their bonds, debentures or other obligations shall be deemed to be shares of stock, for the purpose of any provision of this chapter which requires the vote of stockholders as a prerequisite to any corporate action and the certificate of incorporation may divest the holders of capital stock, in whole or in part, of their right to vote on any corporate matter whatsoever, except as set forth in § 242(b)(2) of this title.

8 Del. C. 1953, § 221; 56 Del. Laws, c. 50; 57 Del. Laws, c. 421, § 6; 65 Del. Laws, c. 127, § 6.;

§ 222 Notice of meetings and adjourned meetings.

(a) Whenever stockholders are required or permitted to take any action at a meeting, a written notice of the meeting shall be given which shall state the place, if any, date and hour of the meeting, the means of remote communications, if any, by which stockholders and proxy holders may be deemed to be present in person and vote at such meeting, the record date for determining the stockholders entitled to vote at the meeting, if such date is different from the record date for determining stockholders entitled to notice of the meeting, and, in the case of a special meeting, the purpose or purposes for which the meeting is called.

(b) Unless otherwise provided in this chapter, the written notice of any meeting shall be given not less than 10 nor more than 60 days before the date of the meeting to each stockholder entitled to vote at such meeting as of the record date for determining the stockholders entitled to notice of the meeting. If mailed, notice is given when deposited in the United States mail, postage prepaid, directed to the stockholder at such stockholder's address as it appears on the records of the corporation. An affidavit of the secretary or an assistant secretary or of the transfer agent or other agent of the corporation that the notice has been given shall, in the absence of fraud, be prima facie evidence of the facts stated therein.

(c) When a meeting is adjourned to another time or place, unless the bylaws otherwise require, notice need not be given of the adjourned meeting if the time, place, if any, thereof, and the means of remote communications, if any, by which stockholders and proxy holders may be deemed to be present in person and vote at such adjourned meeting are announced at the meeting at which the adjournment is taken. At the adjourned meeting the corporation may transact any business which might have been transacted at the original meeting. If the adjournment is for more than 30 days, a notice of the adjourned meeting shall be given to each stockholder of record entitled to vote at the meeting. If after the adjournment a new record date for stockholders entitled to vote is fixed for the adjourned meeting, the board of directors shall fix a new record date for notice of such adjourned meeting in accordance with § 213(a) of this title, and shall give notice of the adjourned meeting to each stockholder of record entitled to vote at such adjourned meeting as of the record date fixed for notice of such adjourned meeting.

8 Del. C. 1953, § 222; 56 Del. Laws, c. 50; 58 Del. Laws, c. 235, § 3; 71 Del. Laws, c. 339, § 40; 72 Del. Laws, c. 343, §§ 11–13; 77 Del. Laws, c. 14, §§ 7–9.;

§ 223 Vacancies and newly created directorships.

(a) Unless otherwise provided in the certificate of incorporation or bylaws:

(1) Vacancies and newly created directorships resulting from any increase in the authorized number of directors elected by all of the stockholders having the right to vote as a single class may be filled by a majority of the directors then in office, although less than a quorum, or by a sole remaining director;

(2) Whenever the holders of any class or classes of stock or series thereof are entitled to elect 1 or more directors by the certificate of incorporation, vacancies and newly created directorships of such class or classes or series may be filled by a majority of the directors elected by such class or classes or series thereof then in office, or by a sole remaining director so elected.

If at any time, by reason of death or resignation or other cause, a corporation should have no directors in office, then any officer or any stockholder or an executor, administrator, trustee or guardian of a stockholder, or other fiduciary entrusted with like responsibility for the person or estate of a stockholder, may call a special meeting of stockholders in accordance with the certificate of incorporation or the bylaws, or may apply to the Court of Chancery for a decree summarily ordering an election as provided in § 211 or § 215 of this title.

(b) In the case of a corporation the directors of which are divided into classes, any directors chosen under subsection (a) of this section shall hold office until the next election of the class for which such directors shall have been chosen, and until their successors shall be elected and qualified.

(c) If, at the time of filling any vacancy or any newly created directorship, the directors then in office shall constitute less than a majority of the whole board (as constituted immediately prior to any such increase), the Court of Chancery may, upon application of any stockholder or stockholders holding at least 10 percent of the voting stock at the time outstanding having the right to vote for such directors, summarily order an election to be held to fill any such vacancies or newly created directorships, or to replace the directors chosen by the directors then in office as aforesaid, which election shall be governed by § 211 or § 215 of this title as far as applicable.

(d) Unless otherwise provided in the certificate of incorporation or bylaws, when 1 or more directors shall resign from the board, effective at a future date, a majority of the directors then in office, including those who have so resigned, shall have power to fill such vacancy or vacancies, the vote thereon to take effect when such resignation or resignations shall become effective, and each director so chosen shall hold office as provided in this section in the filling of other vacancies.

8 Del. C. 1953, § 223; 56 Del. Laws, c. 50; 63 Del. Laws, c. 25, § 10; 73 Del. Laws, c. 298, § 8; 77 Del. Laws, c. 253, §§ 24, 25.;

§ 224 Form of records.

Any records administered by or on behalf of the corporation in the regular course of its business, including its stock ledger, books of account, and minute books, may be kept on, or by means of, or be in the form of, any information storage device, method, or 1 or more electronic networks or databases (including 1 or more distributed electronic networks or databases), provided that the records so kept can be converted into clearly legible paper form within a reasonable time, and, with respect to the stock ledger, that the records so kept (i) can be used to prepare the list of stockholders specified in §§ 219 and 220 of this title, (ii) record the information specified in §§ 156, 159, 217(a) and 218 of this title, and (iii) record transfers of stock as governed by Article 8 of subtitle I of Title 6. Any corporation shall convert any records so kept into clearly legible paper form upon the request of any person entitled to inspect such records pursuant to any provision of this chapter. When records are kept in such manner, a clearly legible paper form prepared from or by means of the information storage device, method, or 1 or more electronic networks or databases (including 1 or more distributed electronic networks or databases) shall be valid and admissible in evidence, and accepted for all other purposes, to the same extent as an original paper record of the same information would have been, provided the paper form accurately portrays the record.

8 Del. C. 1953, § 224; 56 Del. Laws, c. 50; 57 Del. Laws, c. 148, § 15; 72 Del. Laws, c. 343, § 14; 81 Del. Laws, c. 86, § 7.;

§ 225 Contested election of directors; proceedings to determine validity.

(a) Upon application of any stockholder or director, or any officer whose title to office is contested, the Court of Chancery may hear and determine the validity of any election, appointment, removal or resignation of any director or officer of any corporation, and the right of any person to hold or continue to hold such office, and, in case any such office is claimed by more than 1 person, may determine the person entitled thereto; and to that end make such order or decree in any such case as may be just and proper, with power to enforce the production of any books, papers and records of the corporation relating to the issue. In case it should be determined that no valid election has been held, the Court of Chancery may order an election to be held in accordance with § 211 or § 215 of this title. In any such application, service of copies of the application upon the registered agent of the corporation shall be deemed to be service upon the corporation and upon the person whose title to office is contested and upon the person, if any, claiming such office; and the registered agent shall forward immediately a copy of the application to the corporation and to the person whose title to office is contested and to the person, if any, claiming such office, in a postpaid, sealed, registered letter addressed to such corporation and such person at their post-office addresses last known to the registered agent or furnished to the registered agent by the applicant stockholder. The Court may make such order respecting further or other notice of such application as it deems proper under the circumstances.

(b) Upon application of any stockholder or upon application of the corporation itself, the Court of Chancery may hear and determine the result of any vote of stockholders upon matters other than the election of directors or officers. Service of the application upon the registered agent of the corporation shall be deemed to be service upon the corporation, and no other party need be joined in order for the Court to adjudicate the result of the vote. The Court may make such order respecting notice of the application as it deems proper under the circumstances.

(c) If 1 or more directors has been convicted of a felony in connection with the duties of such director or directors to the corporation, or if there has been a prior judgment on the merits by a court of competent jurisdiction that 1 or more directors has committed a breach of the duty of loyalty in connection with the duties of such director or directors to that corporation, then, upon application by the corporation, or derivatively in the right of the corporation by any stockholder, in a subsequent action brought for such purpose, the Court of Chancery may remove from office such director or directors if the Court determines that the director or directors did not act in good faith in performing the acts resulting in the prior conviction or judgment and judicial removal is necessary to avoid irreparable harm to the corporation. In connection with such removal, the Court may make such orders as are necessary to effect such removal. In any such application, service of copies of the application upon the registered agent of the corporation shall be deemed to be service upon the corporation and upon the director or directors whose removal is sought; and the registered agent shall forward immediately a copy of the application to the corporation and to such director or directors, in a postpaid, sealed, registered letter addressed to such corporation and such director or directors at their post office addresses last known to the registered agent or furnished to the registered agent by the applicant. The Court may make such order respecting further or other notice of such application as it deems proper under the circumstances.

8 Del. C. 1953, § 225; 56 Del. Laws, c. 50; 63 Del. Laws, c. 25, § 11; 65 Del. Laws, c. 127, § 7; 74 Del. Laws, c. 84, § 9; 76 Del. Laws, c. 252, § 3; 77 Del. Laws, c. 14, § 10; 77 Del. Laws, c. 253, § 26.;

§ 226 Appointment of custodian or receiver of corporation on deadlock or for other cause.

(a) The Court of Chancery, upon application of any stockholder, may appoint 1 or more persons to be custodians, and, if the corporation is insolvent, to be receivers, of and for any corporation when:

(1) At any meeting held for the election of directors the stockholders are so divided that they have failed to elect successors to directors whose terms have expired or would have expired upon qualification of their successors; or

(2) The business of the corporation is suffering or is threatened with irreparable injury because the directors are so divided respecting the management of the affairs of the corporation that the required vote for action by the board of directors cannot be obtained and the stockholders are unable to terminate this division; or

(3) The corporation has abandoned its business and has failed within a reasonable time to take steps to dissolve, liquidate or distribute its assets.

(b) A custodian appointed under this section shall have all the powers and title of a receiver appointed under § 291 of this title, but the authority of the custodian is to continue the business of the corporation and not to liquidate its affairs and distribute its assets, except when the Court shall otherwise order and except in cases arising under paragraph (a)(3) of this section or § 352(a)(2) of this title.

(c) In the case of a charitable nonstock corporation, the applicant shall provide a copy of any application referred to in subsection (a) of this section to the Attorney General of the State of Delaware within 1 week of its filing with the Court of Chancery.

8 Del. C. 1953, § 226; 56 Del. Laws, c. 50; 77 Del. Laws, c. 253, § 27.;

§ 227 Powers of Court in elections of directors.

(a) The Court of Chancery, in any proceeding instituted under § 211, § 215 or § 225 of this title may determine the right and power of persons claiming to own stock to vote at any meeting of the stockholders.

(b) The Court of Chancery may appoint a Master to hold any election provided for in § 211, § 215 or § 225 of this title under such orders and powers as it deems proper; and it may punish any officer or director for contempt in case of disobedience of any order made by the Court; and, in case of disobedience by a corporation of any order made by the Court, may enter a decree against such corporation for a penalty of not more than $5,000.

8 Del. C. 1953, § 227; 56 Del. Laws, c. 50; 77 Del. Laws, c. 253, § 28.;

§ 228 Consent of stockholders or members in lieu of meeting [For application of section, see 81 Del. Laws, c. 86, § 40]

(a) Unless otherwise provided in the certificate of incorporation, any action required by this chapter to be taken at any annual or special meeting of stockholders of a corporation, or any action which may be taken at any annual or special meeting of such stockholders, may be taken without a meeting, without prior notice and without a vote, if a consent or consents in writing, setting forth the action so taken, shall be signed by the holders of outstanding stock having not less than the minimum number of votes that would be necessary to authorize or take such action at a meeting at which all shares entitled to vote thereon were present and voted and shall be delivered to the corporation by delivery to its registered office in this State, its principal place of business or an officer or agent of the corporation having custody of the book in which proceedings of meetings of stockholders are recorded. Delivery made to a corporation's registered office shall be by hand or by certified or registered mail, return receipt requested.

(b) Unless otherwise provided in the certificate of incorporation, any action required by this chapter to be taken at a meeting of the members of a nonstock corporation, or any action which may be taken at any meeting of the members of a nonstock corporation, may be taken without a meeting, without prior notice and without a vote, if a consent or consents in writing, setting forth the action so taken, shall be signed by members having not less than the minimum number of votes that would be necessary to authorize or take such action at a meeting at which all members having a right to vote thereon were present and voted and shall be delivered to the corporation by delivery to its registered office in this State, its principal place of business or an officer or agent of the corporation having custody of the book in which proceedings of meetings of members are recorded. Delivery made to a corporation's registered office shall be by hand or by certified or registered mail, return receipt requested.

(c) No written consent shall be effective to take the corporate action referred to therein unless written consents signed by a sufficient number of holders or members to take action are delivered to the corporation in the manner required by this section within 60 days of the first date on which a written consent is so delivered to the corporation. Any person executing a consent may provide, whether through instruction to an agent or otherwise, that such a consent will be effective at a future time (including a time determined upon the happening of an event), no later than 60 days after such instruction is given or such provision is made, if evidence of such instruction or provision is provided to the corporation. Unless otherwise provided, any such consent shall be revocable prior to its becoming effective.

(d)(1) A telegram, cablegram or other electronic transmission consenting to an action to be taken and transmitted by a stockholder, member or proxyholder, or by a person or persons authorized to act for a stockholder, member or proxyholder, shall be deemed to be written and signed for the purposes of this section, provided that any such telegram, cablegram or other electronic transmission sets forth or is delivered with information from which the corporation can determine (A) that the telegram, cablegram or other electronic transmission was transmitted by the stockholder, member or proxyholder or by a person or persons authorized to act for the stockholder, member or proxyholder and (B) the date on which such stockholder, member or proxyholder or authorized person or persons transmitted such telegram, cablegram or electronic transmission. No consent given by telegram, cablegram or other electronic transmission shall be deemed to have been delivered until such consent is reproduced in paper form and until such paper form shall be delivered to the corporation by delivery to its registered office in this State, its principal place of business or an officer or agent of the corporation having custody of the book in which proceedings of meetings of stockholders or members are recorded. Delivery made to a corporation's registered office shall be made by hand or by certified or registered mail, return receipt requested. Notwithstanding the foregoing limitations on delivery, consents given by telegram, cablegram or other electronic transmission, may be otherwise delivered to the principal place of business of the corporation or to an officer or agent of the corporation having custody of the book in which proceedings of meetings of stockholders or members are recorded if, to the extent and in the manner provided by resolution of the board of directors or governing body of the corporation.

(2) Any copy, facsimile or other reliable reproduction of a consent in writing may be substituted or used in lieu of the original writing for any and all purposes for which the original writing could be used, provided that such copy, facsimile or other reproduction shall be a complete reproduction of the entire original writing.

(e) Prompt notice of the taking of the corporate action without a meeting by less than unanimous written consent shall be given to those stockholders or members who have not consented in writing and who, if the action had been taken at a meeting, would have been entitled to notice of the meeting if the record date for notice of such meeting had been the date that written consents signed by a sufficient number of holders or members to take the action were delivered to the corporation as provided in this section. In the event that the action which is consented to is such as would have required the filing of a certificate under any other section of this title, if such action had been voted on by stockholders or by members at a meeting thereof, the certificate filed under such other section shall state, in lieu of any statement required by such section concerning any vote of stockholders or members, that written consent has been given in accordance with this section.

8 Del. C. 1953, § 228; 56 Del. Laws, c. 50; 56 Del. Laws, c. 186, § 14; 57 Del. Laws, c. 148, § 16; 58 Del. Laws, c. 235, § 4; 66 Del. Laws, c. 136, §§ 12–14; 67 Del. Laws, c. 376, §§ 7, 8; 70 Del. Laws, c. 349, § 4; 72 Del. Laws, c. 343, § 15; 73 Del. Laws, c. 82, § 11; 77 Del. Laws, c. 14, § 11; 79 Del. Laws, c. 327, § 5; 81 Del. Laws, c. 86, §§ 8–10.;

§ 229 Waiver of notice.

Whenever notice is required to be given under any provision of this chapter or the certificate of incorporation or bylaws, a written waiver, signed by the person entitled to notice, or a waiver by electronic transmission by the person entitled to notice, whether before or after the time stated therein, shall be deemed equivalent to notice. Attendance of a person at a meeting shall constitute a waiver of notice of such meeting, except when the person attends a meeting for the express purpose of objecting at the beginning of the meeting, to the transaction of any business because the meeting is not lawfully called or convened. Neither the business to be transacted at, nor the purpose of, any regular or special meeting of the stockholders, directors or members of a committee of directors need be specified in any written waiver of notice or any waiver by electronic transmission unless so required by the certificate of incorporation or the bylaws.

8 Del. C. 1953, § 229; 56 Del. Laws, c. 50; 57 Del. Laws, c. 148, § 17; 72 Del. Laws, c. 343, § 16.;

§ 230 Exception to requirements of notice.

(a) Whenever notice is required to be given, under any provision of this chapter or of the certificate of incorporation or bylaws of any corporation, to any person with whom communication is unlawful, the giving of such notice to such person shall not be required and there shall be no duty to apply to any governmental authority or agency for a license or permit to give such notice to such person. Any action or meeting which shall be taken or held without notice to any such person with whom communication is unlawful shall have the same force and effect as if such notice had been duly given. In the event that the action taken by the corporation is such as to require the filing of a certificate under any of the other sections of this title, the certificate shall state, if such is the fact and if notice is required, that notice was given to all persons entitled to receive notice except such persons with whom communication is unlawful.

(b) Whenever notice is required to be given, under any provision of this title or the certificate of incorporation or bylaws of any corporation, to any stockholder or, if the corporation is a nonstock corporation, to any member, to whom (1) notice of 2 consecutive annual meetings, and all notices of meetings or of the taking of action by written consent without a meeting to such person during the period between such 2 consecutive annual meetings, or (2) all, and at least 2, payments (if sent by first-class mail) of dividends or interest on securities during a 12-month period, have been mailed addressed to such person at such person's address as shown on the records of the corporation and have been returned undeliverable, the giving of such notice to such person shall not be required. Any action or meeting which shall be taken or held without notice to such person shall have the same force and effect as if such notice had been duly given. If any such person shall deliver to the corporation a written notice setting forth such person's then current address, the requirement that notice be given to such person shall be reinstated. In the event that the action taken by the corporation is such as to require the filing of a certificate under any of the other sections of this title, the certificate need not state that notice was not given to persons to whom notice was not required to be given pursuant to this subsection.

(c) The exception in paragraph (b)(1) of this section to the requirement that notice be given shall not be applicable to any notice returned as undeliverable if the notice was given by electronic transmission.

8 Del. C. 1953, § 230; 56 Del. Laws, c. 50; 65 Del. Laws, c. 127, § 8; 71 Del. Laws, c. 339, § 41; 72 Del. Laws, c. 343, § 17.;

§ 231 Voting procedures and inspectors of elections.

(a) The corporation shall, in advance of any meeting of stockholders, appoint 1 or more inspectors to act at the meeting and make a written report thereof. The corporation may designate 1 or more persons as alternate inspectors to replace any inspector who fails to act. If no inspector or alternate is able to act at a meeting of stockholders, the person presiding at the meeting shall appoint 1 or more inspectors to act at the meeting. Each inspector, before entering upon the discharge of the duties of inspector, shall take and sign an oath faithfully to execute the duties of inspector with strict impartiality and according to the best of such inspector's ability.

(b) The inspectors shall:

(1) Ascertain the number of shares outstanding and the voting power of each;

(2) Determine the shares represented at a meeting and the validity of proxies and ballots;

(3) Count all votes and ballots;

(4) Determine and retain for a reasonable period a record of the disposition of any challenges made to any determination by the inspectors; and

(5) Certify their determination of the number of shares represented at the meeting, and their count of all votes and ballots.

The inspectors may appoint or retain other persons or entities to assist the inspectors in the performance of the duties of the inspectors.

(c) The date and time of the opening and the closing of the polls for each matter upon which the stockholders will vote at a meeting shall be announced at the meeting. No ballot, proxies or votes, nor any revocations thereof or changes thereto, shall be accepted by the inspectors after the closing of the polls unless the Court of Chancery upon application by a stockholder shall determine otherwise.

(d) In determining the validity and counting of proxies and ballots, the inspectors shall be limited to an examination of the proxies, any envelopes submitted with those proxies, any information provided in accordance with § 211(e) or § 212(c)(2) of this title, or any information provided pursuant to § 211(a)(2)b.(i) or (iii) of this title, ballots and the regular books and records of the corporation, except that the inspectors may consider other reliable information for the limited purpose of reconciling proxies and ballots submitted by or on behalf of banks, brokers, their nominees or similar persons which represent more votes than the holder of a proxy is authorized by the record owner to cast or more votes than the stockholder holds of record. If the inspectors consider other reliable information for the limited purpose permitted herein, the inspectors at the time they make their certification pursuant to paragraph (b)(5) of this section shall specify the precise information considered by them including the person or persons from whom they obtained the information, when the information was obtained, the means by which the information was obtained and the basis for the inspectors' belief that such information is accurate and reliable.

(e) Unless otherwise provided in the certificate of incorporation or bylaws, this section shall not apply to a corporation that does not have a class of voting stock that is:

(1) Listed on a national securities exchange;

(2) Authorized for quotation on an interdealer quotation system of a registered national securities association; or

(3) Held of record by more than 2,000 stockholders.

67 Del. Laws, c. 376, § 9; 71 Del. Laws, c. 339, § 42; 72 Del. Laws, c. 343, § 18.;

§ 232 Notice by electronic transmission.

(a) Without limiting the manner by which notice otherwise may be given effectively to stockholders, any notice to stockholders given by the corporation under any provision of this chapter, the certificate of incorporation, or the bylaws shall be effective if given by a form of electronic transmission consented to by the stockholder to whom the notice is given. Any such consent shall be revocable by the stockholder by written notice to the corporation. Any such consent shall be deemed revoked if (1) the corporation is unable to deliver by electronic transmission 2 consecutive notices given by the corporation in accordance with such consent and (2) such inability becomes known to the secretary or an assistant secretary of the corporation or to the transfer agent, or other person responsible for the giving of notice; provided, however, the inadvertent failure to treat such inability as a revocation shall not invalidate any meeting or other action.

(b) Notice given pursuant to subsection (a) of this section shall be deemed given:

(1) If by facsimile telecommunication, when directed to a number at which the stockholder has consented to receive notice;

(2) If by electronic mail, when directed to an electronic mail address at which the stockholder has consented to receive notice;

(3) If by a posting on an electronic network together with separate notice to the stockholder of such specific posting, upon the later of (A) such posting and (B) the giving of such separate notice; and

(4) If by any other form of electronic transmission, when directed to the stockholder.

An affidavit of the secretary or an assistant secretary or of the transfer agent or other agent of the corporation that the notice has been given by a form of electronic transmission shall, in the absence of fraud, be prima facie evidence of the facts stated therein.

(c) For purposes of this chapter, "electronic transmission" means any form of communication, not directly involving the physical transmission of paper, including the use of, or participation in, 1 or more electronic networks or databases (including 1 or more distributed electronic networks or databases), that creates a record that may be retained, retrieved and reviewed by a recipient thereof, and that may be directly reproduced in paper form by such a recipient through an automated process.

(d) [Repealed.]

(e) This section shall not apply to § 164, § 296, § 311, § 312, or § 324 of this title.

72 Del. Laws, c. 343, § 19; 73 Del. Laws, c. 82, § 12; 77 Del. Laws, c. 253, § 29; 81 Del. Laws, c. 86, § 11.;

§ 233 Notice to stockholders sharing an address.

(a) Without limiting the manner by which notice otherwise may be given effectively to stockholders, any notice to stockholders given by the corporation under any provision of this chapter, the certificate of incorporation, or the bylaws shall be effective if given by a single written notice to stockholders who share an address if consented to by the stockholders at that address to whom such notice is given. Any such consent shall be revocable by the stockholder by written notice to the corporation.

(b) Any stockholder who fails to object in writing to the corporation, within 60 days of having been given written notice by the corporation of its intention to send the single notice permitted under subsection (a) of this section, shall be deemed to have consented to receiving such single written notice.

(c) [Repealed.]

(d) This section shall not apply to § 164, § 296, § 311, § 312 or § 324 of this title.

73 Del. Laws, c. 298, § 9; 77 Del. Laws, c. 253, § 30.;

---

15 PENNSYLVANIA CON. STATUTES ANN. CH. 33

CHAPTER 33

BENEFIT CORPORATIONS

Subchapter

A. Preliminary Provisions

B. Corporate Purposes

C. Accountability

D. Transparency

Enactment. Chapter 33 was added October 24, 2012, P.L. 1228, No. 152, effective in 90 days.

SUBCHAPTER A

PRELIMINARY PROVISIONS

Sec.

3301. Application and effect of chapter.

3302. Definitions.

3303. Formation of benefit corporations.

3304. Election of benefit corporation status.

3305. Termination of benefit corporation status.

§ 3301. Application and effect of chapter.

(a) General rule. —This chapter shall apply to all benefit corporations.

(b) Application of business corporation law generally. —The existence of a provision of this chapter shall not of itself create any implication that a contrary or different rule of law is or would be applicable to a business corporation that is not a benefit corporation. This chapter shall not affect any statute or rule of law that is or would be applicable to a business corporation that is not a benefit corporation.

(c) Laws applicable to benefit corporations. —Except as otherwise provided in this chapter, Part I (relating to preliminary provisions) and this subpart shall apply generally to benefit corporations. The provisions of this chapter shall control over inconsistent provisions of this title. A benefit corporation may be simultaneously subject to this chapter and one or more other chapters of this article.

(d) Organic rules may not be inconsistent. —A provision of the articles or bylaws of a benefit corporation may not relax, be inconsistent with or supersede any provision of this chapter.

(Oct. 22, 2014, P.L. 2640, No. 172, eff. July 1, 2015; Nov. 21, 2016, P.L. 1328, No. 170, eff. 90 days)

2016 Amendment. Act 170 amended subsec. (d).

2014 Amendment. Act 172 amended subsec. (c).

§ 3302. Definitions.

The following words and phrases when used in this chapter shall have the meanings given to them in this section unless the context clearly indicates otherwise:

"Benefit corporation." A business corporation that is subject to this chapter.

"Benefit director." The director designated as the benefit director of a benefit corporation as provided in section 3322 (relating to benefit director).

"Benefit enforcement proceeding." A claim or action for:

(1) failure to pursue or create the general public benefit purpose of the benefit corporation or any specific public benefit purpose set forth in its articles; or

(2) violation of any obligation, duty or standard of conduct under this chapter.

"Benefit officer." The individual, if any, designated as the benefit officer of a benefit corporation as provided in section 3324 (relating to benefit officer).

"General public benefit." A material positive impact on society and the environment, taken as a whole and assessed against a third-party standard, from the business and operations of a benefit corporation.

"Independent." When a person has no material relationship with a benefit corporation or any of its subsidiaries, other than the relationship of serving as the benefit director or benefit officer. A material relationship between an individual and a benefit corporation or any of its subsidiaries will be conclusively presumed to exist if:

(1) the person is or has been within the last three years an employee of the benefit corporation or any of its subsidiaries, other than as a benefit officer;

(2) an immediate family member of the person is or has been within the last three years an executive officer, other than a benefit officer, of the benefit corporation or any of its subsidiaries; or

(3) the person, or an association of which the person is a governor or officer or in which the person owns beneficially or of record 5% or more of the outstanding interests, owns beneficially or of record 5% or more of the outstanding shares of the benefit corporation. The percentage of ownership in an association shall be calculated as if all outstanding rights to acquire interests in the association had been exercised.

"Minimum status vote." As follows:

(1) In the case of a business corporation, in addition to any other required approval or vote, the satisfaction of the following conditions:

(i) The shareholders of every class or series must be entitled, as a class, to vote on the corporate action regardless of a limitation stated in the articles of incorporation or bylaws on the voting rights of any class or series.

(ii) The corporate action must be approved by a vote of the shareholders of each class or series entitled to cast at least two-thirds of the votes that all shareholders of the class or series are entitled to cast on the action.

(2) In the case of a domestic association other than a business corporation, in addition to any other required approval, vote or consent, the satisfaction of the following conditions:

(i) The holders of every class or series of interest in the association that are entitled to receive a distribution of any kind from the association must be entitled as a class to vote on or consent to the action regardless of any otherwise applicable limitation on the voting or consent rights of any class or series.

(ii) The action must be approved by vote or consent of the holders described in subparagraph (i) entitled to cast at least two-thirds of the votes or consents that all of those holders are entitled to cast on the action.

"Specific public benefit." Includes:

(1) providing low-income or underserved individuals or communities with beneficial products or services;

(2) promoting economic opportunity for individuals or communities beyond the creation of jobs in the normal course of business;

(3) preserving the environment;

(4) improving human health;

(5) promoting the arts, sciences or advancement of knowledge;

(6) promoting economic development through support of initiatives that increase access to capital for emerging and growing technology enterprises, facilitate the transfer and commercial adoption of new technologies, provide technical and business support to emerging and growing technology enterprises or form support partnerships that support those objectives;

(7) increasing the flow of capital to entities with a public benefit purpose; and

(8) the accomplishment of any other particular benefit for society or the environment.

"Subsidiary." An association in which a person owns beneficially or of record 50% or more of the outstanding interests. The percentage of ownership in an association shall be calculated as if all outstanding rights to acquire interests in the association had been exercised.

"Third-party standard." A standard for defining, reporting and assessing overall corporate social and environmental performance which is:

(1) Comprehensive in that it assesses the effect of the business and its operations upon the interests listed in section 3321(a)(1)(ii), (iii), (iv) and (v) (relating to standard of conduct for directors).

(2) Developed by an organization that is independent of the benefit corporation and satisfies the following requirements:

(i) Not more than one-third of the members of the governing body of the organization are representatives of any of the following:

(A) An association of businesses operating in a specific industry the performance of whose members is measured by the standard.

(B) Businesses from a specific industry or an association of businesses in that industry.

(C) Businesses whose performance is assessed against the standard.

(ii) The organization is not materially financed by an association or business described in subparagraph (i).

(3) Credible because the standard is developed by a person that both:

(i) Has access to necessary expertise to assess overall corporate social and environmental performance.

(ii) Uses a balanced multistakeholder approach, including a public comment period of at least 30 days to develop the standard.

(4) Transparent because the following information is publicly available:

(i) About the standard:

(A) The criteria considered when measuring the overall social and environmental performance of a business.

(B) The relative weightings, if any, of those criteria.

(ii) About the development and revision of the standard:

(A) The identity of the directors, officers, material owners and the governing body of the organization that developed and controls revisions to the standard.

(B) The process by which revisions to the standard and changes to the membership of the governing body are made.

(C) An accounting of the sources of financial support for the organization, with sufficient detail to disclose any relationships that could reasonably be considered to present a potential conflict of interest.

(Nov. 21, 2016, P.L. 1328, No. 170, eff. 90 days)

2016 Amendment. Act 170 amended the defs. of "benefit corporation," "benefit director," "independent," "minimum status vote" and "subsidiary."

Cross References. Section 3302 is referred to in section 8892 of this title.

§ 3303. Formation of benefit corporations.

A benefit corporation shall be formed in accordance with Article B (relating to domestic business corporations generally) except that its articles shall also state that it is a benefit corporation.

§ 3304. Election of benefit corporation status.

(a) Amendment. —An existing business corporation may become a benefit corporation by amending its articles so that they contain, in addition to the requirements of section 1306(a) (relating to articles of incorporation), a statement that the corporation is a benefit corporation. The amendment shall not be effective unless it is adopted by at least the minimum status vote.

(b) Fundamental transactions. —If an association that is not a benefit corporation is a party to a merger or division or is the exchanging association in an interest exchange, and the surviving, new or any resulting association in the merger, division or interest exchange is to be a benefit corporation, then the plan of merger, division or interest exchange shall not be effective unless it is adopted by the association by at least the minimum status vote.

(Oct. 22, 2014, P.L. 2640, No. 172, eff. July 1, 2015)

2014 Amendment. Act 172 amended subsec. (b).

Cross References. Section 3304 is referred to in sections 321, 322, 323, 324, 325, 326, 327, 328, 3305 of this title.

§ 3305. Termination of benefit corporation status.

(a) Amendment. —A benefit corporation may terminate its status as a benefit corporation and cease to be subject to this chapter by amending its articles to delete the provision required under section 3304 (relating to election of benefit corporation status) to be stated in the articles of a benefit corporation. The amendment shall not be effective unless it is adopted by at least the minimum status vote.

(b) Fundamental transactions. —If a plan would have the effect of terminating the status of a business corporation as a benefit corporation, the plan shall not be effective unless it is adopted by at least the minimum status vote. Any sale, lease, exchange or other disposition of all or substantially all of the assets of a benefit corporation, unless the transaction is in the usual and regular course of business, shall not be effective unless the transaction is approved by at least the minimum status vote.

Cross References. Section 3305 is referred to in section 321 of this title.

SUBCHAPTER B
CORPORATE PURPOSES

Sec.

§ 3311. Corporate purposes.

(a) General public benefit purpose. —A benefit corporation shall have a purpose of creating general public benefit. This purpose is in addition to its purpose under section 1301 (relating to purposes).

(b) Optional specific public benefit purpose. —The articles of a benefit corporation may identify one or more specific public benefits that it is the purpose of the benefit corporation to create in addition to its purposes under section 1301 and subsection (a). The identification of a specific public benefit does not limit the obligation of a benefit corporation to create general public benefit.

(c) Effect of purposes. —The creation of general and specific public benefit as provided in subsections (a) and (b) is in the best interests of the benefit corporation.

(d) Amendment. —A benefit corporation may amend its articles to add, amend or delete the identification of a specific public benefit that it is the purpose of the benefit corporation to create. The amendment shall not be effective unless it is adopted by at least the minimum status vote.

(e) Professional corporations. —A professional corporation that is a benefit corporation does not violate section 2922(a) (relating to stated purposes) by having the purpose to create general public benefit or a specific public benefit.

SUBCHAPTER C
ACCOUNTABILITY

Sec.

§ 3321. Standard of conduct for directors.

(a) Consideration of interests. —Without regard to whether the benefit corporation is subject to section 1715 (relating to exercise of powers generally) or 1716 (relating to alternative standard), in discharging the duties of their respective positions, the board of directors, committees of the board and individual directors of a benefit corporation, in considering the best interest of the benefit corporation:

(1) shall consider the effects of any action upon:

(i) the shareholders of the benefit corporation;

(ii) the employees and work force of the benefit corporation and its subsidiaries and suppliers;

(iii) the interests of customers as beneficiaries of the general or specific public benefit purposes of the benefit corporation;

(iv) community and societal considerations, including those of any community in which offices or facilities of the benefit corporation or its subsidiaries or suppliers are located;

(v) the local and global environment;

(vi) the short-term and long-term interests of the benefit corporation, including benefits that may accrue to the benefit corporation from its long-term plans and the possibility that these interests may be best served by the continued independence of the benefit corporation; and

(vii) the ability of the benefit corporation to accomplish its general public benefit purpose and any specific public benefit purpose; and

(2) may consider:

(i) matters listed in section 1715(a); and

(ii) any other pertinent factors or the interests of any other group that they deem appropriate; but

(3) shall not be required to give priority to the interests of any person or group referred to in paragraph (1) or (2) over the interests of any other person or group unless the benefit corporation has stated in its articles its intention to give priority to certain interests related to its accomplishment of its general public benefit purpose or of a specific public benefit purpose identified in its articles.

(b) Coordination with other provisions of law. —The consideration of interests and factors in the manner required under subsection (a):

(1) shall not constitute a violation of section 1712 (relating to standard of care and justifiable reliance); and

(2) is in addition to the ability of directors to consider interests and factors as provided in section 1715 or 1716.

(c) Exoneration from personal liability. —

(1) A director shall not be personally liable, as such, for monetary damages for any action taken as a director in the course of performing the duties specified in subsection (a) unless the action constitutes self-dealing, willful misconduct or a knowing violation of law.

(2) A director shall not be personally liable for monetary damages for failure of the benefit corporation to pursue or create general public benefit or a specific public benefit.

(d) Limitation on standing. —A director does not have a duty to a person that is a beneficiary of the general public benefit purpose or a specific public benefit purpose of a benefit corporation arising from the status of the person as a beneficiary.

(Nov. 21, 2016, P.L. 1328, No. 170, eff. 90 days)

2016 Amendment. Act 170 amended subsec. (c).

§ 3322. Benefit director.

(a) General rule. —

(1) The board of directors of a benefit corporation which is a registered corporation shall include a director who:

(i) shall be designated as the benefit director; and

(ii) shall have, in addition to all of the powers, duties, rights and immunities of the other directors of the benefit corporation, the powers, duties, rights and immunities provided in this subchapter.

(2) The board of directors of a benefit corporation which is not a registered corporation may include a director who:

(i) shall be designated as the benefit director; and

(ii) shall have, in addition to all of the powers, duties, rights and immunities of the other directors of the benefit corporation, the powers, duties, rights and immunities provided in this subchapter.

(b) Election, removal and qualifications. —The benefit director shall be elected and may be removed in the manner provided under Subchapter C of Chapter 17 (relating to directors and officers). Except as set forth in subsection (e)(2)(i) or (g), the benefit director shall be an individual who is independent. The benefit director may serve as the benefit officer at the same time as serving as the benefit director. The articles or bylaws of a benefit corporation may prescribe additional qualifications of the benefit director not inconsistent with this subsection.

(c) Annual compliance statement. —The benefit director shall prepare, and the benefit corporation shall include in the annual benefit report to shareholders required under section 3331 (relating to annual benefit report), a statement whether, in the opinion of the benefit director, the benefit corporation acted in accordance with its general and any specific public benefit purpose in all material respects during the period covered by the report and whether the directors and officers complied with sections 3321(a) (relating to standard of conduct for directors) and 3323(a) (relating to standard of conduct for officers), respectively. If, in the opinion of the benefit director, the benefit corporation or its directors or officers failed so to act, then the statement of the benefit director shall include a description of the ways in which the benefit corporation or its directors or officers failed so to act.

(d) Status of actions. —The acts of an individual in the capacity of a benefit director shall constitute for all purposes acts of that individual in the capacity of a director of the benefit corporation.

(e) Alternative governance arrangements. —(Deleted by amendment).

(f) Exoneration from personal liability. —Regardless of whether the bylaws of a benefit corporation include a provision eliminating or limiting the personal liability of directors authorized under section 1713 (relating to personal liability of directors), a benefit director shall not be personally liable for any act or omission in the capacity of a benefit director unless the act or omission constitutes self-dealing, willful misconduct or a knowing violation of law.

(g) Professional corporations. —The benefit director of a professional corporation does not need to be independent.

(July 9, 2013, P.L. 476, No. 67, eff. 60 days; Nov. 21, 2016, P.L. 1328, No. 170, eff. 90 days)

2016 Amendment. Act 170 deleted subsec. (e).

2013 Amendment. Act 67 amended subsecs. (a) and (b) and added subsec. (g).

Cross References. Section 3322 is referred to in sections 3302, 3331 of this title.

§ 3323. Standard of conduct for officers.

(a) General rule. —Each officer of a benefit corporation shall consider the interests and factors described in section 3321(a) (relating to standard of conduct for directors) in the manner provided in that subsection when:

(1) the officer has discretion to act with respect to a matter; and

(2) it reasonably appears to the officer that the matter may have a material effect on the creation by the benefit corporation of general public benefit or a specific public benefit identified in the articles of the benefit corporation.

(b) Coordination with other provisions of law. —The consideration of interests and factors in the manner described in subsection (a) shall not constitute a violation of section 1712(c) (relating to standard of care and justifiable reliance).

(c) Exoneration from personal liability. —

(1) An officer shall not be personally liable, as such, for monetary damages for any action taken as an officer in the course of performing the duties specified in subsection (a) unless the action constitutes self-dealing, willful misconduct or a knowing violation of law.

(2) An officer shall not be personally liable for monetary damages for failure of the benefit corporation to pursue or create general public benefit or a specific public benefit.

(d) Limitation on standing. —An officer does not have a duty to a person that is a beneficiary of the general public benefit purpose or a specific public benefit purpose of a benefit corporation arising from the status of the person as a beneficiary.

(Nov. 21, 2016, P.L. 1328, No. 170, eff. 90 days)

2016 Amendment. Act 170 amended subsec. (c).

Cross References. Section 3323 is referred to in section 3322 of this title.

§ 3324. Benefit officer.

A benefit corporation may have an officer designated as the benefits officer who shall have such authority and shall perform such duties in the management of the benefit corporation relating to the purpose of the corporation to create general or specific public benefit as may be provided by or pursuant to the bylaws or, in the absence of controlling provisions in the bylaws, as may be determined by or pursuant to resolutions or orders of the board of directors. If a benefit corporation has a benefit officer, the duties of the benefit officer shall include preparing the benefit report required under section 3331 (relating to annual benefit report).

Cross References. Section 3324 is referred to in section 3302 of this title.

§ 3325. Right of action.

(a) Limitations. —

(1) Except in a benefit enforcement proceeding, no person may bring an action or assert a claim against a benefit corporation or its directors or officers with respect to:

(i) failure to pursue or create general public benefit or a specific public benefit set forth in its articles; or

(ii) violation of a duty or standard of conduct under this chapter.

(2) A benefit corporation shall not be liable for monetary damages under this chapter for any failure of the benefit corporation to pursue or create general public benefit or a specific public benefit.

(b) Parties with standing. —A benefit enforcement proceeding may be commenced or maintained only:

(1) directly by the benefit corporation; or

(2) derivatively by:

(i) a shareholder that owned at least 2% of the total number of shares of a class or series outstanding at the time of the act complained of;

(ii) a director;

(iii) a person or group of persons that owns beneficially or of record 5% or more of the interests in an association of which the benefit corporation is a subsidiary at the time of the act complained of; or

(iv) such other persons as may be specified in the articles or bylaws of the benefit corporation.

(c) Cross reference. —The provisions of Subchapter F of Chapter 17 (relating to derivative actions) shall apply to derivative actions under this section.

(July 9, 2013, P.L. 476, No. 67, eff. 60 days; Nov. 21, 2016, P.L. 1328, No. 170, eff. 90 days)

2016 Amendment. Act 170 amended subsec. (b).

SUBCHAPTER D
TRANSPARENCY

Sec.

§ 3331. Annual benefit report.

(a) Contents. —A benefit corporation must deliver to each shareholder an annual benefit report including:

(1) A narrative description of:

(i) the ways in which the benefit corporation pursued general public benefit during the year and the extent to which general public benefit was created;

(ii) the ways in which the benefit corporation pursued any specific public benefit that the articles state is the purpose of the benefit corporation to create and the extent to which that specific public benefit was created;

(iii) any circumstances that have hindered the creation by the benefit corporation of general or specific public benefit; and

(iv) the process and rationale for selecting or changing the third-party standard used to prepare the benefit report.

(2) An assessment of the overall social and environmental performance of the benefit corporation against a third-party standard applied consistently with any application of that standard in prior benefit reports or accompanied by an explanation of the reasons for any inconsistent application. The assessment does not need to be audited or certified by a third-party standards provider.

(3) The name of the benefit director and the benefit officer, if any, and the address to which correspondence to each of them may be directed.

(4) The compensation paid by the benefit corporation during the year to each director in that capacity.

(5) (Deleted by amendment).

(6) The statement of the benefit director described in section 3322(c) (relating to benefit director).

(7) A statement of any connection between the organization that established the third-party standard, or its directors, officers or any holder of 5% or more of the governance interests in the organization, and the benefit corporation or its directors, officers or any holder of 5% or more of the outstanding shares of the benefit corporation, including any financial or governance relationship which might materially affect the credibility of the use of the third-party standard.

(8) (Deleted by amendment).

(b) Timing of report. —A benefit corporation shall annually send a benefit report to each shareholder either:

(1) within 120 days following the end of the fiscal year of the benefit corporation; or

(2) at the same time that the benefit corporation delivers any other annual report to its shareholders.

(c) Internet website posting. —A benefit corporation must post all of its benefit reports on the public portion of its Internet website, if any, except that the compensation paid to directors and any financial or proprietary information included in the benefit report may be omitted from the benefit report as posted.

(d) Availability of copies. —If a benefit corporation does not have an Internet website, the benefit corporation shall provide a copy of its most recent benefit report, without charge, to any person that requests a copy, but the compensation paid to directors and financial or proprietary information included in the benefit report may be omitted from the copy of the benefit report provided.

(e) Filing of report. —Concurrently with the delivery of the benefit report to shareholders pursuant to subsection (b), the benefit corporation must deliver a copy of the benefit report to the department for filing, except that the compensation paid to directors and any financial or proprietary information included in the benefit report may be omitted from the benefit report as filed under this section. The department shall charge a fee of $70 for filing a benefit report.

(July 9, 2013, P.L. 476, No. 67, eff. 60 days; Nov. 21, 2016, P.L. 1328, No. 170, eff. 90 days)

2016 Amendment. Act 170 deleted subsec. (a)(8).

2013 Amendment. Act 67 deleted subsec. (a)(5).

Cross References. Section 3331 is referred to in sections 3322, 3324 of this title.

INDEX

References are to Pages